CW01466579

Haunted
Liverpool 19

Tom Slemen

The Tom Slemen Press

ISBN-10: 1547003936
ISBN-13: **978-1547003938**

DEDICATION

For The Vamps

CONTENTS

The Vengeful Spinster	1
Say Who You Are	8
Somewhere Only We Know	18
Buried Alive	36
The White Dot	41
The Phantom Monks of Childwall	50
Time Out of Joint	63
Anonyma	74
The Mint Green Car	80
Who's That Girl?	92
Sleepy Gene	101
Huyton's Ghostly Highwayman	110
Mimic	118

Silhouettes	127
A Grim Premonition	140
The Trojan Sofa	147
More Liverpool Timeslips	159
The Man Who Wasn't There	172
The Unexplainables	176
Encounter with a Zombie	186
The Family of Souls	195
Strangers in the Night	206
Nanny's Secret	213
Pet Hole	228
The Elemental	233
The Witch of County Road	240
Sathan	247
Father Murphy	254
The Beast	259
Ghostly Smells	264

Skirmishes with Supernatural Abductions   271

Eve & Liv   277

Eavesdropping on Hell   280

Some Carnate and Discarnate Ghosts   291

THE VENGEFUL SPINSTER

The following story is true in every respect, No names or places have been changed.

Many years ago in the 1970s, a 19-year-old lad from Woolton named Des began to see a 17-year-old girl from Childwall named Debbie (whose surname was very unusual). One gloriously uplifting summer's day around 1.30pm, Debbie was walking up Hartsbourne Avenue dressed in a white tee shirt featuring a yellow smiley face and a short bottle green skirt. On her feet she wore no socks, just a pair of Dunlop tennis shoes. Her long golden hair was stirred by a zephyr, and in the eyes of Des, Debbie was a wonderful sight to behold. He asked her if she knew what time it was, and Debbie said, 'Around half one now I think.'

'Where are you going?' Des asked, walking alongside of the girl.

'To my friends,' Debbie answered meekly, and actually blushed.

1

'Can I walk with you?' Des asked, cheekily.

There was a pause as Debbie's greenish blue eyes looked away. Then she said, 'If you want.'

A week later the couple were 'necking' – kissing intimately in the back row of the Abbey Cinema, and after the film had ended at 10.20pm, Des persecuted Debbie to have sex with him. She kept saying no, but even as the couple walked along hand in hand, Des was consciously steering her towards Trinity Churchyard in Wavertree's Fir Lane, where he intended to carry out the act he had dreamt of each night since he had met Debbie. The girl relented when Des said to her, 'I thought we had something really special, Debbie; I thought that. I love you so much and want to marry you as soon as I get a job.'

The couple embraced, and there was an out-of-season roll of thunder in the heavens. There was a sweet scent in the air from the flowers of the cemetery, and the atmosphere seemed to be laden with desire. Des led Debbie into the churchyard and here, he laid the girl out on one of the old long gravestones that lie flat against the ground.

'I'm a virgin,' Debbie whispered in Des's ear, but he just said: 'Shush!' and kissed her face all over.

As Des made love to his girlfriend, lightning flashed through the summer skies, and then as the thunder rolled, the ground vibrated with so much force, Debbie had strange mental images of the dead being shook out of their graves. She felt so much pain and yet so much pleasure as she lay there, but a few minutes into the lovemaking act, heavy rain began to fall, soaking the teens to the bone. Debbie felt her open mouth filling up with the rain, and she tried to push Des off.

There was a purple flash of light, and in that millisecond, Debbie saw someone standing over Des, looking over his left shoulder. The figure was of a woman with a shock of white wiry straw-like hair, and her eyes were wide and bulging, a green greyish colour with no pupils, and her jaw looked skeletal. Debbie tried to push Des off her when she saw the figure, but at that moment he cried out and pinned the girl down with tremendous strength. His hands left red marks on Debbie's sensitive skin around her wrists, and after a minute, Des got to his feet, adjusted his trousers and walked away. He left Debbie there stretched out on the grave. She started to cry. She realised all his promises of undying love had been nothing but sweet-talk. Debbie picked herself up, put her panties back on, and shouted Des's name. He stopped, delved into his pocket, and treated himself to the last cigarette from a crumpled packet. He lit up, puffed on the ciggy, and said to Debbie: 'Well, what did you think?'

Debbie swore at him and called him a bastard. 'You just used me,' she sobbed. 'I thought you loved me.'

'I do love you, you stupid get,' Des told her, and he climbed over the short railings and walked off in a huff.

Debbie cried and tried to follow him, but almost fell as she climbed over the railings. She walked home to Childwall, soaked and disappointed. The emptiness she felt inside and the coldness temporarily blotted out the memory of that strange ghoulish figure she had seen looming over her and Des in the graveyard. As Debbie reached Childwall Valley Road, she heard running behind her, and turned to see that it was Des with a smile on his face. He shouted: 'I have been shouting you ever since you crossed over Church Road, didn't you hear me deaf lugs?'

Debbie walked on and tried to ignore him.

'Debbie I love you girl, stop being like this!' Des caught up and seized her forearm.

Debbie slapped his hand and pulled her arm away. 'You're really horrible, and you couldn't even do it properly!' she said, marching along as the thunder rolled again.

'Well that's because you're a virgin!' Des shouted, and stopped in his tracks. He shouted all sorts of insults at the girl as she walked on into the night. Debbie put it all down to experience; this was to be just the first encounter with the many male scumbags in her life, all out for one thing, and it wasn't romance. She felt as if her innocence had been robbed.

That night, Des watched the television until around midnight, and when his parents went to bed, he sneaked into the hallway and stole a few cigarettes from the box of twenty Embassy in his father's inside coat pocket. He then lay in bed, smoking and listening to the *Night Owl* music programme on Radio City. He thought about the act in the cemetery, and then he dozed off. Des woke around 3am, and opened the window. It was sweltering in the bedroom with the close summer air. Des took off his underpants and lay under just a thin nylon sheet. He quickly drifted off into the strange territory of dreams, and he had one of the worst nightmares in his life. A skeletal naked woman with a shock of white hair was stretched out on the ceiling above his bed, and her saliva was drooling out of her open mouth and falling in vile strings onto Des's face. Then this woman let out an ear-splitting scream and fell from the ceiling onto Des. As she landed on him, he saw her face close up, and saw that her eyes had no pupils. They were bulging like boiled eggs stripped of their shells, only they had a green-grey tinge to them. The old hag began to utter the most disgusting language to Des and told him she was about to make love to him. Des screamed and tried to get her off him, but the zombie-like woman laughed and said: 'I'm a *virgin too*! Yes, you despicable little [expletive delted]! Make love to me or I'll claw your eyes out!'

And she lifted her bony, skeletal fingers to Des's face. She had long thick dirty fingernails, and they clawed at Des's right cheek, drawing blood. Her other cold claw-like hand was sliding down past the teenager's navel. Try as he may, Des could not push the living corpse off him, and somehow she managed to start making love to him. He felt her bristly tongue snaking around in his mouth and when it touched his tonsils he almost threw up. The woman started to shake and scream with laughter, and the two of them rolled over – and off the bed.

Des woke up, startled with thunder booming in the skies outside. The curtains were blowing wildly in the stormy wind. He recalled the old hag, then got back into bed, and he felt *so* relieved it had all been a dream, but then he felt something trickle down his right cheek like a tear. It was blood. He stroked the wetness and looked at the blood on his middle fingertip, then realised the old hag had not been a dream, and he felt the end of the bed move as if someone was there. In the semi-darkness he saw her there on all fours. Her bare breasts hung, triangular and deflated, and even in the poor light he could see the saliva drooling from the open mouth onto the bed cover.

Des ducked under the thin blanket and screamed for his mother and father as the ghoul pounced. She shrieked with laughter as she tore into the blankets with her strong appalling muck-encrusted nails, tearing the fabric apart and inflicting wounds on Des's arms, legs and torso. The attack seemed to go on for ever, until the light came on in the bedroom, and Des felt the blanket being torn off his bed. His mother stood there with a look of sheer horror on her face as she saw her naked son laying there, his face and body lacerated and scored with red glistening scratches. 'Des, what – oh my God!' she muttered, and then the teenager's father came into the room.

No one could explain what had happened. Des's father said he had heard of foxes getting into houses and inflicting injuries to children, but such a fox would have to negotiate the stairs to reach Des's bedroom, after gaining entry into the house. Des's mother wondered if some Bob cat – a wild feral feline – had climbed in through his open window, but quickly dismissed the idea. In the end, she thought a maniac had shinned up the drainpipe outside to get into the bedroom to attack her son, perhaps with some knife.

But Des felt the old hag had visited him because he had made love in the cemetery, and he recalled the words she said about her being a 'virgin too' – *just like Debbie*. When he met Debbie a few weeks later, he told her about the ghoulish woman who had attacked him in his bed, and with great delight, Debbie told him what she had seen in the cemetery that night as Des had his wicked way with her, and Des went cold. Debbie then said she was now seeing someone and that he was much better at lovemaking than Des. Des refused to sleep in his room after that night, and slept in a spare room surrounded by Holy water, crucifixes and a large old leather-bound edition of the Bible. This seemed to do the trick, and he had no further encounters with the old hag.

Des's story soon did the rounds in Woolton, and came to the attention of a local investigator into the paranormal named John Finnegan, and this researcher asked Des to show him the gravestone he had made love to Debbie on. Des was not sure what gravestone it was but narrowed it down to a row of three such gravestones. John researched the names on the gravestones and made a chilling discovery: Debbie, having a very unusual surname, was undoubtedly a descendant of a woman who had been buried in one of the graves that Des had pointed out. The woman with the same unique surname as Debbie had died late in her life, and had never married. The sisters of this woman had all married and had children, but this particular woman had died a spinster. When Des discovered this, he put a huge bunch of flowers on the grave and said a prayer. In his mind he asked the ancestor of Debbie to forgive him, and after that day, Des also began to attend church each Sunday.

SAY WHO YOU ARE

The Liverpool district of Fazakerley has the distinction of being a unique place-name in the country; there is nowhere else with that name, and the meaning and origin of the name Fazakerley remains a mystery. The ancient Fazakerleigh family took their name from the district, and speculated that the name might be Anglo-Saxon, but this doesn't seem to be the case. Fazakerley is not only a name of mysterious origins, the whole district is one of the most haunted on Merseyside, and the following story is just one tale about the supernatural goings-on in the area.

Just a stone's throw from University Hospital Aintree, there is a certain Fazakerley factory which has been going through thick and thin, through boom-time and recession, and of course, most factories have a security guard or two, and this factory had two men who we shall call Greg and Nick, both in their thirties. Nick had been a guard at the factory for almost four years in 2002, and had quite a chequered work history. He had worked in a casino in Turkey, then left to be a farm labourer in the south of France for a few years before gradually gravitating back to his home town of Liverpool, where he found work as a doorman on a city centre club. After sustaining a few violent attacks by coked-up club goers, Nick opted for a job at the Fazakerley factory, and found the nocturnal hours rather conducive and beneficial to his state of mind. Nick would read books he'd wanted to study for years, and sometimes listened to Classic FM between doing rounds. Greg was a rather brash, in-your-face type of character, the type who could cadge money from a bailiff, but it was understood that he would never try to invade Nick's bubble of personal space or try and order him about – even though Greg was a few years older than his colleague and had been a guard for fifteen years.

It was a Friday morning at 2.30am, and Greg did his rounds at the factory, and when he came back to the office, which was basically just a glorified garden hut at the end of a huge yard dotted with crates, he saw Nick doing *The Times* crossword. 'God, it's a bit King Billy out there.'

'Bit what?' Nick asked without looking up from the newspaper.

'Chilly,' moaned Greg, 'Chilli beans.'

'Just made some coffee for you,' Nick said, and he nodded to the cluttered desk then tapped the top of the Parker pen against his bottom lip as he dwelt on a cryptic clue to a twelve-letter word with three U's in it.

'Ta,' replied Greg, and he grabbed the large black ceramic mug of hot Nescafé, took a sip, then located an unopened packet of custard creams. Greg dunked one biscuit after another and slurped the coffee, and Nick finally said, 'Can you stop that?'

'Stop what?' Greg asked, perplexed.

'Slurping,' Nick told him, and shook his head as he

filled in the wrong squares in the crossword.

'Is it okay if I breathe?' asked Greg, 'Or does that get on your nerves as well?'

'Listen!' Nick looked beyond the panes of the office out into the blackness of the yard.

'What?' Greg followed his gaze, and looked out into the yard.

'Can you hear it?' Nick put the newspaper and ballpoint down and went to the door. He opened the door, admitting an icy breeze, then looked out into the blackness. 'Here!' he said to Greg, 'Listen!'

Greg came to the doorway slurping the coffee.

'Sssh!' Nick put his index finger to his lips and then he said, 'Can you hear it?'

The two guards stood in silence, and sure enough, in the midst of the faint howling of the wind around the crates and high walls of the yard, they both heard someone singing.

'I can hear it,' Greg said, and yawned. 'It's a radio somewhere in the distance.'

Nick shook his head twice. 'It's not a radio, that's someone singing, but where's it coming from?'

'Sound travels further of a night,' Greg explained, and his eyes darted about because the singing voice sounded eerie.

'What is that song?' Nick tilted his head so his good ear – his right one – faced the end of the yard.

Greg squinted as the wind buffeted his eyes. 'Seal,' he suddenly said.

Nick's eyes became animated and he gave a slight smile. 'Yeah, that's it; that song by Seal. *Kiss From a Rose.*'

'*I've been kissed by a rose on the grey* – ' Greg tried to sing

10

a line from the song.

But the singer was not singing those words, and as the two guards listened in the dead of night, the unknown vocalist suddenly belted out a strange version which went: '*I've been kissed by a rose on the grave…*'

'He's making his own words up now,' said Nick, with a very nervous laugh, because he thought the mention of a grave at that time in the morning was eerie. And the singing stopped dead. Just the wind was moaning now, and suddenly a huge moth flew into the office and hit Greg in his left eye – and the guard had a terrible phobia about moths, especially overgrown velvet-winged ones with golden bug eyes. Greg let out a yelp and tried to hurl the hot coffee over the fluttering stout-bodied insect as it circled his head, but the coffee just missed Nick and went out into the yard. Nick picked up his copy of *The Times* and batted the moth out into the night and slammed the door. Greg shuddered and when he rolled up his sleeves and went to the sink to wash his eye, Nick could see the goosepimples raised on his forearms.

At a quarter to four, another sinister sound was heard by the two guards; the sound of a spade, digging into stony soil. This time, Greg heard the unusual sound first and drew Nick's attention to it. They opened the office door. Nick was due to do his rounds in ten minutes and seemed quite nervous. He listened in the yard, and once again, he heard that song again with its twisted lyrics, and the sound of a shovel digging away, spading earth. Nick swore under his breath, then went to a cupboard and got a new battery out and fitted it to his torch. He also located his old

MagLite torch in his locker and was glad to see it still had some power in it.

'I've never seen you like this,' Greg said to his colleague. 'You look all on edge. It's just sound travelling of a night, echoing from miles away.'

Nick didn't even reply. He put on his coat, looked at the screen of his mobile to see if the battery was in need of charging, and as usual its indicator showed it only had 14% power left. The walkie-talkie was switched on, and Nick whistled a random tune to take his mind off the situation.

'Do you want me to go round with you?' Greg asked.

'Nah, it's okay, I'm not that scared mate,' Nick told him and smirked, but Greg could tell his friend was very unnerved by the strange sounds they'd both heard.

'There it is again;' Greg said, holding his hand out with his index finger pointing upwards. 'Be a laugh if someone was tunneling in here.'

'Wouldn't be a laugh,' Nick said, and he went to the door. 'See you in a mo.' He left the office and walked down the long dark yard and into the labyrinth of walkways between towering stacks of crates, portakabins and pallets. At the very bottom of the yard, he turned left, with both torches shining the way, and here he could hear that creepy singer quite clearly, and Nick could literally feel the hairs on the back of his neck rising up.

'I've been kissed by a rose on a grave...'

Then he saw the singer. He wasn't sure if it was a he or a she, because all he could see was a shadowy figure, and it was either the silhouette of a nun or someone

12

wearing a hood and the cowl of a monk, but they were close up to a wire-link fence, and even when the two torchbeams were aimed at the figure, Nick could see nothing but blackness in it, as if he was shining a torch down a bottomless pit. He was so afraid of the weird "thing" he could hardly breathe, and when Greg's voice came across the walkie-talkie, joking about ghosts, Nick couldn't even reply. The guard turned on his heels and he walked back the way he had come with the sounds of his heart pounding through his carotid artery. When he got back to the office, he said to Greg, 'There's something all in black by the fence.'

'What?' Greg could see that all the colour had drained from his colleague's face.

Nick realised he still had the torches on and he switched them off as he gave a garbled reply. 'There's a thing, all in black, like a monk or a nun, in a long robe, and it's just all shadow, by the wire fence.'

'Shurrup!' Greg said, thinking – or hoping – that Nick was pulling his leg.

'I swear on our Michael's life,' Nick said, referring to Michael, his 3-year-old son, 'there's a ghost out there. It was singing, and I could hear that sound of a spade digging dead clear when I got by it.'

Greg suddenly turned towards the window panes of the office and swore loudly.

Nick turned to see what he was swearing at – and there it was – the thing he had seen by the fence a few minutes ago. It was moving out of the darkness up the yard, only visible because it contrasted against a block of light-coloured crates. The thing moved as if it was on wheels, slowly but steadily towards the office. 'That's it!' Nick said, and he looked at Greg's face. He

13

had never seen his friend as scared in all the time he'd worked with him. Greg had tackled an intruder at the factory once in the bravest manner, even though the prowler had a knife, but this was different – it was something unearthly – and that terrified the guards.

The creature of shadow halted about thirty feet away. Greg found his high-powered lantern torch and shone it at the figure, lighting up the yard, and Nick shone his two torches, but still the guards could see not one bit of detail within the entity. It was pure blackness, as dark as the interior of a coffin.

Greg suddenly picked up his mobile and started to dial.

'Who you calling?' Nick asked.

Greg never answered. He looked back through the windows at that uncanny visitor, then to the faint tinny voice on his phone he said, 'Police, police!'

Nick wasn't keen on him phoning the law because he thought they'd laugh at the idea of two guards reporting a ghost, but Greg didn't mention the ominous figure.

'Hiya. I'm a guard at a factory in Fazakerley, and there's a dangerous intruder on the premises – could you send someone round please a-s-a-p?' Greg told the woman on the police switchboard, and gave the name of the factory, his own name and the postcode of the premises.

Less than ten minutes later – and those minutes felt like hours to the guards – a blue flashing light could be seen down by the gates of the factory – but to unlock those gates, the guards would have to pass the apparition, which was still standing in the same spot, radiating pure menace. Greg estimated that it looked as if it was about five-feet-seven in height.

'We'll have to just run past it,' Nick said, opening the door of the office, looking down the yard with the high-beam of the lantern sweeping left to right across the ghostly figure.

'Okay, mate,' said Greg, and the two guards ran as fast as their legs could carry them, and straight away, the black figure moved slowly towards the left – intending to intercept them, and Nick flew past it first, and then Greg passed within inches of the thing, and he thought he heard a voice cry out from it. As Nick panicked and inserted the key into the gate's padlock the wrong way round, the shadowy creature began to move down the yard towards them faster and faster.

'Hurry up!' shouted Greg, ready to climb the gate to get away from the entity if need be. Two policemen were getting out of their car about twenty feet away outside. At last the padlock clicked and Nick and Greg yanked at the gate and pulled it open. They ran to the police and said, 'Look at this thing!'

The policemen trotted to the gates and looked into the yard.

And they saw nothing.

One of the policemen shone his own torch into the yard, and then he went into the yard and said, 'Where is he?'

Another police car turned up, and soon the yard was occupied by four policemen plus Greg and Nick, and when the guards described what had happened, the policemen just looked at one another without saying a word, until finally, one of the officers said, 'It's probably been a hoody. With this bad lighting here you'd probably think you'd seen all kinds. You should have a floodlight down here and maybe get the bosses to stick a camera up near the front of the place.'

The police then departed, and not long afterwards, the milky pale light of dawn infiltrated the skies over the Fazakerley factory. The guards went home at 7am, and that morning at 10.15 am, Greg left his bed to go the toilet, and his wife heard him scream, then shout out: "Say who you are!" and this was followed a loud thud. She called out to her husband, then sensed something was wrong. She got up, hurried along the landing, and found Greg on the floor outside the toilet. He was laying there on his back with his hands clutching his chest – with his eyes wide open. He looked as if he was dead, but his wife called an ambulance, and she saw the ambulance men look at one another after they tried to resuscitate him. One of the ambulance men quickly put his index and middle fingers over Greg's eyes to close the lids. Greg's wife then let out a terrible scream. Her husband had died of a heart attack. He'd smoked forty cigarettes a day until a few month back when he took to wearing nicotine patches.

Nick never mentioned the sinister entity which had stalked him and Greg at the factory on the very morning his friend had died, and when Greg's wife said she had heard her husband cry out: "Say who you are!" before he collapsed, Nick felt a shiver run down his spine. He wondered if that thing had paid a visit to Greg – and had called to 'collect' him, knowing that his time was near perhaps.

Nick went to the funeral, and after the service, they played a recording of a song that meant a lot to Greg's wife, for she had started dating Greg in the summer of

1995 when the song was in the charts. It was Seal's *Kiss From a Rose*. Nick went stone cold inside when he heard this song, and recalled the occasion when he and his late friend had heard that song being sung by that entity all hours in the morning. And Nick also recalled the sound of a spade digging. Did it symbolise the grave that would be dug for Greg? Greg had often talked about death in the wee small hours, and he had always told Nick that he wanted to be cremated if he "bit the big one" – a phrase he often used about meeting his end. And yet Greg's wife had decided he would be buried for some reason.

Nick saw all of the roses on Greg's coffin before it was lowered into the ground forever, and immediately thought about the eerie line of that song sung by God knows what: '*kissed by a rose on a grave...*'

Understandably, Nick later handed in his notice at the factory in Fazakerley, but I have heard that the reaper-like figure is still occasionally seen in the vicinity, and in 2009, I received an email from a man who reported seeing a black hooded silhouette gliding down Sandy Lane, which is not a thousand miles away from that factory.

SOMEWHERE ONLY WE KNOW

Have you ever suddenly recollected some unusual occurrence from your childhood, then thought, did that really happen or was it something I dreamt or some memory of an incident that happened on a television programme? I recall being visited by what I can only describe as a shadow-being when I was about two. It would sneakily slide out of the wall of my bedroom, almost immediately after my mum or dad had tucked me in and I vaguely remember pressing the tip of a butter-knife against my chest after some information was imparted to me from the silhouetted being which convinced me that I'd be okay if I died 'and went back'. My mother stopped me from doing any self-injury – or even worse – just in time. I think the shadow stopped visiting me some time after that. I have had the opportunity through my unusual work to talk to many people from all walks of life about the paranormal, and a lot of folk have told me of similar recollections of some very odd things which have lain buried in their memories for years. What follows is based on the recollections of two men who are, at the time of writing, what we imprecisely term as middle-aged. See what you think.

In the summer school holidays of 1972, two ten-year-olds from Bootle named Davy and Barry, were invited to go and stay with Barry's old Auntie Agnes, or "Aggie" as Barry called her, at a crumbling old house on Cambridge Street, just around the corner from the Oxford Street Maternity Hospital (now converted to house a suite of apartments known as Lennon Studios, as John Lennon was born there when it was a maternity hospital, as I was myself). Davy was from a rather clean home, and was quite shocked when he saw his first cockroach at Aggie's house, crawling on the floor of the kitchen, and he felt sick when Aggie halted in the middle of frying some sausages to stoop down and pick up the roach before tossing it out the kitchen window. When Davy told Barry about the disgusting way his auntie had continued cooking without washing her hands, Barry said, 'Don't start calling Auntie Aggie or you'll go home!'

Aggie was a widow who lived with a much older brother named Alf, who immediately struck Davy as a rather enigmatic man who knew something. 'Knows what?' Barry asked his best friend, but Davy just said, 'I don't know, it's hard to explain. I just think *he knows things.*'

And that teatime, Aggie and Alf and some jangling next-door neighbour named Queenie sat with the boys around the big table, eating fish, chips and peas, when Barry said, 'Hey Uncle Alf, Davy says you know things.'

Davy's face went pinkish-red, and he said to Barry, 'No I didn't, you.'

Barry grinned wickedly and said: 'You did, you said he knows things and you've gone all red, ha!'

'Stop talking at the table and eat your tea, Barry!' Aggie told her nephew sternly.

Barry licked the tip of his index finger and then

placed it on his own face as he made a hissing sound as he looked at red-faced Davy. 'You've gone like a tomato!' he told Davy.

'Hey, Barry, be quiet and leave Davy to eat his tea!' said Alf, and he smiled at Davy and winked.

After tea, Barry and Davy left the house to go gallivanting. They played with a few children of an Irish family called the Ryans who lived locally, then went to explore the rocks outside the crypt section of the Roman Catholic Cathedral, which lay just a few hundred yards away. Around 10pm, as twilight fell, Queenie – Aggie's neighbour – could be heard, shouting for Barry in a yodelling type of voice. The two boys went to Aggie's house, and they were treated to cordial, jelly and cream, and then told to go upstairs to share the bath. The boys sat in the bath with their underpants on, flicking water and hurtling Crazy Bath Foam at one another, until Aggie came in and told them to dry and go to bed immediately. The boys did, and had to share an old double bed in a room with mildewed wallpaper and old fashioned furniture. Just after midnight, Davy and Barry were still awake, and telling one another stories, when Barry decided to go and root about in an ancient-looking mahogany cabinet. The two doors of the cabinet were adorned with what antique dealers would describe as foliate fretwork panels. Barry knelt down, opened the doors, and looked inside at the bundles of old yellowed newspapers. He shifted the bundles out the way and saw another door set into the back of the cabinet, and so he turned the handle to reveal a small flight of steps that went down into the darkness. 'Wow! Look at this Davy! It's a secret passage.'

Davy got out the bed and went to see what his friend was talking about. When he saw the steps, he had a bad feeling about the discovery, and advised Barry to close the inner door and put the newspapers back in place, but Barry was already crawling into the cabinet towards the stairs. 'Don't Barry, you might fall down a hole down there!' Davy warned, and then he saw an old candle in a holder on the cabinet, and he told Barry they should light it to show the way. Barry came back out the cabinet, and after he and Davy went downstairs to the kitchen to light the candle from the pilot light on the cooker, they returned to the bedroom and went inside the cabinet. Each boy was barefooted and Barry only wore his underpants, whereas Davy had old baggy pyjama bottoms on. They descended the ice-cold sandstone steps and came to a number of doors of different shapes and sizes. Barry carefully opened the first door, which was only about one-and-a-half feet high and two feet across, and the boys found themselves looking down at someone's parlour. An old woman was asleep in a high-backed chair in front of a fire, and her cat on the fireside rug was gazing up at the boys, who began to giggle. 'Whose house is this?' Barry asked and sniggered. The old woman started to snore, and Barry shouted: 'Hey love!' startling the poor elderly thing. And then he slammed the door shut and went to look at the other doors. 'We should go back now,' Davy said nervously, his hand cupped around the candle, guarding it from draughts.

'No, this is great!' said Barry excitedly, and he pulled open a bigger door which was about three feet square to reveal a tunnel. The boys crawled down the tunnel and saw light streaming from a square on the wall which turned out to be a ventilator grille. They looked through it and saw a woman, aged about forty or less, sitting in the bath, reading a book. Davy was terrified of being caught as some Peeping Tom, and tried to back away on his knees, but Barry put his fingers to his mouth and whistled loudly through the ventilator, startling the woman. The boys heard an almighty splash and the woman shouted: 'Who's that? Who's there?'

The boys returned to the steps which led to the cabinet and fled up them to the bedroom. The inner cabinet door was slammed shut and the bundles of newspapers were put back in place. The boys laughed about their bizarre discovery until well after 1am, and then they both fell fast asleep. The next morning when they awoke they agreed not to mention the "secret passage" and the doors and tunnels to anyone. As the boys sat at the table for a breakfast of boiled eggs and fried bread (made with lard), Aggie said to them: 'What was that racket about in your room last night eh?'

'Wasn't us auntie,' Barry replied with a slight telltale grin on his face, 'we went to sleep straight away.'

'Well the bugs must have clogs on in this house then,' Aggie replied in a sarcastic tone.

That evening at 7pm, Alf gave Barry and Davy a drawing pad each and some felt tip pens. The boys said they were going upstairs to their room to draw a comic strip, but this was just a pretence to go up to the bedroom to explore the tunnels leading from the cabinet again. On this occasion, the boys travelled some distance down a tunnel until they came to a normal-sized door, and when they opened it, they found themselves in a room lined with expensive-looking leather-bound books. The carpet was dark red, and from the ceiling hung an elaborate crystal chandelier. The boys entered the room and went to another door, and from behind this door came the most peculiar-sounding music they had ever heard. It sounded just like a piano playing in reverse. 'Let's go, quick, come on Barry,' Davy whispered as he watched his over-intrepid friend reach for the handle of the door.

Barry turned the handle, and there was a man sitting at a grand piano dressed in a black coat with hammer tails. His face looked very strange. He had a long aquiline nose, bulging eyes with dark circles around them, and protuberant teeth which stuck out as he grinned. He was hammering the keys with his hands and making an unholy racket. All of a sudden, the odd-looking pianist happened to glance over at the door, and he spotted Barry looking in on him. He stopped playing, got to his feet, and ran towards the boys. Davy was out of the library like a shot, and soon scrambling along the tunnel to the flight of steps. He heard Barry's screams echoing behind him and a man's gruff voice. Davy fell out of the cabinet and ran downstairs to tell Aggie what had happened but he collided with Barry's Uncle Alf on the bottom step.

'Hey! What's all this?' Alf said, leaning against the newel post with his hands clutching his stomach where Davy's head had winded him.

Davy rattled off an almost incoherent attempt at explaining what had just occurred and Alf ran up to the room, followed by Davy, who took slow, reluctant steps to reach the bedroom. When Davy entered the bedroom it was empty, and the cabinet door was wide open. He could hear Alf arguing with someone and the sound of Barry crying his eyes out. A few minute later, Barry came running out the cabinet with his shirt torn and his face was slicked with tears. He ran past Davy and out of the room. Then Alf came out of the cabinet on all fours with a cut lip, and without a word of explanation, he closed the inner door of the mahogany cabinet, then put all of the newspaper bundles back in place in the cabinet, and slammed the two doors shut with quite a temper. He then pushed Davy out of the room and said, 'You're going home!'

Down in the kitchen there was a blazing row between Alf and Aggie.

'They're nothing but trouble and they're going home tonight, so help me God!' bawled Alf.

'Over my dead body they are!' countered Aggie, and she hugged a sobbing Barry and said to him, 'Stop crying pet, you and your friend are staying here! Take no notice of your uncle!'

Alf stormed off out of the house but later returned and remained sulkily silent for an hour. After supper, the boys went up to their room and Davy asked Barry what had happened when the man who had been playing the piano had caught him. Barry said he had tried to bite his arms and legs but he had punched him and hit him with a chair, and Barry had hidden under the piano at one point, but then Uncle Alf came upon the scene and the two men started to punch one another. As Barry was telling an engrossed Davy about the incident, three raps sounded on the double doors of the mahogany cabinet, and Davy let out a yelp and sat up in bed, gazing at the source of the sounds. The doors opened, and a boy of around 7 or 8 years of age came out. He wore a dirty pale shirt with ho collar and a pair of trousers that ended just under the knees. He looked at Davy and Barry from the interior of the cabinet, and then he and Barry posed the same question simultaneously: 'Who are you?' they said.

'You first,' said Barry, and he got out the bed and stooped down to look past the stranger in case that man was around, but the boy was alone.

'I'm Billy,' said the boy.

'Where are you from, Billy?' Barry asked him.

'From in there,' Billy said, pointing into the dark passageway behind him.

'Do you know who that man is who plays the piano?' Barry queried.

'Mr Wroot plays the piano,' said Billy, 'and he's trying to kill me.'

'Trying to kill you?' said Davy, feeling very unsafe all of a sudden.

'You'd better come in here then,' Barry advised Billy, and the young boy came into the bedroom and Barry went into one of the drawers in an dresser and found a pair of old brown nylon stockings that must have belonged to Aggie. He used one of the stockings to tie together the door handles of the mahogany cabinet – just in case Mr Wroot tried to get into the room.

'Do you live next door?' Davy asked Billy, and the boy returned a puzzled expression.

'No, in there,' Billy nodded towards the cabinet.

'Yeah, we know you came out there, but where's your house?' Barry asked the barefooted boy. 'Is it in this street? Who made all those secret passages?'

Billy shrugged. 'I don't know. I live in there; that's where I live.'

'You can stay here if you like,' Barry told Billy, and pointed to the bed.

Billy nodded enthusiastically and soon the three boys were sitting on the bed, and Davy was showing Billy how to draw with the felt tips. Billy seemed fascinated by the pens, and he also seemed mesmerised by the bedside lamp, and burnt his fingers twice touching the bulb. At half-past one in the morning, there came a gentle tapping on the doors of the cabinet, and all three boys awoke with a start. Billy was sleeping at the bottom of the bed, top-tail fashion to the other two. He sat up with a look of fear on his face and gazed at the cabinet doors, which were bulging now as someone behind them pushed against them. Then a smarmy-sounding voice said, 'Billy? Are you in there?'

Billy recoiled with a yelping sound and backed away from the cabinet until he was seated between Davy and Barry.

'Is that him?' Davy whispered to Billy. 'Is that Mr Wroot?'

Billy was so afraid of the man behind those doors, he never heard Davy's question, and Barry, seeing how terrified the boy was, led him out of the room. All three went downstairs to the kitchen, where Barry armed himself with a huge carving knife, and Davy grabbed the heavy cast iron poker out the fire grate.

Billy started to sniffle, and tears rolled from his eye as he trembled.

'Don't be scared, Billy, he won't get you I promise,' Barry tried to reassure his new friend. 'Davy and I will kill him.'

All of a sudden, there came the sound of movement behind the walls of the kitchen, and the boys froze as they realised that Wroot was using some hidden passages leading to the kitchen. They heard loose powdery plaster behind the damp wallpaper trickling down, and it sounded like sand falling on the skin of a drum.

'He's here!' little Billy sobbed, looking about at the walls.

Davy and Barry were speechless with fear, and they were confused. How could this man move around the house behind the walls?

A deadly silence descended, and the only sound to be heard came from cats hissing and screeching at one another in the distance somewhere. The door of the cupboard under the sink flew open and that man Davy had seen playing the piano in that secret room – the one who had captured Barry and tried to bite him on the arms and legs – reached out with his arm and his large hand grabbed Billy by his left ankle. Before Billy could even cry out, Mr Wroot yanked at Billy's ankle and the boy fell forwards and cracked his forehead on the hard tiles as he fell face down. Billy was knocked clean out by the fall, and Wroot laughed as his other arm reached out and seized the other ankle of the unconscious boy.

'No!' Barry screamed and he wanted to stab Wroot but was too afraid to even try, and he and Davy watched in horror as the little boy was dragged into the cupboard under the sink. Wroot closed the door behind him, and then Barry and Davy heard the maniac move behind the wall as he returned to what was presumably his lair.

The door of the kitchen burst open, and Davy let out a scream. Aggie came in wearing a hairnet and nightgown, followed by her brother Alf, who was wearing red and white striped pyjamas. 'What's all this noise, eh?' Aggie yelled. Her eyes were all bloodshot.

Barry opened the door of the cupboard under the sink and pointed to the cylinder of Vim and bottles of disinfectant and Windolene laying on their sides in disarray. He spouted out the story of Billy coming out of the cabinet on the run from a Mr Wroot, and Alf stopped the boy's conversation stone dead by shouting at him to: 'Stop!'

'Come on you two, get to bed!' Aggie hollered at Barry and Davy. 'And put that knife back in the drawer,' she said to Barry, then took the poker from Davy's grip.

The boys begrudgingly went up the stairs to their room, and Davy whispered to Barry: 'I want to go home in the morning, I've had enough of this.'

'We can't go home and leave Billy with that man,' Barry told his friend, recalling the way he had tried to sink his teeth into him when he captured him in that room.

'I don't care about Billy, I hate this house!' Davy confessed.

At a quarter to four in the morning, the boys awoke from their very light sleep, and heard distant screams. Alf knocked on the wall and shouted, 'I won't warn you two again!'

'It isn't us!' Barry shouted to the wall.

'Get to sleep now!' Alf cried out.

'Those screams,' Davy whispered, and his eyes seemed full of terror now; 'they sounded like Billy's screams.'

'We've got to help him,' said Barry, and he said this

three times to Davy and elicited three shakes of Davy's head. 'Well I'm helping him!' Barry said, and he sneaked out of the room again and took ages tiptoeing down the stairs, avoiding the creaky steps, until he reached the kitchen, where he looked for some candles. The boy was terrified because he imagined Wroot would emerge from some cupboard and seize him in a flash, but he managed to obtain two candles and some matches before sneaking at a snail's pace back up the stairs to the room. He undid the stockings on the door handles of the mysterious mahogany cabinet and removed the newspaper bundles. The silver handle on the inner door was turned and the two boys bravely went in search of the little lad Billy.

They tried the door that led to that library, where the man they assumed to be Wroot attacked Barry, but it was locked. The duo tried another door, and looked in on the darkened parlour where they had seen the old woman dozing in the high-backed chair, but there was no sign of the woman, and the chiming of the clock on the mantelpiece striking the hour of four startled the boys. On the way back down the passage, Davy noticed a peephole in the door to the locked library, but it was too far up the door for either boy to look through, so Barry bent over and rested his hands on his kneecaps as Barry stood on his back, using him as a human step. Barry steadied himself, and looked through the hole. What he saw was so horrific, so shocking, he fell from Davy's back and ran off, unable to speak or cry out, leaving his candle in the holder on the floor.

'Wait for me!' Davy shouted after his terror-stricken friend, and he had the good sense to pick Barry's candle up off the floor before he ran after him. When Davy reached the bedroom he found it empty, and he heard a commotion downstairs. When Davy went down to the hallway he came upon Barry in tears, and he was illuminated by the light shining through the doorway of the parlour. In the doorframe, silhouetted, stood the boy's Uncle Alf with his coat on over his pyjamas, and he roared: 'Enough is enough! As soon as it's light, you two pests are out of here and I don't care what Aggie says this time! You could have caused a fire going round the place with candles all hours in the morning! Now get back to bed!'

And he lurched towards Davy, who backed away in fright. Alf snatched the candles from each of the boy's hands and told him to get to bed. 'Pronto! Go on! Get up there!' he barked.

Up in the room, Davy asked his friend what he had seen through the peephole in the door, and as Barry tied not one, but three stockings around the handles of the mahogany cabinet, he started to sniffle again.

'What did you see?' Davy pressed his friend, but soon wished he hadn't asked him.

Barry knelt there after tying the third knot of the stockings, and said: 'That weird man was sitting at a table, and he had one of those things tied round his neck under his chin...'

'You mean a napkin?' Davy asked.

Barry nodded, and tears came streaming down his face. 'And there was all blood on it, and he had a knife and a fork and on the plate was Billy's head...' Barry started to cry again, and he buried his face in his hands.

Uncle Alf started knocking on the wall, and faint

cries of: '*Shut up and get to sleep!*' could be heard through the thin wall.

'What? Billy's *head?*' Davy recoiled in horror. A nervous twitch played in his cheek.

'He'd cut his nose off and he had it on the end of the fork, and Billy's eyes were gone as well…' Barry's voice trailed off into a whisper.

'Why would he do that to Billy?' Davy began to shake, and he looked at the cabinet then backed away and sat on the end of the bed – the end furthest from that portal to a very strange world of tunnels, doors and strange characters.

'Listen!' Barry suddenly said, and his eyes widened and turned right towards the bound doors of the cabinet.

Davy tried to stop breathing so he could listen more intently. Yes, he could hear it too. That peculiar piano and its odd-sounding music was playing faintly. Wroot was tinkling the ivories.

'Maybe we should leave,' Barry suggested, and Davy nodded enthusiastically.

The faint piano music stopped.

'How can we get home though?' Barry pondered, 'Bootle's miles away.'

'We should go to the police and tell them about Billy, and they'll lock that man up,' Davy said, still shaking from that mental image of Billy's severed head on the plate with no eyes and the bloody napkin and carved-off nose.

There came faint footsteps on the stairs outside. Barry and Davy looked at one another – two pallid faces barely visible in the bedroom, where the only light came from an old sodium light burning outside in

31

the entry. 'Who's that?' Davy whispered.

The footfalls halted outside the bedroom door. The floor creaked outside that door.

Davy went to the dresser and picked up an old vase, ready to throw it at whoever was outside. He somehow knew – somehow sensed – that it wasn't Barry's Uncle Alf out there.

'Who is it?' Barry said to the door.

The doorhandle squeaked as it slowly turned, and the door opened a few inches.

'Uncle Alf, is that you?' Barry asked, and began to blink rapidly.

No reply came.

'Uncle Alf?' Barry asked once more.

'Get to bed!' came Uncle Alf's faint voice from next door. So, if Alf was in bed, who was coming into the room?

The door opened steadily and Barry and Davy backed away to the other side of the room, near to the window.

That man – the cannibal who had been seen eating Billy's head on the plate, looked around the door and even in the darkened room, the whites of the maniac's eyes seemed almost to fluoresce. He smiled, and ran the tip of his tongue around his lips.

'Uncle Alf!' Barry screamed at the top of his voice, 'Help! Murder! Murder!'

The man who the late Billy had referred to as Mr Wroot, gritted his teeth at the yelling boy and gave a threatening cut-throat gesture by drawing his index finger-tip across his fat adam's apple.

All of a sudden, Davy hurled the vase at Wroot and it smashed squarely in his face, and the fragments of the vase scattered everywhere. Wroot let out a loud grunt, and blood blossomed from a large cut on his forehead, just over his right eyebrow. He lunged across the room at the boys, and Barry dived onto the floor and scrambled under the bed, and a second later, Davy did the same. They then bolted like rats from under the bed and ran to the doorway with Wroot a few feet behind them. The boys ran downstairs and across the hall and tried to get out via the front door, but the old rusty bolt on the bottom of the door wouldn't budge. Davy slammed the vestibule door behind him and sandwiched between that door and the front door, he and Barry tried to yank back the bolt. Davy looked at the frosted glass of the vestibule door, expecting to see Wroot's evil sinister face peer through that pale glass at any moment.

'Help us open it, come on!' Barry groaned, putting all his might into shifting the damned bolt.

There came a steady thump on the carpeted stairs.

'He's coming!' cried Davy, and he tried with every ounce of his strength to pull that bolt back, and it seemed to be slowly moving.

Barry looked back at the vestibule door and saw a shadow on the pale glass pane of the vestibule door. That door opened.

Both boys cried out in discordant skew-whiff harmony.

But thankfully it was only Alf, and although he was furious at the screams, he had obviously seen Wroot's blood from the injury he had sustained from the vase. 'Who's hurt himself?' he said, and he reached to the light switch and clicked it on. A small sixty-watt tungsten bulb burned its yellow light above.

The boys gave their account of the cannibal at large in the house and when Davy said, 'The man who gave you a fat lip is a cannibal Alf,' Alf became enraged and said to him, 'You will never, and I mean, never, set foot in here again! Pack your things you little runt!' This abreaction to Davy's comments was incomprehensible to the lads.

And that morning, despite Aggie's loud and colourful protestations, Alf marched the boys to the house of a neighbour who had a car, and he got this neighbour to drive the boys to their homes in Bootle.

Barry's parent simply couldn't believe the far-fetched story of secret passages in Aggie's house and the cannibal who ate the little boy. Davy's parents just laughed and said he had a very vivid imagination when he gave his account of the strange and terrifying goings-on at the house on Cambridge Street, and gradually, over the years, the boys drifted apart, and whenever they told anyone about the goings on at that house in the summer of 1972, their accounts were met with scepticism, and who could really blame anyone for disbelieving such a incredible and fanciful story? A few years ago, Barry, now a father of four in his forties, wrote to me to tell me about the extraordinary incidents from all those years ago, and he and I tracked down Davy, who was working in a call centre in Kent. Barry wasn't very computer savant, and never even bothered with email, and he wasn't aware that Davy had a Facebook page. When we caught up with Davy, he confirmed the story and the two men now stay in touch. I talked to a psychologist, and he told me that he knows of many people who suddenly recall very bizarre incidents from their childhood which they often dismiss as a faulty memory or a memory of a dream which has been filed away as a real occurrence. I mentioned this case briefly on a radio programme and did not mention Cambridge Street, and a woman later contacted me with a strange story which seemed to add some credence to Barry and Davy's frightening experiences. The woman, in her fifties, named Tina, who lived on Crown Street, Edge Hill, in the 1970s, said she used to be friends with a girl named Maureen who lived on Cambridge Street in the early 1970s, and she had heard the story of the secret passages under houses on Cambridge Street and once heard Maureen's grandmother talk about 'a dirty old man' named Wroot who was a well-known landlord of several house in the area around Cambridge Street. Wroot – and Maureen's grandmother would always emphasise the silent 'W' at the beginning of the man's surname, was said to lurk in the cellars of his house and stand under the aria grids so he could look up women's skirts. The other depraved things this man got up to could not be put into print in a book such as this or I would risk prosecution under the Obscene Publications Act. I asked Tina if Maureen's grandmother ever mentioned Wroot playing a piano, but Tina said she couldn't recall any mention of this. The period when this man was carrying out his disgusting activities would probably be around Edwardian times, and this leads me to believe that Barry and Davy, and Uncle Alf, must have been dealing with ghosts, so this makes me to wonder if the secret passages were also ethereal, or whether a timeslip situation was the cause of the nightmarish phenomena.

BURIED ALIVE

One unusually sunny Sunday afternoon in the October of 1892, a middle-aged joiner named Bill Eckersley left his house at 51 Chester Road in Tuebrook and headed for nearby Newsham Park, where he liked to walk on Sundays after his usual roast dinner. On this afternoon, he saw a rather sinister-looking black four-wheeled carriage, known as a "growler" coming along West Derby Road from the east. Eckersley waited for the carriage to pass, but instead it pulled up at the kerb six feet in front of him and two tall men in bowlers alighted from it and hurried towards the joiner, who was naturally startled by their quick approach.

'Mr Eckersley sir,' said one of the tall pair. He seemed to be about thirty and sported a large black walrus moustache. Before the carpenter could utter a word the men came to each side of him and seized him by his arms. Eckersley was bundled into the carriage where a third man pointed a pistol at the joiner. The man with the walrus moustache then produced a bag made of some dark canvas-like material and put it over Eckersley's head. The joiner sat there in an understandably terrified state, and he felt the carriage swerve around and go back the way it had arrived. 'What's the meaning of this?' Eckersley asked, trembling as he thought of the gun pointed at him. Why was he being abducted? He hoped that it was perhaps some jest, but as the growler trundled on for a long time that was very difficult to gauge, Eckersley thought he'd never see his wife and children again. At one point in the journey, the joiner heard the peel of church bells, and sometime after that he heard the distinctive sound of an Italian street musician's barrel organ, and whenever he asked where he was being taken, he'd feel the barrel of the gun between his ribs.

At last the growler came to a halt and Eckersley was guided out of the carriage and taken into a house with an echoing hallway. He was taken down stone steps which felt hard and cold beneath the joiner's shoes, and here the bag was removed from his head. Billy Eckersley found himself in a cellar workshop illuminated by six oil lamps. There were stacks of quality wood and carpentry tools of every sort, and the centre of the cellar was dominated by a large workbench equipped with several vices.

The man with the walrus moustache unfurled a long roll of paper on the desk and placed boxes of tacks and nails at each corner of the sheet to prevent it from curling up. Eckersley could see this paper featured the blueprint of a very strange item indeed – an unusually broad coffin that was almost heart-shaped. 'We have a friend who would like you to make this as soon as possible,' walrus moustache said in a well-spoken accentless voice, and he tapped the index finger of his black leather-gloved hand on the unusual design.

'Why have I been brought here? What's going on?' Billy Eckersley demanded to know.

'You were brought here to make this coffin,' said walrus moustache, 'that's what's going on. The sooner you make this the sooner we will return you to your home.'

'Why couldn't you have just asked me to make this instead of resorting to kidnapping me?' asked the carpenter.

The second abductor, who also wore a bowler, said to the carpenter: 'You're not in any position to question what we say Mr Eckersley. Now, you must do what we say or meet your fate.'

Billy Eckersley reluctantly worked around the clock sawing the wood and fitting together the bizarrely-shaped coffin, and after eight hours, he was given a meal and a glass of beer. And then he resumed his work, and when he had finished the job, a few hours after the break, he asked the two men if they required the coffin to be varnished, and they said they didn't. They inspected the coffin, which measured a little over six feet in length and four and a half feet in width, and both agreed that Eckersley had done an excellent job. The man with the heavy moustache took the bag from his pocket, ready to put it on the joiner's had for the return journey, when the door to the cellar burst open, and in ran a young barefooted lady of about twenty to twenty-five years of age, dressed in a long white nightgown. She had dark circles around her bulging mad-looking eyes, and she threw her arms out to Eckersley and tried to run to him but the two abductors intercepted her and began to drag her out the room.

'Help me!' she screamed, 'They're going to bury me alive!

Eckersley shook with fear when he heard the woman, and he felt so helpless as he watched the two men drag the poor young lady out of the cellar. Her small white hands tried to grip at the architrave of the door but they peeled her fingers from the doorframe and shouted profanities at her. Then came the sound of a door being slammed and locked, and the two men returned to take the joiner back to his neighbourhood – or would they perhaps shoot the joiner and dump his body in some remote spot, thereby insuring that their dastardly intentions would never be discovered?

Billy Eckersley sweated copiously under his hood during the return journey, for he expected to receive a bullet-hole in his skull at any moment. At last the growler came to a halt on Snaefell Avenue, off West Derby Road. It was night-time, and there was a torrential downpour. Eckersley was thrown out of the carriage with the bag still on his head, and almost immediately, the growler tore off into the night. The carpenter took the bag off his head and looked for the carriage but it was gone, although he thought he could hear it rattling round the corner of Sutton Street, headed for the Green Lane thoroughfare. Eckersley went home, where his frantic wife and children were so glad to see him. He told his wife what had happened and she urged him to go to the police – which he did – later that night. The police sergeant Eckersley talked to was very sceptical of the story, and he said there was little he could do when he had so little information to go on. Eckersley told him he recalled the peel of a church bells and the sounds of an Italian street musician's barrel organ during the journey, but the sergeant just shook his head and said all that was too vague to serve as a clue. Billy Eckersley left the police station in Tuebrook bitter, and disillusioned, but then came a surprising development.

A local coachman named David Rees was going up West Derby Road a week after the abduction and pulled up his carriage when he saw Eckersley to tell him that he had witnessed him being abducted on the previous Sunday. Rees said he had tried to follow the growler, but lost it near Deysbrook Lane when a hansom cab collided with the coach he was driving. Rees had seen the mysterious black growler several times since and felt is was connected to Croxteth Hall – which lay in the general direction the growler was headed that Sunday.

When Eckersley told the coachman about the special coffin he was forced to build and the claims of the woman in the white gown, Rees vowed to track down the abductors, but found his quest thwarted by the police who seemed to warn him off from delving into the strange goings-on. Both Eckersley and Rees were visited in the dead of night by shadowy men who warned them to stop prying into matters that did not concern them. Around this time there were rumours circulating that a woman had been buried alive next to the body of her wealthy lover in a special coffin in a grave in Anfield cemetery. The burial had taken place at three in the morning. The bizarre ritual was said to have been carried out by disciples of the dead man, an aristocrat who had worshipped the Devil. The thought of the young lady who had begged for help from Billy Eckersley being buried alongside the corpse of her lover, haunted the joiner for many years. The earth beneath our feet holds many such macabre secrets, and this has been just one of them.

THE WHITE DOT

There are certain things, certain phenomena, reported to me regularly by the readers of my books and columns, which I have a hard time explaining, and the following story belongs to this class of inexplicable mystery.

One rainy evening in the October of 1963, a woman in her mid-thirties named Rita, was recovering from a bout of the flu, and she sat in her armchair, which had been dragged close to the two-bar electric fire with her hands cupped around a mug of cocoa as she watched an episode of the popular western series *Bonanza* on her little 16-inch black and white television. Perhaps I should point out at this point that Rita's husband was working nights at a factory, and had set off to work around 8pm, and would not be due back home until around six in the morning. The couple's two children, Tina, aged 13, and Susan who had just turned 15, were staying with Rita's sister Ann, over on Leyfield Road, West Derby. Rita's home was situated on Melwood Drive, and she and her family had lived there for almost five years. Rita was not a woman who entertained the thought of anything supernatural, nor could she acknowledge the existence of ghosts. She was a down-to-earth housewife of that day and age, and so, when the strange incidents which I am about to document took place, Rita was naturally shocked and left unnerved by the experiences.

After *Bonanza* had finished at around 8.55pm, Rita got up from her armchair, gripped the large silvered tuning wheel and turned it away from the Granada channel towards BBC1, just in time to catch the last few minutes of the medical drama series *Doctor Finlay's Casebook*. After that came the news, and then *The Dick Van Dyke Show*, which Rita was fond of, but the flu was making her feel drowsy, and about half way through the American comedy show, she fell asleep, and when she awoke, *The Dick Van Dyke Show* had ended and a boring piano recital was being shown, so Rita turned the tuner back to Granada, and watched the programmes there for a while, but again dozed off. Rita awoke around ten to midnight, and then a few minutes later, the television stations closed down. Remote control consoles were very rare in those days, and so, Rita got up and switched off the television, then, feeling drained by her cold, she sat on the armchair near to the television set for a moment and saw the white dot appear. This dot is never seen today because of the advanced screens we have in modern televisions, but in the 1960s, when a TV set was switched off, the picture on screen would collapse and shrink to a bright luminous dot a bit smaller than a decimal penny. This came about as the capacitors (which store power in the set) discharged and the cathode-ray tube would continue to emit electrons without the beam being moved horizontal or vertically. People often joked about being so addicted to TV that they watched it all day until the white dot appeared at night when the stations closed down.

Well on this night, Rita happened to look at the little luminous dot, and normally it faded after about fifteen seconds, but on this occasion, the dot persisted and did not change for about a minute, and Rita felt as if there was something almost hypnotic about the glowing point. It began to expand, and as it did a face appeared within it – a grinning face set in a head – a bald head. Rita was more stunned than scared, and she looked away for a moment, squeezed her eyes shut, thinking the flu was making her see things that weren't there. She looked back at the TV screen, and the grinning face was still there, and seemed more sharply defined now. As the West Derby housewife looked on, she saw that the tiny mouth of the luminous face was opening and closing as if words were being spoken, and suddenly, as clear as a bell, she heard a voice which sounded as if it was far off, and this voice was calling to her.

'Rita…Rita…'

This really unnerved the woman, and she stood up and left the living room to go into the hall in a confused manner. She didn't know whether to call on her neighbour June, who lived next door, and tell her what she had just seen and heard, or whether to stay put. Rita went to the doorway of her living room, peeped in, and saw that the luminous dot had now faded from the screen of the television set. She hurried into the room and unplugged the telly, then went up to bed, where she thought of the strange incident for a while until she drifted off into an uncomfortable sleep because of her flu.

At 6.20am, Rita's husband Hugh came home, and when he got into bed, she told him what had

43

happened, and predictably, he said she'd seen the face in the dot and heard her name being called because she'd probably had a temperature because of her illness. Hugh was soon snoring, and Rita got up soon afterwards. Despite having no appetite, she tried to have a bowl of cornflakes, and then she went into the living room and looked at the television set in the cold light of morning. She decided she probably had been seeing and hearing things – or at least she hoped she had.

That evening again at 8pm, Hugh set off for the factory night shift, and once again the girls stayed over at their aunt's house on Leyfield Road. Rita's flu seemed a bit lighter, and she sat there drinking tea and enjoying a Turkish Delight her husband had bought her as she sat in her usual armchair watching the telly. She watched a film which started around 8.10pm, and then smoked a few cigarettes as she enjoyed *Comedy Playhouse*. During the news at 10pm, Rita browsed the *Liverpool Echo*, and then around half-past ten she watched one of her favourite shows on the box – *That Was The Week That Was*, a satirical programme presented by David Frost. The show ended around a quarter past eleven, and not long afterwards the television channels closed down for the night. Rita switched off the telly, and once again she saw the usual white dot appear in the centre of the screen – and it quickly transformed itself into that grinning, impish face.

'Oh God,' Rita gasped, and put her hand to her mouth in shock.

'*Rita…Rita…*' said the voice in the distance. This time Rita could gauge just where the voice coming from – the direction of the TV set.

The housewife suddenly found herself unable to move, and she fell into what she could only describe as a dreamy state, rather like the state of consciousness the mind shifts into between waking and sleeping. The luminous bald head on the screen expanded as it went out of focus, and a circle opened up with images within it, and those images were very eerie indeed. Two silhouettes of men sitting at a desk in a huge luxurious office swam into view, and in American accents, they chatted to one another. Rita hear one of the men say to the other: 'He wants us to join up with the commies and we can't do that. We can never do that.'

And then the scene before Rita dissolved, and she saw a man in an open-topped car moving along through what looked like a pleasant green park. Somehow, Rita knew what was going to happen. One of the men she had seen in the office was lying in some sort of underground den, and he was aiming an unusually long rifle at the man in the car. The barrel of the rifle was protruding from a flower-bed in a garden or some sort to the left of the man in the car, who had a lady beside him – possibly his wife. Rita heard the loud, ear-piercing crack from this rifle after a number of other gunshot sounds had echoed throughout the living room – and then what she witnessed was truly horrific. The head of the man in the car exploded as the bullet from the sinister rifle hit him from behind and just to his left. The front of the head flew open and a cloud of blood and atomised brain matter billowed into the sunlight.

Rita suddenly regained the power to move, and she

let out a scream, and then she ran out of the living room and stayed in the kitchen for a while, where she trembled as she thought of the significance of what she had just witnessed. She wondered if she was going mad, and knew now that the flu was not to blame, as her appetite had returned and she had felt a lot better than the day before. Rita didn't dare tell her husband what she had seen and heard, because he'd naturally think she was going insane.

A month later, Rita, like millions across the world, was shocked and saddened to learn of the mysterious murder of US President John Fitzgerald Kennedy at Dallas on 22 November. Only then did Rita recognise who the man had been in that 'vision' which was seemingly induced by the white dot on the television – it had been the head of JFK she had seen exploding. But the Press and television reports made no mention of a violent explosion of blood from the President's head – most people who watched the television reports and read the newspaper articles had the impression that bullets had merely entered the President's back and head and killed him. Many years later, the controversial footage of the actual assassination of Kennedy, is routinely viewed by members of the public via YouTube, and this footage – shot by Abraham Zapruder on a Bell & Howell 8mm cine camera, and therefore known as the Zapruder Film - clearly, and quite graphically, shows the front of Kennedy's head explode as a high-velocity bullet seems to enter from behind the President and to the left. This bullet then leaves the President's head from the front-right area, leaving a ghastly flap of skin and other tissue dangling from the exit wound. This is exactly what Rita saw that October night, a month before the assassination took place. The official verdict is that Lee Harvey Oswald single-handedly shot the President with a rifle from the window of a nearby building, but the angle of the exit wound in the final head shot to Kennedy hints that the assassin was to the left and behind the President – almost diagonally opposite to the "Grassy Knoll" area so favoured by conspiracy theorists – but is there any evidence to back up the presence of a gunman in the aforementioned location? The House Select Committee of Assassinations – the official investigating body assigned to the assassination – concluded that Oswald was solely responsible, but a lot of evidence said otherwise, including the alleged accidental recording of the gunshots by a police motorcyclist's dictabelt recorder. The recording of shots came from a motorcycle police officer who was travelling about 200 feet behind the Presidents car, and puts the source of the gunshots to the left and back of Kennedy. A very mysterious woman was also standing near this area as Kennedy was shot, and she has never been identified, but is nicknamed the Babushka Lady, because she resembles a Russian woman in her attire – a dowdily-looking mac and headscarf which is tied under her chin. This individual, who seems to be using a cine camera, is apparently filming the assassination of Kennedy from much closer quarters than Abraham Zapruder, who captured the Babushka Lady in his own film for a second or so. The whole assassination has spawned countless books, movies and documentaries, and a recent poll in the United States has shown that most Americans believe that President Kennedy was not killed by Lee Harvey Oswald, but hired hitmen (who were possibly military-trained) for some political reason. The truth behind the Kennedy assassination will come out in time to come, when most of the conspirators are dead, and in the meantime, theories abound as to why the 35th President of the United States was murdered in Dallas on that eventful Friday in November 1963. In Rita's strange vision, she said she had clearly seen two silhouetted Americans, and one of them had said to the other: 'He wants us to join up with the commies and we can't do that. We can never do that.'

The idea of Kennedy wanting the Russians to join up with the Americans may seem ludicrous, but there is a little-known fact concerning JFK that may tie in with this paranormal mystery and even throw some light on the Dallas assassination. In October 1963, shortly before Rita had her weird premonition, which was seen in the white dot of the TV screen, President Kennedy came out with a curious proposal which he put to the Soviet Premier Nikita S. Khrushchev: he asked the Russians if they would be willing to join forces with the US to explore the Moon. The strongly-worded proposal of a joint American-Russian manned lunar programme was put forward by Kennedy in a speech before the United Nations General Assembly on 20 September, 1963 in New York, and many right-wingers in the US Senate were horrified when Kennedy stated that joint missions to the moon with Russians and American astronauts working together "would require a new approach to the Cold War". Many of those right-wingers breathed a sigh of relief when Khrushchev's government rejected Kennedy's proposal – but then, unknown to most of us in the West at that time, Khrushchev told his closest comrades in private that perhaps the USSR should accept Kennedy's offer – but weeks later, the US President was murdered in very sinister circumstances, and of course, the person who was widely publicised as the assassin – Lee Harvey Oswald – was himself murdered before he could even stand trial. Had the Soviet Union teamed up with the United States, a lot of armament dealers and manufacturers of Cold War missiles would have undoubtedly lost billions of dollars.

After Rita recovered from her flu, she never again saw anything strange in her television screen, but for some time, whenever show switched off her TV set, she would deliberately avoid looking at that white dot.

THE PHANTOM MONKS
OF CHILDWALL

At a little ad hoc booksigning after a talk on ghosts in October 2011, an obsessive man who has stalked me for many years approached with his head bowed and put a copy of my *Haunted City* on the table for me to sign for his daughter. This man is often found on a certain well-known Liverpool forum, where he constantly criticises me and accuses me of all sorts. Not only has he visited places where I have been living, he also once visited a friend's street under the pretence of being lost, just to see if he could catch a glimpse of me there. Whenever I am at a public event, be it an appearance at the history fair at St George's Hall or a talk I am giving somewhere, you can guarantee that the stalker will be waiting there in the shadows with his mobile phone, waiting to take a sneak picture (which he often publishes on the forum he frequents). I don't mind him taking pictures of me, as that's perfectly legal in a public place, but if there is a niece, nephew present, or some other minor who is related to me, or the little boy or girl of someone getting their book signed in the shot, I dislike people of the stalker's mentality capturing these innocent children on video or in stills, as there are a lot of sick people knocking about nowadays, as evidenced by the stalker. The stalker is so out of touch with reality, he doesn't realise that some fellow members of his forum love winding him up by deliberately mentioning me, just to get him to post a rant, and he falls for it every time. On the following occasion he and a fellow nut from the same forum came to a booksigning, and while his friend videoed me on his phone, the stalker tried to catch me out so he'd have material for his beloved forum life. I know this because someone who frequents the forum of obsessives told me. The stalker said, 'Hey Tom, there are a lot of ghosts knocking about aren't there? How can you write all these books when there must be a limited amount of ghosts, like?'

I addressed him by his first name to give him a little shock, because any psychologist will tell you that the stalker who thinks he hasn't been seen by his prey recoils in horror when he discovers they know his name. I told him that two days back, the United Nations had announced that the world's population had reached seven billion, and I also informed him that whilst this figure is alarmingly high, the dead still outnumber the living. For every living person there are 15 dead ones, with 107 billion dead since written records began. The official figures for the number of people who have lived, if you are interested, are 107,602,707,791 (and obviously this figure will have gone up since the statistics were published by the Population Reference Bureau, and will have risen by thousands by the time you reach the end of this book). So, if many ghost are images – be they sentient or as conscious as a TV picture – then we shouldn't be too surprised there are a lot of them about when we see that the dead still outnumber us by fifteen to one. The stalker and his pocket cameraman fled when they realised they had received a good answer to the question about 'a lot of ghosts knocking about'.

Well, even stalkers can pose some interesting questions, and there are a lot of ghosts "knocking about" – not just in Liverpool, but particularly in Britain; in fact the Guinness Book of Records once stated, some years ago, that Britain had more ghosts per square mile than many other countries, and this is due, no doubt to our long and bloody history. Some ghost are rarely noticed as they walk among us because they are the carnate manifestations of people who have recently died, and so their clothing, being fairly modern, does not seem out of the ordinary, but Victorian ghosts – males with their top hats and women with their long black dresses (often "sticky-out" crinoline ones) are immediately noticed if they appear amongst modern folk. Regency-period ghosts in white periwigs have been seen around Liverpool, and several medieval-looking ones as well, and these latter types are the subject of the following story, related to me many years ago by a Childwall woman named Louise.

In 1995, 29-year-old Louise and her 39-year-old husband Duncan were elated to move out of a crumbling damp house in Kensington and into a lovely semi-detached house in Childwall. Duncan had received compensation from a serious accident at his workplace the year before, and Louise's auntie had died, leaving her a lot of money in the will, and so the couple decided to go house-hunting, and Louise found the house of her dreams in Childwall, just a stone's throw from the Childwall Abbey pub. The couple moved into the house in the summer of 1995, and

Duncan got a job working nights at a factory near Haydock, and although Louise was not happy sleeping alone at nights, Duncan assured her he would have a word with the boss at his works soon to see if he could get onto the day shift, and if the boss said that wasn't possible, Duncan would find another job someplace where he could work days.

It was a humid July night when Louise first slept alone at the new house. She felt okay, even though she was on her own. She sat reading a teenage magazine called *Sugar* which her young sister Jenny had left during her visit in the afternoon, and Louise found the teen magazine rather amusing; full of personality tests, advice on first-time sex and so on. It was around one in the morning when Louise finally dropped off, and although Duncan had advised her not to, she had left the window open a few inches. Who would be able to get up to an upstairs window, Louise had reasoned, and she preferred the night-time breeze filtering into the stuffy room rather than an electric fan which had started to make an irritating clicking sound as it swept left and right. Around 2.20am, something woke Louise; she wasn't sure if it was a noise in the room, or somewhere outside in the suburban Childwall night, but she looked around the room and most of the light shining into the bedroom was from the moon, which was full that night. There was also a faint glow from a bluish mercury-vapour lamp shining into the room from the street, about a hundred yards distant.

Louise turned in the bed and her left hand pounded the pillow to soften it up a bit. She tried to relax and drive thoughts about being alone, and away from Duncan, when she suddenly heard some sort of music in the distance. She opened her eyes and listened. It sounded like monks chanting. Immediately, Louise thought someone had a radio or a CD player on in the distance somewhere, and the music sounded just like 'Enigma' – the musical project founded by Michael Cretu, David Fairstein and Frank Peterson. Enigma was storming the charts around that time and the music used Gregorian chants to give the hits a monastic ambience. Louise, however, was something of a music fan, and when she listened to the distant chanting monks she became quite sure that the sound they were producing was not like any Enigma CD she had heard, and she found the deep liturgical voices quite unsettling.

The chanting seemed to fade away after a few minutes, and Louise convinced herself that she had merely heard the audio to some film on a television somewhere, and she fell asleep.

She was rudely awakened around 3am by someone with an ice-cold hand grabbing at her right wrist as she lay on her back in bed. Louise's eyelids flew open when she realised there was someone there, and to her utter horror, she saw two figures wearing the attire of hooded monks, standing at the bottom of her bed. The cowls they wore looked of a darkish brown material, and Louise could hardly see the faces of the monks in their pointed hoods. One of these eerie bedroom visitors said something in a rich deep voice, and the words sounded as if they were in Latin. The only one of these words that Louise could make out was "Albion" – which is an archaic name for Britain (in fact it's the oldest known name for Britain). Louise screamed at the intruders, who had been standing side by side, but now they parted – and one went round the left side of the bed and the other came round the right hand side. The face of the one on the right could now be partially seen as faint lamplight from a mercury-vapour streetlight outside caught the right side of his face. This 'monk' was a smooth-featured man with pallid skin who seemed to be about thirty. Louise's screams did not provoke the least reaction in the hooded prowlers, and simultaneously they bent over her and one of them clamped an icy hand over her mouth and grabbed her forearm to drag her towards he bottom of the bed as the other monk seized Louise's other arm and dragged her in a likewise fashion. Louise was wearing nothing on this humid night, and as her stomach slid across the cold brass piping at the end of the bed, she began to cry, thinking she might be raped or perhaps murdered by two men who were obviously unbalanced to be dressing up as monks. At this point, Louise saw that the wall facing the bed, where she was being dragged towards, was not there. In its place was a dark passageway of some sort, and Louise seems to have a faint recollection of sandstone carvings along the walls and cold wide stony steps. At the end of this passageway, Louise could make out a cluster of candles burning on a tall stand. She also recalled detecting a sweet scent which reminded her of church incense. Louise passed out as she entered the passageway, and vaguely recalls being carried by the hooded men. She woke up screaming on her bed around five in the morning with the blankets and pillow in disarray. By the welcome light of that summer morning, Louise saw that her heavy mahogany chest of drawers, which had stood against the right wall – as seen from the bed – had been dragged a few feet away towards the door, and the middle drawer was open. Louise got up, threw on some underwear and a nightie, and went downstairs to smoke numerous cigarettes in the kitchen as she tried to fathom out what had happened. She rooted through the drawer in the kitchen trying to find the work number her husband had left her, but was unable to find the scrap of paper anywhere. She realised he'd be back at 7am anyway, and how on earth could she expect him to believe what had taken place earlier in the morning anyway? But she did tell him what had happened as soon as he got home, and he knew his wife was not lying from the look of fear in her eyes as she related what had happened. Duncan believed the house was haunted and said that they should perhaps start looking for somewhere else, but Louise shook her head and said, 'No, we're staying put. I think if I saw those figures again I'd kill them. No one's making us leave here, not even ghosts.'

'How can you kill them if they're already dead?' joked Duncan nervously, and he asked to have a look at his wife's body to see if the intruders were flesh and blood characters who had perhaps belonged to some cult. 'If they've touched you in any way, I'll bleedin' kill them myself, never mind *you* killin' them!' Duncan said through clenched teeth. There wasn't a mark on Louise's body, and Duncan said he'd have to pack in his job rather than have his wife go through another weird episode at the house. Louise said she'd bring her younger sister Jenny over, and Duncan was angry at the suggestion. 'And what's a young girl going to do if those things do come back? I'll find a decent daytime job, love,' Duncan told her.

But as the day developed into a hot and sunny affair, Louise convinced her husband that the whole thing with the monks had been some lucid dream. 'What about the chest of drawers? Something pulled them out,' Duncan realistically reasoned.

'Ah, sleepwalkers move things about,' retorted Louise, 'it's well known. My cousin used to leave his bed all hours in the morning and sleepwalk around starkers adjusting the paintings in his lounge.'

Duncan got some sleep and reluctantly agreed to go to work at 8pm. By then, 17-year-old Jenny had arrived, and of course, her big sister Louise never said anything about the monks.

Jenny watched MTV and sat talking about boys and Take That and which Spice Girl she looked like, and she also had a voracious appetite for such a slim girl. She ate every Magnum ice cream in the freezer and even ate the remainder of Duncan's birthday cake. At one in the morning, Jenny admitted she smoked cigarettes and asked Louise if she could have one of hers. Louise said, 'No, they're bad for your health Jenny; you're not smoking.' Louise then muted the television because Jenny had switched over to The Box channel and had the volume on full.

'Oh go on, don't be an 'arld arse – pretty please Louise,' the girl begged, and Louise saw the funny side of the unintentional rhyme of 'please Louise' – and she relented, and said, 'Okay – just this once – and I mean it, no more after this.'

Jenny lit an Embassy Regal cigarette and kept giggling because Louise was watching her. 'It's mad, you watching me, oh I feel mad smoking in front of you,' the girl said, blushing.

All of a sudden in the silence (because of the muted television) both females heard faint chanting somewhere.

'What's that?' Jenny asked her sister, somehow reading the concern on Louise's face.

Louise was quite scared, and she went into the hallway and checked that the security chain had been put on the front door.

'Louise, what's up? You're scaring me?' Jenny asked, following closely behind her sister as she went to the kitchen – to get a huge carving knife from the cutlery drawer.

'Nothing, it's okay Jen,' Louise said, and her trembling hand took the knife from the drawer and placed it on the draining board.

'Louise what's going on?' Jenny raised her voice and coughed as she accidentally inhaled the ciggy smoke too far back into her lungs.

There were thuds upstairs.

Both girls looked up at the kitchen ceiling with expressions of utter surprise.

Jenny yelped. 'Who's that?' she asked, and then she said to her sister: 'Did you just hear that?' There was a thump on the ceiling of the hallway – which meant someone was coming along the landing upstairs. By now, the sounds of monks chanting – that very same chanting that Louise had heard the night before – could clearly be heard in the rooms upstairs.

'Come on Jenny!' bawled Louise at her sister, and she picked up the knife with one hand and with the other hand she dragged Jenny to the front door and began to unfasten the chain.

Both sisters saw male sandaled feet appear at the top step of the stairs, and the Jenny screamed. Louise opened the door and she and her sister hurried out into the cool summer night and trotted down the drive. Louise looked up at her bedroom window and saw that something was glowing in the room and casting shadows against the lace curtains – it looked like a procession of monks in their cows and pointed hoods, moving from right to left.

The sisters ran off down the street, and bumped into an elderly man, a Mr Serridge, who was out walking his dog because of a bout of insomnia. Mr Serridge, seeing the large knife in Louise's hand, thought he was about to be mugged, and knew his little Jack Russell would not be of any use to repel his imagined mugger, so he was greatly relieved when he learnt that the girls were fleeing from something and not about to attack him. When Mr Serridge heard Louise mention monks, the word seemed to strike some chord in the elderly dog-walker, and he inhaled sharply then said, 'Oh, they're back then are they?' And he looked in the direction of Louise's house, which was just visible through the trees.

'You know about them?' Louise asked, hoping the old man could somehow help her or at least explain what was going on. What he said in reply only served to tighten the nerves of the two sisters.

Serridge said that as far back as he could remember, there had been stories about Devil-worshipping monks who came up from some subterranean abbey that lay somewhere beneath the ground close to that mysterious stretch of land known as "Bloody Acre". This traditionally accursed field, which runs alongside the graveyard of All Saints Church, has been known as Bloody Acre since time immemorial, and no one – not one historian – has ever found out why, but many supposedly learned local historians have claimed that the field obtained its sanguineous title because of some mere unreported skirmish in the English Civil War – but long before the days of Cromwell, that field was said to be a place to avoid and respect. All sorts of things have been seen and heard over, on and beneath Bloody Acre – phantom explosions, strange subterranean bells and weird incantations, and some have even claimed to have seen the emergence of a huge black vaporous Angel of Death who shows himself before a major war on the Acre.

As the old man talked about Bloody Acre, Jenny bent down and stroked the Jack Russell, and she smiled as the dog rolled onto his back with his head back so she could stroke under his chin. Then all of a sudden the dog let out a loud yelp, which started Jenny and Louise, and then the animal looked at something further down the suburban drive. It was one of those monks, silhouetted by the feeble lamp post shining behind him. 'Oh my God! Oh!' shrieked Louise, and Jenny cowered behind her.

'Don't be afraid,' said Mr Serridge, and he said to Louise, 'Hold him a minute,' and handed the dog's lead to her. The old man then walked towards the monk, and the figure stopped.

'Mr Serridge halted about six feet away from the figure and spat on the ground between himself and the baleful-looking entity. 'In the name of the Lord, what do you wish?' Mr Serridge shouted to the apparition, and as Louise and Jenny, and the little frightened dog looked on, the monk instantly vanished. Mr Serridge then walked back to the trembling sisters and said, 'Stay at my house until morning if you want. Someone must have conjured them up.'

Louise was speechless for a while, and then she said, 'We can't, we've left the front door open.'

'I'll go and shut it, what number is it?' the brave old man asked.

'I haven't got the keys or nothin' – oh I don't know what to do,' replied Louise, and then she said, 'Are you sure we can stay in yours?'

'Yes,' said Mr Serridge, 'I'm a widower, and I live on my own.'

'My husband will be back around seven,' Louise recalled, and Mr Serridge nodded and said, 'Well you'll be okay in my place till then. Are you sure you haven't left the cooker on or anything?'

Louise hugged Jenny, who seemed very afraid, and said: 'No, there's nothing switched on. Thanks mate.'

And the elderly man went off as his dog let out a yelp and tilted its head as it watched its master walk away. Serridge returned about three minutes later and said, 'Hope you don't mind, but I went in the house and found your keys, just in case you want to go home.'

'Ah, thanks,' Louise said, 'what's your name? My name's Louise and this is my sister Jenny.'

'Jacob,' Mr Serridge answered, 'call me Jake if you want.'

Serridge looked after the sisters until 7am. He gave Jenny glass after glass of Vimto and every flavour of crisp, bag after bag. He told Louise that someone in the area was known to dabble in witchcraft 'and that sort of stuff' and this irresponsible person had caused these monks to walk before. Serridge hinted that this person – who he would not name – might have even targeted Louise because she was a newcomer. 'They're a real clique round here,' Serridge said with a dismissive shake of his head, 'well some of them anyway.'

'Well I think I'll be moving,' Louise admitted defeat at last. 'I couldn't put up with another night like this.'

'You've got a real bad rash on the back of your neck Louise,' Jenny noted, and pulled back the flimsy collar of her sister's nightie to get a better look at it. 'I always get that with nerves,' said Louise.

Serridge said he would make a number of crosses out of rowan branches later in the morning and bind them with red thread, and he explained that such crosses had always been used as 'ghost repellents'. Louise told him not to bother, but later that day, Mr Serridge came to Louise's home while her husband was fast asleep in bed, and gave her six of the crosses. He told her to put one in each room. He would also ask a local nun he knew to say prayers to protect the house. That night, Louise pretended she was going to stay at her mother's house, and she even visited her mum over in Huyton, but when Duncan was at work, Louise got a taxi back to the house. She decided that if anything supernatural took place, she'd go and stay at Mr Serridge's home, but that night, nothing remotely paranormal took place, and Louise and Duncan stayed at the house, where they still live today.

TIME OUT OF JOINT

The following story fascinates me because of two reasons. Firstly, it hints that our reality is but one version of reality, and that many worlds similar to our own exist next to one another in layers, rather like the pages of a very thick book. I also find this story fascinating because I am referenced in it, and that is rather rare in these stories.

In the winter of 2009, a 21-year-old Indian-born student named Indra, who was studying economics and sociology at Liverpool University, began to suffer from intense headaches. Indra's friends constantly advised him to go and see his doctor, but the student had always had a long-standing phobia of being diagnosed with various terminal conditions, and was well-known as the hypochondriac of his family. He decided to hide his head in the sand regarding his headaches and tried his best to carry on with his studies by periodically taking paracetamol every four hours. This regime of self-medication went on for weeks. Then Indra started to take Co-Drydamol and eventually stronger analgesics. The headaches became more severe, and during one particularly bad headache at a library at the university, Indra began to sniffle, and fresh bright red oxygenated blood dripped from his nose and blotted the pages of the book he was reading. The student almost hyperventilated with shock when he saw the blood, because he was convinced that such nosebleeds accompanied with such crippling headaches were a sure sign of an aggressive brain tumour.

Indra left the library and went to the toilet, where he mopped his nose with tissue and held back his head as he panted with anxiety in the toilet cubicle. Once he was sure the nosebleed had stopped, he left the library and walked aimlessly among the city centre of Liverpool, convinced he was dying. Indra was walking up Ranelagh Street, passing a shop called Dawsons, which sold musical instruments, when he saw a former college friend named Craig coming out of the shop in his wheelchair, which was being pushed by Craig's girlfriend, Jaclyn. Indra didn't want to talk to Craig, because he felt so down regarding his 'terminal' condition, and so he crossed the road and nipped down Fairclough Street, which leads on to Lawton and Cropper Streets – back streets behind the former Lewis's building. Indra thought he heard Craig shout after him as he crossed Ranelagh Street but he never turned round. As Indra was walking from the back street towards Newington, which leads onto Renshaw Street, he had a 'funny turn'. He felt dizzy, out of breath, and also experienced a weird tingling sensation in his head. The sensation passed after less than a minute, and Indra was now convinced he was seriously ill, and when he reached Renshaw Street, his heart was palpitating and his mouth was bone dry. He went to a newsagents on that street to get a bottle of Evian, and it was here, in the midst of his hyper-anxiety, that he noticed something odd. On the front of all of the tabloid newspapers, there were headlines stating that Liam Gallagher had been knifed to death in a brawl with a 'fan'. Being a former Oasis fan in his younger days, Indra bought a copy of the *Daily Mirror*, and thought it'd be something to read in an effort to take his mind of his illness, and when he left the shop he headed for his home, which was a flat on Falkner Street. Upon reaching the junction of Hope Street, he noticed that the modern street 'scuptlure' – A Case History – a collection of concrete casts of suitcases and luggage near to the former Liverpool Art College – was nowhere to be seen. Indra walked on to his flat on Falkner Street, and when he reached the house in question, he discovered that his key would not fit the lock on the door. He decided he'd have to buzz the number of the old Swedish woman who lived underneath his flat – Number 3. He pressed the buttom for Number 3, and a gruff male voice answered. 'Hello?' said the unknown man.

'Hi, is Ingrid there? It's Indra,' the student said into the intercom.

There was a pause as Indra heard the faint white noise hiss from the intercom speaker.

'No. You've got the wrong address mate,' a crotchety voice replied, and with a click the intercom became silent.

Indra looked at the label next to button number 3 – but it didn't say Ingrid's surname; instead it said 'FLAT 3 - M. MURRAY.' Indra had never heard of anyone of that surname living in any of his neighbouring flats, and he looked at the number on the door, just to make sure he hadn't gone to the wrong house. No, he was at the right house of course, and this really puzzled him. He put his key in the door once again, but it wouldn't turn. He walked away from the house, utterly confused. He heard a noise above, and when the student looked up, he saw the face of a shaven-headed man of about fifty looking from Ingrid's window at him with a suspicious expression. Indra walked on, and things became even stranger. When he reached Hope Street, he took out his mobile phone and decided to call his former girlfriend Vanessa. She answered the call and when Indra began to tell her about the mysterious disappearance of Ingrid, Vanessa said: 'I think you've got the wrong number.'

'No, it's me, Indra,' the student told her with a smile.

'Who, sorry?' Vanessa asked.

'Indra,' he laughed, and then asked, 'have you been drinking.'

'I haven't a clue who you are,' Vanessa said.

'It's me – Indra! Your ex. Stop messing about. I've just –'

Vanessa hung up. Indra called her again. The phone rang for a while and then the automated voice irritatingly announced: 'The person you are calling is not available.'

As Indra swore to himself, he happened to look up. Immediately he noticed there was something wrong with the Anglican Cathedral. Instead of the usual squarish shape of the building's tower, it was much longer and rounded at the top, and the stonework looked much darker, as if it had been subjected to the type of long-term air pollution that once turned the Liver Building and St George's Hall soot-black. This didn't make any sense at all. Indra had passed the cathedral just two days ago and it had looked as it always did, and it was impossible for builders to have altered the shape of the cathedral since then, so what was going on? An eerie thought crossed Indra's disoriented mind: had he died and somehow passed into some parallel world? That would explain why the street sculpture had vanished and also throw some light on the sudden disappearance of his Swedish neighbour. And it could explain why Vanessa, a girl he had dated for four years, had never heard of him. Indra wandered back into town, and decided to visit a café he often frequented on Bold Street. He was greatly relieved when the people running the café welcomed him. 'Where are you up to, Indra?' said Di, one of the waitresses as he walked in.

'Oh, not so bad,' Indra replied, taking his usual window seat. 'I've been having some really bad headaches.'

Di loved talking about medical matters, and after she had asked Indra to move his head in certain directions, and after she had felt his neck and looked into his eyes and asked him if he was eating okay, she gave him a bill of clean health. 'You know what you've got?' she said to him, as she went to make his cappuccino.

'No,' said Indra, imagining she'd say 'cancer of the brain' or something.

'Sinusitis,' Di said from the other side of the counter. 'My sister had it really bad. Had nose bleeds and everything.'

'I had them! That's what I had!' Indra said, rising from his seat. He went over to the counter and discussed all of his symptoms with the petite blonde, and she nodded to each description of his illness.

'Just go to your doctors Indra, or even go to Holland and Barrett and get these – ' Di ripped a page from her orders pad and wrote down the name of two products she believed the student could effectively treat his sinusitis with.

'Oh, thanks, Di,' Indra said gratefully as she handed him the scribbled note. 'I'd marry you if you weren't already spoken for.'

Di blushed and said she *wasn't* spoken for. She was single.

Indra went cold, because he had met Di's husband and had even bought her 3-year-old daughter an ice cream when he bumped into Di and her family at the Albert Dock in the previous summer.

Indra gave a troubled smile and sat down in his window seat as Di eyed him, and she still wore a blush on her face. She asked him if he was still with that girl he had come into the café with a few months ago. Indra assumed she was talking about Vanessa, and he said, 'Ah, so you remember her then?'

'Yes, she was very pretty. I could tell her hair was naturally red. Are you not with her now then?'

Indra was puzzled at Di's remarks about his red-headed girlfriend, because Vanessa's hair was raven black, and she had never once coloured her locks. Four women, all office workers in their thirties who were known to Di, came into the café and Di served them, and then she brought over Indra's cappuccino, and went to talk to him, but one of the office workers distracted Di and called to her. Indra only took a few sips of his coffee before leaving the money on the table before he headed for the door.

'You got to go?' Di asked, with disappointment in

her eyes.

Indra nodded, and before he stepped out onto Bold Street, he said: 'I'll probably be back in later Di.'

'Oh, okay, bye Indra,' Di said, and went to collect his money from the table.

Indra walked down Bold Street and went into the Holland & Barrett health store to buy the items Di had recommended for his sinusitis. Upon leaving the health shop, the student decided to call into Waterstones. It was a random choice. He felt so confused and perplexed at the events that were unfolding behind him. He decided he'd go upstairs to the coffee shop on the first floor of the bookstore and take the pills from the health store. The ground floor was packed with people, young and old, and they were all gathered around a table where an author named Robin Brown was signing copies of his book, which was called *Liverpool is Haunted*. Indra saw that the book's design looked very similar to the *Haunted Liverpool* books in font and graphical style, as well as thickness. Then came a shock which stunned the student.

Among the people standing around, waiting for a signed copy of *Liverpool is Haunted*, was Craig, who had been a college friend of Indra for three years. Craig had been born with cerebral palsy, and was wheelchair bound – and yet, here he was, standing up, and his hair had a slight reddish tint to it. But what really shocked Indra was the presence of the young man standing next to Craig. It was an old friend named Barry, who had died in a car crash five years ago – and yet here he was, looking slightly older and in a very healthy and tanned condition. Indra called his old best friend's name. 'Barry?' he said, but Barry didn't react as if he hadn't heard him. So Indra moved in closer and tentatively raised his hand to tap Barry on the shoulder. He tapped him. Barry turned to look at him with an expression that was a mixture of annoyance and bafflement.

'Sorry?' Barry said.

'I thought you were dead,' Indra said, and he could almost feel tears welling in his eyes.

Barry looked him up and down and uttered the four-lettered swear-word as he told Indra to go away.

Indra recoiled in shock at the profanity, and backed away, out of Waterstones. Indra hurried up Bold Street, breathing heavily, with his heart pounding. He passed the café where Di worked, and moments later, he heard a female voice call out his name. Indra halted, and turned.

A beautiful young lady with long straight red hair stood there. Had she called his name?

'Where are you going?' she asked.

Indra slowly realised that this was the 'pretty' girl Di had referred to. In this version of reality, she was his girlfriend.

'I was just going home,' Indra said, and found himself stuck for words.

'How can you be if you're going in *that* direction?' the redhead asked, and she smiled.

'I live in that direction,' Indra told her. He looked at her face and figure. She was absolutely perfect.

'No you don't, we live down at the dock,' she said, and she beckoned Indra to her with her curling index finger. Indra walked towards her, and as he came nearer she said: 'I've told you to stop buying things for me; you don't have to.'

Indra could smell her lovely perfume now, and he saw the blueness of her eyes, and the cute freckles which her foundation couldn't hide. She embraced him, kissed his cheek and hugged him hard, then led him by his hand into the café, where Di the waitress gave him daggers. The couple sat in the window seat, and the unknown red-haired girl talked and talked without giving Indra a chance to say anything. His 'partner' stopped chatting at one point and said, 'Aw, you're nose is bleeding,' and she dabbed his nose with a napkin.

The vivid bright scarlet blood dripped onto the front of Indra's tee-shirt.

'You'd better go and clean up,' the redhead told him, and Indra rose from the table and went to the toilets downstairs. He looked at himself in the mirror above the wash basin and said, 'What the hell is going on?'

And that tingling sensation returned in his head. He shuddered, and gripped the rim of the porcelain basin. He somehow knew that everything had now returned to normal, and one part of him hoped that the beautiful girl with red hair would still be around upstairs – but when Indra went upstairs, he saw that the window seat was empty. He looked for his copy of the *Daily Mirror*, but it was nowhere to be seen, and through the window, he saw a rain-slicked Bold Street. Passers-by were hurrying along in the downpour. Indra turned to look for Di, and a waitress named Angela told him that Di was on a short holiday and not due in till next week. Angela then said, 'I didn't see you come in here before. Have you just come up from the toilet?'

71

Indra nodded, and his sadness showed in his face. He ordered a cappuccino and sat down and thought hard and long about the past few hours. He tried to rationalise what he had experienced but was unable to. He recalled the tabloid headlines about the death of Liam Gallagher, and asked Angela if she knew anything about it. She said she hadn't, and she took out her phone and searched Google News for any items about the Oasis vocalist, but there was no news of his death listed.

When Indra returned to his flat on Falkner Street, he saw that Ingrid's surname was listed on the intercom, and on this occasion, his key fitted the door. He phoned Vanessa as soon as he got to his flat, and she answered and said, 'Hiya Indra, what's up?'

He told her about all of the strange incidents – of seeing Craig walking about without his wheelchair and of meeting Barry, five years after he had died in a horrific car crash. Vanessa sounded very concerned and urged Indra to see a doctor. 'No, I'm fine,' Indra reassured her, 'the nosebleeds were just because of sinusitis.'

Vanessa was so worried about Indra's health, she paid him a visit within the hour and preached to him until he visited the A&E of the Royal Teaching Hospital. His head was x-rayed and a specialist treated him – for a rare form of sinusitis which was managed with several pills for a few months. The headaches and nosebleeds never returned. Vanessa began to date Indra again, and the student began to have a series of strange dreams about the red-haired lady he had somehow encountered from some parallel version of his life. Indra would often wake up in tears, because he found that he loved the girl from his 'other life' more than Vanessa and felt she was his soulmate. The dreams eventually became less frequent, and today, Vanessa and Indra are happily married.Indra mentioned the strange 'slip' into what seems to have been some alternate life to Di, and she confirmed what he already knew; the waitress had never set eyes on any red-headed girlfriend of his. Perhaps this red-haired beauty exists in this version of Indra's life but maybe her path and his simply never crossed.

I am a great believer in parallel worlds – versions of our planet that are dislocated dimensionally from this world but sometimes overlapping, allowing us to visit them. These alternative worlds may be the places we glimpse in dreams where we discover people who are dead in our world, walking about in the dream world. Perhaps there are – as quantum physics hints – an infinite number of planet Earths which we could one day visit, where slightly different versions of ourselves and others exist. As you read this book, another version of you may be reading the same book in a world close by in time and space. In that world, the *Titanic* sits in some Californian harbour as a floating museum (having never hit any iceberg in 1912), President Kennedy was never assassinated, and the Beatles never broke up, and you are married to someone else. Parallel worlds are a fascinating possibility, and may well be proven to exist one day.

ANONYMA

Late one night in the summer of 2002, a young couple entered Central Station on Ranelagh Street and rode the escalator down to the platform where the train would take one of them under the river to Wirral's Eastham Rake. The time was 11.25pm and the train as due any minute. Hannah stood on her tiptoes to kiss the face of her 6-foot-2 boyfriend Brandon. As the couple, both aged 17, embraced, Brandon thought he heard something to his left. The platform was deserted except for a drunken old man who had been talking to himself, and he was to the left of Brandon. Brandon broke away from his lover's kiss for a moment to turn to face the black mouth of the tunnel.

'The train comes from the other direction,' Hannah told him.

'I know,' Brandon replied, and he squinted at the arch of darkness with its ruby red light and a line of grimy neon panel lamps which stretched into a curve. 'I thought I heard a whistling sound.'

'Mmm, come here you,' Hannah grabbed the collar of his tee shirt and dragged Brandon down to her level to continue the kissing. This time she broke off the kiss, shot a startled look at her boyfriend of three months, then turned her face left. 'I heard it then' she said, 'what is it?'

As the two teenagers looked towards the gaping tunnel, they saw three faint white spots floating towards them. As these things got nearer, Hannah thought they resembled dandelions, and Brandon said, 'Are they daddy-bunchies?'

Hannah giggled and said: 'What's a daddy bunchy?'

Brandon blushed and said: 'They're like sort of dandelions and they eat sugar, or at least that's what my Nan used to say.'

'Dandelions aren't alive you dickhead,' laughed Hannah, 'they're just fluffy things that come off plants with seed thingies in them.'

Brandon wasn't listening. He had a look of terror in his eyes that made Hannah swing her face to the left again to see what was exerting such a look on her partner's face. The 'dandelions' were flying about like white bumble bees now, and making a faint whistling sound as they darted through the air. 'What are they?' she gasped.

'Let's go, come on!' Brandon said, with a mounting sense of foreboding, and he backed away towards the wide corridor leading to the escalators.

'They're just flies, Brandon,' Hannah resisted his pulls, 'and I'll miss my train you soft get!'

'They are not flies! Arrgh!' Brandon ducked. One of the white things whizzed within inches of his head and hit the Perspex cover of a tubeway advert with a clicking sound. These things sounded as if they had a hard shell.

Hannah let out a yelp, and then she tried to put her arms up her back – they way people do when they are trying to scratch that itchy part of the back that's almost out of reach. 'It bit me!' she yelled. 'It's on me!'

Brandon put his hands on his girlfriend's shoulders and spun her around. She was wearing a black Pantera tee shirt, and there on the centre of her back, clinging to the shirt, was a white thing that looked just like a dandelion, but the arms were hard like needles, and the needles that were stuck into Hannah's back were red – as if they were miniature transparent hair-thin tubes siphoning off blood. Hannah let out a string of swear-words and screamed in agony as Brandon tried to pull the barbed creature from her back. The lad let out an agonising cry as the think razor-like "hairs" of the thing dug painfully into his index finger and thumb as he tried to grab it.

'Get it off me!' Hannah sobbed, and seemed ready to faint as she staggered forward. She went onto her knees and her hands rested on the rubbery black-grey tiles of the floor. Brandon took his orange railway ticket from his jeans pocket, and bent it in two, and then he got the ghastly unidentified thing between the folded ticket and at last, he managed to pull it out. He tried to throw it onto the track, but the white hairy looking creature flew off – back towards the tunnel it had come from.

Hannah lay on the floor, crying, and Brandon helped her up then lifted her shirt. Blood was trickling down the long bulge of her spine from the small cluster of tiny incisions. Brandon dabbed at the droplets of blood which kept popping out of the tiny wounds but they wouldn't stop bleeding. The train arrived, and Brandon insisted that he should accompany Hannah home in the state she was in. Even after the girl had reached her home, the wound was still pouring with blood, and wouldn't stop bleeding until amost one in the morning. Other people have encountered these "bloodthirsty dandelions" over the years. A construction engineer on a Liverpool One building site once told me how, in 2008, he saw something white and fluffy drift past him like a snowflake, and then he felt something sting his right cheek. Another white airborne object had inflicted a cut to the engineer's face, and it looked just like the fluffy seed ball of a dandelion. It floated towards Church Street, and seemed to be under intelligent control at one point. I mentioned this incident and the one which had taken place on the underground on a radio station, and later received a letter from a man named Hammond who said he had studied these unidentified creatures – which he termed "Anonyma" (derived from the word *anonymous*) - for many years, and he was of the opinion that some of the unidentified creatures were alien and others were manmade, created in laboratories by scientists who were meddling with DNA. I do not believe Mr Hammond is a crank. Even the most prominent scientists are discovering new species of microbes all of the time, and some viruses which have come to light are providing microbiologists with a headache. A case in point is the virus that was originally labelled the Bradford coccus, discovered by Timothy Rowbotham, a microbiologist working for the UK's Public Health Laboratory Service. In 1992, Rowbotham was attempting to trace the outbreak of pneumonia in Bradford, and the trail led him to sample some water at the base of a hospital cooling tower. He took his samples back to his laboratory and discovered that they contained amoebae, and the amoebae seemed to have been infected with something – and this something was thought to be a microbe which Rowbotham had never encountered before, so he called it the Bradford coccus. With more pressing matters to attend to, the microbiologist put the Bradford coccus into deep freeze and there it remained for eleven years, until a fresh pair of eyes with an electron microscope took another look at the microbe, and what they saw was astounding. The Bradford coccus was a freak of nature. It is an unheard-of giant - thirty times bigger than the rhinovirus – and what's more, it is very hard to kill. It looks alien. It seems to be a bacterium, but it isn't, even though it passed the established test for bacteria – the Gram stain. This is a widely-used test in which various chemicals are applied to the sample which is suspected of containing bacteria. If the stain produced is purple, then it's a bacterium, if its pink its something else. The Bradford coccus produced a purple stain, as if it was a bacterium. The Gram stain test, named after the Danish bacteriologist who first described it - Hans Gram (1853-1938) is generally seen as an infallible method to differentiate bacteria – and yet this test was telling the scientists that a virus was a bacterium. The most eminent bacteriologists in the world took a closer look at the Bradford coccus, and all agreed that it was a giant virus. In human terms, imagine a man standing next to a giant who is twelve storeys high – that's the size difference with this strange virus. The head of the giant virus is a polyhedron having twenty plane faces (which makes it an icosohedron) and it contains 1,262 complex genes in a finely structured body. Most viruses have only 10 to a 100 genes. To this day, no one knows what the Bradford coccus is – it may be an alien virus to this planet or perhaps some missing link between viruses and bacteria, but perhaps it forms part of that shadowy group of unidentified creatures

Hammond terms as Anonyma. This mysterious group could include the Surrey Puma, the Beast of Bodmin, the Loch Ness Monster, Sasquatch, the Yeti and so on, as well as some of the more local unidentified creatures I have detailed in the *Haunted Liverpool* books: the ghastly-looking snake-like insect with no eyes and razor teeth which lived in the rubbish chute of various tenements in Liverpool in the 1960s, the tripodal creatures that were alleged to have attacked people across the city in the 1970s (see the chapter entitled "Parasitic Things" in *Haunted Liverpool 17*), as well as the dandelion-like spores that inflict wounds.

THE MINT GREEN CAR

This story came my way many years ago when I first started to collect strange tales. I have had to change a few of the details but I can assure you that, unfortunately, all of the events described in the account happened exactly as I describe. I am at a loss to offer a rational explanation regarding the incidents in the story, but I'm sure some readers will form their own theories in this respect.

Around the mid-Seventies, there stood a used cars lot in Liverpool, not a stone's throw from Seel Street, and it was run by a very atypically honest man in his sixties named Vince. With his pencil thin moustache and prominent gap between his front teeth, Vince bore a certain resemblance to the ultra-debonair actor Terry Thomas. One beautifully sunny day in early March, a 20-year-old secretary named Johanna – but who went by the shortened form of Jo –visited the used car lot, with its tricolour bunting and a six-foot-tall Michelin tyre man (which wore a sandwich board bearing the name "Vince's Used Cars" upon it). Vince had his back turned to Jo as he was in the middle of a blazing row with a long-haired man of about thirty who wore a denim jacket and a matching pair of jeans. He was saying to Vince, 'I want a refund,' and other things Jo couldn't make out because Vince was talking over the disgruntled customer's heated comments. The blonde secretary found it all quite funny, even the colourful language, and as the men argued away, Jo went to look for a car. She'd recently passed her test and she was in a good mood. The Equal Pay Act had been passed a few months ago and that meant her salary was now the same as her male counterparts – a significant wage-rise in Jo's circumstances: she now earned £3,500 per year. Jo decided on a mint green car at the lot – but it had no price on it. She reasoned that surely, the car she wanted could not be more than the one that looked like the same model next to it in pillar box red, and that was £150. By now, Vince had paid the dissatisfied customer his money back, and was shaking his head with dismay as the denim-clad man strutted off.

'How much is this car?' Jo asked, and Vince's jaw dropped when the secretary directed his attention to it.

'It's a tun – ' Vince replied, and seemed suddenly stuck for words.

'A what, sorry?'

'A hundred quid – er, pounds, miss,' Vince told her, but then he gave a feeble attempt at a smile and said: 'But look at this one here – in romantic red – and £150. It's more reliable; only had one previous owner you see.'

'I want the mint green one,' Jo insisted, 'I don't like that type of red, it's too gaudy, too showy.'

'Yes, but, well, I'll tell you what, seeing as you're a petite lady, how about that Egyptian-blue mini over there? I wouldn't even mind that car myself to be quite honest – '

'Well take it then,' Jo replied as quick as a flash, 'because I'll have the mint green car. Now how much did you say? A hundred pounds?'

'Very well miss. I tell you what – just give me eighty, okay?' Vince told his customer, and he seemed a little sad. Jo had the feeling he liked the car for some reason and didn't want to part with it.

'What model is it?' Jo asked, stroking the bonnet – which felt warm. It wasn't warm from the feeble English March sun, but smelt warm as well – as if the car had been in use minutes ago.

'It's a Hillman,' Vince told her, watching Jo reach into her handbag for her purse. 'A Hillman Super Imp.'

Jo giggled. 'Imp?'

'Yes, don't let the name fool you though; does eighty, no problem, and it's got a very nice 875 c.c. engine – rear mounted as well. You'll get about forty-five miles to the gallon, and it seats four. Real luxurious car. Wish you'd take the red one though; you deserve it before someone else snaps it up.'

Jo handed him the money. 'No thanks, this one will do just fine.'

She signed a form and received the log book, and then she climbed in the car, beamed a huge smile of satisfaction to Vince, and drove off. No more buses, Jo thought, and she also recalled that invitation from her cousin down in Cornwall to stay in that lovely cottage. Now getting there didn't involve train tables and taxis. Jo lived off Wavertree Road, and wasn't sure whether to drive straight home to show the car off to her neighbour, Winnie, or whether to drive round for a bit. She had to go on a spin; it was irresistible. She drove up Renshaw Street, turned left at Lewis's Corner, and followed the H5 bus (which had come from Warrington) at a sensible thinking distance as it curved from Ranelagh Street into Church Street. She checked the fuel gauge; the tank was half full. Not bad. Then she noticed that the glove compartment was slightly open, and she opened the little door of the compartment further – to reveal a pair of orange knickers. What a strange thing to find in a glove compartment, Jo thought…

Beeeeeep!

A Morris Minor from Hanover Street cut in front of Jo and the driver was beeping his horn manically. She swore at him, checked her mirrors, then slowed down outside the Dolcis shoe store on Church Street. She looked at the orange knickers with a smirk, and then closed the compartment tightly, indicated, and turned right into Parker Street, where she passed Owen Owen and soon found herself in busy traffic on Lime Street. She arrived at the junction just before Commutation Row, intending to travel right up London Road, where a policeman wearing a white coat and gloves stood in a raised box directing the traffic. He beckoned Jo and she swerved into London Road, passing Burton the tailors, Jerome's the photographers and of course, TJ Hughes, and that store was a distraction to Jo, who was a real shopaholic who was always on the lookout for bargains, but she had to try her best to concentrate on the road. Anyway, Jo arrived back home at her terraced house off Wavertree Road, and she showed the car off to her 55-year-old neighbour Winnie. Jo had only left home a year ago and had known Winnie for just under twelve months. Winnie was very motherly towards her and forever giving advice, and on this particular day, Winnie's advice shocked Jo. When Winnie saw the mint green car, she said, 'Jo, I know this sounds funny, but I have a real horrible feeling about that car.'

'Why?' Jo was understandably anxious at her friend's feelings. 'Why, what do you mean?'

Winnie seemed very upset. 'There's just something about it. I'm sorry Jo, I wouldn't say anything like this normally; I'd keep it to myself, but I have a real bad feeling about that car.'

Winnie had something of a reputation in her street for being psychic. She also read tea leaves and had made various predictions over the years which had come to pass. Jo had heard about Winnie's alleged psychic abilities, and this naturally made her very uneasy about driving about in the car – but she tried to dismiss all the talk of bad feelings as mumbo-jumbo.

Three days later, Jo was driving back from an old school friend's house in Widnes, and she ended up driving home along a very lonely narrow lane which would take her through the farmland and fields of Tarbock Green. The lane was not lit at all, and was darker still that summer evening because high hedges bordered the lane on each side. As Jo travelled along this lane at about forty miles an hour, she thought she felt the Hillman Super Imp jolt for a moment, as if someone was moving heavily in the vehicle. Around this time, Jo also realised she had not put on her seatbelt, and decided not to divert her attention from the narrow road just to put it on – even though she knew that wearing a seatbelt or not could be a matter of life or death; she thought about Jimmy Saville's

'Clunk Click every trip' TV advertising campaign to highlight the importance of seatbelt safety, and she smiled inanely. She suddenly detected an aroma of tobacco, and because the side windows were open on this close summer evening, Jo wondered if she had passed a place where someone had been smoking, but she had a horrible feeling that there was a smoker in the car. As she wondered if someone had sneaked into the car to lie in wait for her as it was parked outside her friend's house, she felt a cold clammy hand being cupped hard over her mouth. Jo reacted to the clamped hand with such shock, she involuntarily turned the wheel and the car almost went through a hedge, but she had the mind to keep the vehicle pointed straight as the other hand touched her left breast. In the girl's left ear, a gruff voice said, 'Slow down you bitch!'

Jo slowed down the car, then halted the vehicle, all the while struggling to breathe with the hand pressed against her lips, and she looked into the rear view mirror to see a man with black curly hair, mad staring eyes, and thick eyebrows that met above his long prominent nose.

The man climbed into the front passenger seat and suddenly produced a knife. He told Jo to recline her seat, and when she looked at the knife in shock, he lifted it as if he was about to plunge it in her chest, and she screamed.

The uninvited passenger then adjusted Jo's seat so she was laying back at about forty-five degrees. She then heard him unzip his trousers and start to unfasten the buckle of his belt as he grinned. 'Just be a good girl and I won't have to stick ya, will I?'

'I've got money if you want that instead,' Jo told the would-be rapist in a trembling voice.

'No thanks, I'll just have you instead,' said the disgusting predator. 'Take your stuff off, now!'

'Please don't! You can have the car as well if you want!' Jo said, and she started to cry.

'I could kill you and still *do it* you know!' the man screeched, and his breath reeked of Golden Virginia tobacco.

Just then, Jo noticed a light in the nearside mirror. Another vehicle was approaching. It was a Liverpool man in his thirties named Paul Harris, returning from his girlfriend's house in Widnes on his prized 200 c.c. Ariel Arrow motorcycle.

'Stay still or I'll cut your throat wide open,' the rapist warned Jo, but she slyly reached for the handle on the door, and waited for a few seconds, wondering if she'd soon be dead. She hadn't put her seatbelt on, so there was a chance she'd be able to sprint out of the car as soon as she opened the door. She suddenly pushed the door open and almost fell out the vehicle into the hedge, before running down the road towards the motorcyclist waving her arms in the air as the rapist turned the air blue behind her with some of the coarsest language the secretary had ever heard.

Paul Harris slowed down and came to a halt about ten feet away from Jo. She ran to him and told him how a man with a knife had tried to rape her, and she tried to get onto the motorbike, but Paul pushed her back, and rolled the motorcycle to the side of the road, where he kicked the stand down. He took off his crash helmet, and crept up on the mint green car with the helmet held up slightly, as if he intended to strike the rapist with it. Paul looked in the Hillman and saw nobody there.

'Be careful! He's got a knife!' Jo warned Paul in a hysterical voice.

'There's no one in here, love,' Paul told her, and he even knelt down and looked under the car. He then walked to the hedge at the side of the road and saw that no one could have passed through it. He naturally wondered if the girl who had flagged him down was some attention seeker or a deranged person. 'Well, he's vanished into thin air.'

'He must still be in there!' Jo said, and started to cry.

Paul came up to her and said, 'Look, I swear there is no one in that car. Now, are you going to Liverpool?'

'Yes,' Jo replied, and wiped her eyes, which were now streaked with mascara.

'Well look, I'll drive behind you all the way – how's that?' Paul proposed.

'Are you sure he's gone?' Jo asked, looking at the car with an expression of pure dread.

Paul nodded and patted her left shoulder in a very reassuring manner. 'I'd bet my life on it love. So get in your car now, and I'll go with you, and then I'll escort you home.'

And true to his word, Paul escorted Jo all the way to her home on Wavertree Road, and even came in to have a cup of tea with her and Winnie.

That night, Jo had a series of nightmares about the rapist, and in the morning as she had her cornflakes, she kept going over the assault, and tried to rationalise just how the assailant had entered the car. He must have sneaked into the car as it was parked outside of her cousin's home In Widnes, Jo thought, but even if that was so, how had he escaped from the car after she had flagged down Paul Harris?

Jo felt uneasy about venturing into that car for a while, but on the following morning, the bright Spring sunshine seemed to partly evaporate the fear of the previous evening. Jo decided that the would-be rapist was probably just some opportunist who had somehow sneaked into her car at some point; there was nothing supernatural or weird about his presence in the vehicle. Jo drove to her workplace off Dale Street, and at the end of the usual never-ending typing and Tippexing, she set off for home, braving the madness of the rush hour traffic. She reached home at 5.25pm, after stopping off for a mixed grill at a chippy on Wavertree Road, just around the corner from her place. Jo had had a bit of a falling out with her mother six months ago. Her mum had wanted her to stay at home until she found a decent boyfriend rather than living alone at her own place, and Jo, being the fiercely independent girl she was, deliberately went out and rented a place as far from her Litherland home as possible. But now Jo wondered how her mum - and dad – were doing, and so, on a spare of the moment whim, she decided she'd travel up to her parents' house on Litherland's Hatton Hill Road. Jo intended to set out on the 8-mile journey at 7pm, but she received a visit from an old school friend named Joyce at 6.40pm, and the two girls chatted and caught up on each other's lives, and this delayed Jo's trip. Jo was only too eager to show off her car to Joyce, and she drove her friend to her home in the Dingle that evening at 8pm, then embarked on the journey to Litherland. Twilight was falling by now, and darkness seemed to be gathering by the very minute, which naturally made Jo a little edgy, because she was mindful of the lighting conditions when she had been attacked the night before. Joyce had told Jo she should have reported the attack to the police, and Jo had shook her head and said she thought the would-be rapist would come after her if she did that. She just wanted to forget the whole thing.

As Jo was driving up along Derby Road towards Bootle, a strange silence seemed to fall over everything. To the left were towering grim warehouses, and upon this stretch of road, something terrifying took place. Jo thought she could smell tobacco in the vehicle. She wondered if Joyce had smoked in the car when she had driven her home. She hadn't. Joyce had smoked in Jo's house, and she had smoked Players No. 6 – but this aroma was undoubtedly the same tang as the Golden Virginia tobacco she had smelt seconds before the attack.

Jo looked up to check her rear view mirror.

It was him – again. He was leaning forward in the back seat, but he wasn't looking at Jo; he was watching the passing warehouses as if he was fascinated with the scrolling scenery outside. Jo pulled up at the traffic lights, undid her safety belt, and jumped out of the car. A car horn beeped and tyres screeched behind her as cars braked hard to avoid knocking her down. Jo heard the man in her car shout after her: 'No you don't! Come here!'

But she hurried across the road without even knowing where she was going, as Jo didn't know this part of the city that well. She walked up Millers Bridge in a daze, convinced by now that the man who had attempted to rape her was some ghost. There was no other explanation. Jo waved frantically to a policeman on the other side of the road, and when he came over to see what the matter was, she told him what had happened, but thought it would be unwise to tell him about the previous assault as she had returned from Widnes. The police converged on the abandoned Hillman Super Imp, and found no one in it. Jo refused to get back in that car, and it was sold for £50 via the used cars column of the *Liverpool Echo*. Out of curiosity, Jo went back to Vince's Used Cars lot, and asked the jovial dealer if that car had a history. 'I don't know what you're talking about,' he said.

Jo told him it had been haunted, but she never gave any other details.

'Haunted?' Vince gave a sham chuckle, then asked: 'Well that's a new one, love. You saying you want your money back? Because you can't get a refund on the basis that something is haunted.'

'Oh, it's sold now,' Jo told him, observing the nervous behaviour of the dealer with suspicion, 'but I just wondered if you knew there was something odd about that car.'

Vince raised his eyebrows, feigned a look of innocence, and shrugged. 'It was a perfectly decent car,' he claimed.

'Nah, I think you knew that car had a ghost,' Jo told him, looking Vince right in the eyes. 'That's why you wanted to sell me that red one instead isn't it? And I'll bet that bloke you were arguing with the day I bought the car – the one you gave the money back to – had discovered that car was haunted. I'm right aren't I?'

Vince turned and walked away and went into his hut

without saying a word.

In 1997, a woman from Kirkdale named Sarah told me that she had once owned an old green car which she had used as a "runaround" after she had passed her test in 1976. Whenever this woman drove at night, she said she would start to smell pungent tobacco and then she would feel the 'presence' of someone male in that cab. Sarah had the feeling that this unseen male was violent, and she felt quite threatened when the presence manifested itself. After just a few weeks, Sarah gave the car to a friend. I asked Sarah how she had come into possession of the green car, and she said she had bought it for £50 via the used cars column of the *Liverpool Echo* from a woman in Wavertree...

WHO'S THAT GIRL?

In the summer of 2009 a rather strange and eerie daylight haunting took place off Townsend Lane and Breck Road. It all started when a 45-year-old woman named Donna left her terraced home on Empress Road, off Townsend Lane, in the Cabbage Hall district of the city. Divorcee Donna was going in search of her boyfriend of fifteen months, a 50-year-old man nicknamed 'Buster', who originally hailed from Speke. Buster was normally a selfless man; although a rough diamond in some ways, and never shy when it came to using his fists, should trouble come his way, but that was only one side of him, and Donna and her 17-year-old daughter Avril had come to love Buster in the short time they had come to know him, but every now and then, Buster would go out for a packet of cigarettes and embark on a never-ending pub-crawl. On this sunny day in July 2009, Buster had gone out in the morning to buy twenty cigarettes and a magazine for Avril, and somewhere along the way, he had bumped into an old friend named Gerry Curtayne, because Donna's neighbour Julie had seen the two men talking near Ugly Ben's recycled furniture shop on Townsend Lane, so Donna guessed that Buster and his old school chum had probably gone for a drink in the Stadium pub further up the lane. And so Donna and Avril strolled up Townsend Lane, and various friends and neighbours – some of them nosy parkers and gossipers – and some of them people who genuinely cared for Donna and her daughter – asked where Buster was. Donna had to lie to some of the nosy ones; the janglers who were forever spreading gossip about her (and even about Avril). Donna told them Buster had gone for a drink with a relative who was visiting from Scotland, and Avril almost gave the game away by smirking as her mum told these white fibs. Avril thought she saw Buster coming out of Mio's Mini Market, but it was just someone who looked like him from behind. As mother and daughter were crossing Clarendon Road, which is a little side street off Townsend Lane, Avril noticed a beautiful little girl of about 7 or 8 years of age come out of the mouth of the alleyway at the back of a store called E. G. Doors. This alleyway was alleygated, as many of the entries in Liverpool and other major cities are nowadays. An alleygate is there to prevent and reduce burglaries, criminal damage by vandals, as well as anti-social behaviour – so Avril assumed that the little girl, who wore a blue gingham dress and had long jet-black hair, had not been down the alleyway, but had probably been playing near the top of the entry just round the corner. She would not have been able to climb an alleygate. The little porcelain-skinned child walked towards Donna and Avril, and at closer quarters, Avril saw that the girl had huge dark blue eyes. She smiled faintly at Avril, and because of the little girl's short strides, Donna and her daughter soon outpaced her and overtook her as they headed for the first port of call in the quest for Buster. 'He never drinks in here, mam,' Avril told her mother, as she halted at the entrance to the Winchester pub. Donna went inside anyway and had a quick look about. As Donna was in the pub looking for Buster, Donna put on the earphones of her iPod and started to listen to some songs. Nearby stood the little girl she'd set eyes on a minute or so ago. She was standing near the doorway to the Ryan & Son Bathroom store, and she was looking at the iPod with a fascinated look. Donna came out and said 'He's not in there and no one's seen him anywhere. I hope he hasn't been knocked down or something.'

Donna and Avril walked on up Townsend Lane, and as Avril passed an Indian takeaway, she looked back to see that the girl in the blue gingham dress was still standing by the bathroom fittings shop, apparently gazing at her. Donna reached the Stadium pub a few minutes later, and saw that Buster was not in there, nor had any of the drinkers who knew Buster clapped eyes on him today. Donna and Avril walked along, and coming from the other direction was that little girl again. Donna thought nothing of the child's presence, but Avril wondered how the girl had travelled from that spot outside the bathroom store to the busy junction where Townsend Lane meets Lower Breck Road. The little girl smiled at Avril as she passed her. That girl was now heading north, back in the direction Donna and Avril had come from, towards the Stadium pub. Donna was starting to panic, and she and Avril dashed over the roads at the hectic junction and called in at the Cabbage Hall pub. At first, none of the drinkers Donna talked to said they had seen Buster, but then an old man named Alf said he had seen Donna's fellah going down Breck Road twenty minutes before with 'some little baldy man' – an accurate description of Gerry Curtayne. Donna and Avril came out of the Cabbage Hall pub and crossed back over to the other side, and here, the little girl in the blue gingham dress was standing on that great triangular green, about fifty yards to Avril's left. The girl was standing there, apparently watching Donna and Avril as they now hurried up towards Holy Trinity church. Donna and her daughter passed the church, when all of a sudden, Avril got the shock of her life. The little girl she had first seen on Clarendon Street jumped out from behind a red post office pillar box and yelled: 'Boo!'

Avril was dumbfounded and a little scared by the sudden appearance of the girl because she had just seen her further down the road on that green triangle of grass by Lower Breck Road. It was humanly impossible, without any transport, for anyone to travel from that triangle to the pillar box in such a short time. Avril wondered if she was perhaps seeing the little girl's twin sister, but when she turned to look down the road, she saw that there was no little girl in a blue dress near that triangle. This had to be her. Avril told her mother about the child, who was now following her, in hushed tones, but Donna was more preoccupied with finding Buster, and she said, 'Oh, she's probably just ran up here and you haven't seen her, Avril.'

A voice called out to Donna from nearby St David's Road. It was Donna's elderly uncle, Chad. He called her over, and when she said she was looking for Buster and was really worried about him, Chad clutched her hands and said: 'Donna, you're worrying for nothing girl. I bumped into him before, and he said he's going to a pub called the Round House, and I think he meant the one on Irvine Street, the Mount Vernon. He was with a mate of his –'

'The Mount Vernon?' Donna interrupted, and her eyes rolled to the right as she tried to picture where that pub was. She had drunk there many years ago. 'Isn't that sort of at the edge of Kenny, nor far from the hospital?'

'Yeah, you know where Paddy Comprehensive was don't you?' Chad asked, tracing an imaginary road in the air with the flat of his hand.

'Archbishop Blanch school you mean?' Avril chipped in.

'Don't confuse her Avril,' Chad said, and grinned.

'Yeah, I remember where it is now. Ah, thanks Uncle Chad,' Donna said, and she turned to the roadway as Chad dipped into his wallet and gave Avril a tenner.

'Oi! Taxi!' Donna yelled, and a Hackney cab pulled over on Breck Road.

In the taxi, Donna said, 'I wonder why he's gone to the Mount Vernon? You don't think he's seeing someone do you?'

Avril was looking back at that little girl, who was now standing near the spot where they had met Uncle Chad, and she was looking directly at the taxi. This unnerved Avril, who suddenly heard the mental echo of her insecure mother's question . 'Nah, Buster's not seeing anyone mum. You won't let him go anywhere on his own, so how could he meet someone?'

'I know, because see what happens when he does go out on his own?' Donna told her, trying secretly to justify her reasons for being so clingy with her boyfriend. 'Hey, you don't think he's gone to meet someone off the internet do you? He's seen you in those chat rooms; might have given him ideas.'

'Oh mum please shut up and come back into the real world,' was Avril's plea as she listened to her iPod again.

The taxi soon reached the Mount Vernon pub with its rounded façade, and Donna and Avril went in the establishment, and there was Buster and his friend Gerry, laughing their heads off over something, but when Buster set eyes on Donna and Avril, the smile quickly evaporated from his face.

'Did you get your ciggies then?' Donna asked him, and Buster seemed stuck for words.

'Hiya love, well what it was you see is that, well –'

'Don't "hiya love" me, Bamber,' Donna replied, addressing Buster by his real first name. Avril grinned when she heard her mum utter this name.

'No, wait, give me a word in edgeways will ya?' Buster told her, and he reached first into his left inside pocket, and then searched the right inside pocket.

'It's in *there*,' Gerry said to Buster, and tapped his left coat pocket with the back of his hand.

Buster reached to the indicated pocket and took out a little dark red box. He opened it, and Avril opened her mouth in shock as Buster smiled, and then got down on one knee in front of Donna.

Donna steadied herself. Her left hand leaned on the

vacant tall barstool. Her other hand flew up to her mouth, and she looked as if she was going to cry.

Buster recited Donna's full name – even her confirmation name – and then he said: 'will you marry me?'

'Oh shit,' Avril said unconsciously.

'Yes!' Donna told him, and tears flowed in her eyes as Buster slipped the N-sized white-gold engagement ring onto the third finger of her left hand.

'I thought I'd have a drink before I asked you, Don,' Buster told his fiancée, 'because I was a bag of nerves. That's why I was so restless last night. I had planned to propose to you in the kitchen when you were making breakfast, but my nerve went.'

There was a wave of 'Ahs' from several of the females present – and one from a sarcastic male as well.

Drinks were soon flowing, and Avril got bored, and wandered outside the pub at one point to phone her friend Melissa to tell her about the 'cheesy marriage proposal' – but outside stood that little girl in the blue gingham dress. Avril recoiled in shock as she was in mid-conversation, and she said nothing for a while. Melissa kept asking her if she was still there. The girl gave a sinister smile, and Avril realised that the blueness of the child's eyes had now turned to black. Avril turned and ran back into the pub to tell her mother who was outside, but by now the pub jukebox was booming away and Donna and Buster were dancing like two people possessed as the drinkers clapped in time. Avril shouted for her mother to stop dancing but Donna was on another planet, elated at the proposal, and already the gin and tonic was working its magic in her brain. It was useless. Avril went back into the hallway of the pub and opened the door slightly. There was no sign of the girl. Avril went out into the street and saw the child was nowhere to be seen. The only people about were passers-by and two middle-aged smokers who were forced by the Smoking Ban to risk their lives outside the pub. At this point, Avril decided to walk home all the way to Empress Road, but every now and then she would catch a glimpse of that girl in the blue gingham dress. She was undoubtedly a ghost, for she would come out of phone boxes seconds after Avril had seen her quite a distance away, and she seemed to have the ability to run through alleygates, emerging from the entries of various streets to chase after Avril as she shrieked with laughter. At one point, when Avril finally reached Townsend Lane, she saw the girl standing outside a café called Ann's Pantry. Avril stopped, wondering what the sinister ghost would do next. It ran off down the lane, then sprinted across a patch of grassy wasteland where it seemed to fall. Avril sneaked past this wasteland and halted for a moment to see where the apparition was. All of a sudden, Avril saw the shadow of the girl's head and shoulders inching along the pavement towards her left. Avril ran across the road to avoid the tormenting apparition and just missed a certain death by inches as a van flew past her. Avril stood panting by a carpet store on the corner of Cathedral Road, looking across the road to the girl in the blue dress, who was now standing as still as a statue with an emotionless face. Avril raced off home to Empress Road and went to the house of Julie, her mum's friend. Avril spouted out the seemingly unbelievable account of the creepy stalking girl, but Julie suddenly said: 'I believe you Avril, I've seen her myself.'

Julie said she had seen that same girl in that gingham dress two years ago, and like now, it had been a fine July day. The girl had followed her as far as Clubmoor when Julie went to see her sister. Julie said a few older people in the street had seen the little girl over the years and the general consensus amongst the elders of the neighbourhood is that the child was the ghost of a little girl who was killed during World War Two when a German bomb landed on her house. Avril was not a religious person, but felt moved enough to go to church, where she said an 'Eternal Rest' prayer for the earthbound phantom and also lit a candle for the child as a symbolic gesture. After doing this, Avril saw no more of the ghost in blue gingham.

SLEEPY GENE

As far-fetched as it may seem, the following story is alleged to be true, and it's based on the testimony of three rather simple unpretentious people. One of them has since died. There have been a few name-changes, but otherwise the story is exactly as it was related to me by three people involved in it. The story references the well-reported phenomenon of possession.

Sleep is the greatest thief, for he steals a third of your life, yet in sleep, all are equal; what difference is there between Solomon and a fool when both are in slumbers? Even tyrants like Hitler and Stalin spent a third of their life on holiday from their own egos during the hours of sleep. Mystics say that sleep is the brother of death, that just as we cannot remember the exact point of falling asleep, we will one day be equally oblivious about the point when we slip out of this life. But there are many mysteries concerning sleep; are dreams merely fragments of the waking life, or is there more to them than meets the eye? There was a rather strange case that illustrates what I'm referring to, and it all unfolded in Tuebrook in the infernal late summer of 1976, the year of the Great Drought. On Wednesday, 7 September, 1976, at 5.10pm, 13-year-old Gene Wilson sat down at the family table to have his tea, and as usual his father Ernie told him off because Gene would habitually turn his chair towards the television, because his favourite programme was just starting – a Liverpool-based children's drama series called *Rocky O'Rourke*.

The Wilsons were a big family. There was Gene, of course, his sisters, Sue, fifteen, Michelle 12, Joanne, 9, and brothers Michael, 16, Billy, 10, and Gary, aged 6. There was also Nanny Ann Wilson, in her seventies. Nanny was a lover of wrestling (especially Mick McManus) bingo and horseracing. Nanny would put a bet on Monday to Saturday, it was her only real pleasure, besides her Harold Robbins books. Then there was her husband, Grandad George Wilson, a very active man of 75 who walked miles to the Pier Head and back each day from the family home in Marlborough Road, Tuebrook. Grandad delusionally saw himself as Liverpool's answer to the science historian James Burke, there to explain scientific principles and to translate anything technological into layman's terms for the family. On this very day in fact, he was babbling on about NASA's Viking 2 Lander probe, which had just touched down on Mars, but no one was listening. 'If the world was the size of a beach ball,' he told Gene, 'Mars would be where the Jolly Miller pub is; that's how far space goes up, like.'

Mrs Wilson told her husband to stop reading the broadsheet *Liverpool Echo* at the table while they were 'dining' – a word that always made the girls snigger. Mr Wilson sighed, folded the newspaper, and tackled the plate of scouse. Michael and Billy talked about tomorrow's big game at Wembley between England and the Republic of Ireland, and they discussed the suitability of manager Don Revie, Keegan and Thompson's leg injuries, and who the best footy player in their school was. Sue whispered to Michelle about her ex-boyfriend Richie Ryan, and how he tried to make her jealous by French-kissing Maureen 'Spotty' Muldoon on Lorenzo Drive. Against this typical domestic backdrop, on this particular September day, something very strange took place. After Gene Wilson had finished his tea, he enjoyed the usual slice of sandwich cake for dessert, and a bottle of Cresta lemonade, before retiring to his room for forty winks on this feverishly warm evening. As the family laughed at the contestants' antics on the TV show *It's A Knockout*, downstairs, Gene dozed off for what he expected to be a short nap, but when he awoke, he found himself standing under a full moon in Newsham Park with his arms around a beautiful girl he'd never seen before...

'John, why have you stopped?' Jennifer Danebury asked with a puzzled look in her beautiful eyes.

'Why have I stopped what? And who's John?' Gene Wilson queried, backing away from the girl. What on earth was he doing in a moonlit Newsham Park? Gene wondered, and suspected he was still dreaming, but it all felt too real to be a dream.

'Why have you stopped dancing?' Jennifer asked. There was love in her twinkly eyes, and it scared the virginal Gene. The teenagers gazed at one another in silence for a moment under the full moon, with the distant sounds of traffic and the faint barking of a dog in Rocky Lane heightening the isolation of the park. 'Why has your voice changed?' Jennifer asked. Her face seemed porcelain, doll-like, by the light of the moon.

'I've always talked like this,' said Gene, self-consciously, and he turned and said, 'anyway I better be getting home. Me Mam'll be looking for me.'

As he hurried away from the girl - who was

unknown to him - she shouted after him. 'Why are you going?' But Gene ran off, northwards into the cool night, afraid because he thought he'd been sleepwalking. How else could he have ended up in Newsham Park after going to bed? He heard Jennifer's faint voice drifting on the night breeze: 'John! Don't go!'

All the way home, Gene wondered who this John was that the girl had been referring to. When he reached his home in Marlborough Road at five-past eleven, he found the front door ajar, all the lights on in the house, but no one was about. There came a blast of sound from the television set – the opening bars of the theme to *What the Papers Say* – which startled Gene. He turned the volume down and then went next door to Mrs Folkestone to see if she knew where everyone was.

'Ah, here he is Barbara!' Mrs Folkestone said, when she opened her front door, and his neighbour ushered him into her back parlour, where most of the Wilson family were. Gene's mum was furious, and his father wanted to have words with his son as well, but didn't get a chance. 'Where have you been?' Mrs Wilson shouted, and the boy's sisters, Sue, Michelle and Joanne, told him off, saying how worried they'd all been after finding his bed empty at 8pm. 'Grandad's still walking the streets looking for you!' fifteen-year-old Sue yelled at Gene. 'Where have you been?'

'I don't know,' Gene confessed, 'I woke up in Newsham Park with my arms around some girl!'

Gene's little sister, 9-year-old Joanne, formed a perfect 'O' with her mouth, and said 'Ah! Have you been going out with a girlfriend without telling mum and dad?'

'Who is this girl? What have you been up to, hey?' Mr Wilson wanted to know, but Gene shook his head and said, 'I just told you I don't know! I don't know how I ended up in the park!'

'Liar!' said Gene's other sister, 12-year-old Michelle, and she turned to her mother. 'Mam, I seen him -' she started to say. 'You *saw* him Michelle, not *seen* him,' her father corrected the girl.

'Dad!' Michelle squealed, 'I seen Gene leave the house and I asked him where he was going, and he swore at me in a weird voice!'

'I did not!' Gene denied the claim. Anyway, at 1am, he finally got to bed after enduring a sermon from his father on the 'right way' to find a girlfriend. As soon as Gene slept, "John" took over his body again.

Gene Wilson slipped out of his bed – or, should I say – John Wilson did. He was a 13-year-old who had been born in 1701. Through sheer willpower, his spirit had somehow managed to squat in the attic of Gene Wilson's subconscious, and whenever Gene's conscious mind slept, John would take over the cerebellum neurons of his brain. 'Ah! Life!' John rejoiced, inhaling air, and once again savouring the delights of being alive in a flesh-and-blood body after being a scotch-mist spirit for 262 years. How was this possible? How could one from the Silent Majority (all the dead and unborn people) simply slip into a living body? Any genuine exorcist will vouch for me when I say that spirits can and do occasionally take over one of the living, but they rarely stay in the living for any duration. John Wilson, however, was able to infiltrate Gene Wilson's mind because Gene's DNA and his mindprint were exactly the same as John's and this was due to Gene being a remote descendant of the 18th century teen. When John died in a house fire in 1714, he had been about to elope with Jenny Quidhampton – a poor Lancashire farm girl, and in this time, in 1976, Jenny's exact replica existed in the form of the Tuebrook schoolgirl Jennifer Danebury.

John Wilson came down from Gene's bedroom and explored the house. Watching in the shadows was 9-year-old Joanne Wilson. She had come down for a glass of water on this unbearable summer night, and had hidden when she heard Gene's footsteps. At first she thought it was her brother, but then she heard John Wilson's odd voice. 'Ah, milk of human kindness,' he muttered, and chuckled, after opening the fridge door in the kitchen. He knocked back a whole pint of Unigate milk. 'Milk, I had forgotten the silken taste of thee. In the dark realm of spirits I had dreamed so long of you,' John soliloquized, and he smiled, wiped the milk from his lips, and sighed as he poked his head into the coolness of the fridge. 'Gloriana! Bread, and butter! Yes, I must have them also.'

Joanne watched from the triangle of darkness under the stairs. What's wrong with Gene? She wondered. She saw him grinning at the Mother's Pride loaf. 'A loaf already sliced, how novel!' he said, and used the huge sharp breadknife to spread butter on the slices of bread. Weird raspy voices could be heard in the air in the kitchen, and they scared little Joanne; they were the voices of evil jealous spirits and two mocked John: 'You won't stay alive long, dead man!' whined one, and another deep gruff-voiced spirit warned: 'You'll be punished for entering the world of life!'

John gritted his teeth and swiped the air over the sink with the breadknife – and that really scared Joanne. A tear rolled down her cheek; she wanted the Gene she knew to come back immediately.

John Wilson left the kitchen and sneaked out of the house, into the night.

Joanne woke her parents, sisters and brothers and told them Gene had gone 'bonkers'. The youngest of the family, 6-year-old Gary, didn't understand why everyone was in turmoil, and when he saw the milk bottle John Wilson had emptied on the draining board, the boy sung the jingle that was forever advertising milk on the television: *'Watch out, watch out, watch out, watch out, there's a Humphrey about!'*

Grandad Wilson requisitioned grandson Michael's Ultraviolet Chopper bike and went in search of Gene, while the three Wilson girls and their mum went to the police station. Gene's Dad took his sons Michael and Billy with him to search Newsham Park, while little Gary stayed at home with his Nan.

Then came some shocking news from a neighbour, and Mrs Wilson almost fainted when she heard that news. Her son Gene had been knocked down by a Cortina on West Derby Road, near the junction at Orphan Drive. As the sobbing motorist leaned over Gene, lying inert in the gutter, he saw a ghostly glowing figure of a young man in a huge curly white wig and 18th century-type clothes come out of the unconscious teen. The motorist understandably fled after the apparition slapped him across the face and called him a 'buffoon' and a word that sounded like 'slubberdegullion'.

The dislodged spirit body of John Wilson then ran off to Newsham Park, to the romantic rendezvous with Jennifer Danebury, the girl he had returned to life for. The ambulance arrived and took Gene to hospital, and all of the Wilson family- except Grandad - followed the ambulance in the neighbour's van. Luckily Gene was only concussed but would be kept in hospital for observation. Grandad Wilson, who was not ware of the accident, ironically passed the ambulance in his search for Gene, and decided to steer the Chopper bike into Newsham Park. What he saw, at first scared him, but then intrigued him. He saw the glowing figure of the 18th century counterpart of his grandson.

John Wilson was singing *Greensleeves* as he made his way across the moonlit park to the bridge, where he hoped his lover would be waiting for him. Jennifer Danebury was as romantic as John, but the John she was longing for looked like Gene Wilson, and when she saw the radiant phantom in his huge white 'judge's' wig, embroidered satin coat with turned up sleeves, breeches, and stockings from the knees to his square-toed buckled shoes, the girl felt dizzy with fear. A real live ghost! She clutched the handrail of the bridge, feeling faint, but John Wilson, became so shy, he stopped singing *Greensleeves* and fidgeted with the brass buttons of his ethereal coat as he came quite close to the petrified girl. 'I hath returned from the grave for thy warm love, fair maiden Jenny!' he said in a choked voice. 'I have fended off a legion of unclean spirits and braved the Valley of Death to rejoin you! Of all the numberless dead I alone hath returned to the living side of nature to become thine husband.'

'Yer what?' Jennifer asked, light-headed with shock. And then, John Wilson intended to kiss Jennifer's knuckle but he couldn't lift her hand – because his hand went straight through hers, now that he didn't have Gene Wilson's flesh-and-blood body to operate like a puppeteer. With horror, John realised he was but an insubstantial ghost, and the evil, wicked spirits soon arrived and closed in on him. They gave him a right kicking, and Jennifer screamed. The shadowy gargoyles rose out of the lake and from every shade to torment him. 'Back to the darkness dead man!' said one red-eyed demon with ash-coloured skin.

Grandad Wilson watched the spectacle, and noticed a tall dark figure standing nearby. 'Go and stop them!' said the old man to this silhouette 'Those thugs are beating him! Stop them!' The grandfather got ready to go to the rescue on the Chopper but the dark stranger turned to face the old knight on a bike, and revealed an horrific face with two bright glowing orange eyes and aspects which lead me to believe that he was Abaddon, the patron demon of hate and destruction. 'Leave here or die,' this entity roared.

Grandad Wilson yelped and hurried off, abandoning the Chopper bike. A whirlwind of demonic laughter came down onto the bridge and whisked John Wilson into a spiralling blackness. 'Goodbye sweet Jenny, goodbye my love,' he said, and Jennifer Danebury turned and never stopped running till she reached her Tuebrook home.

HUYTON'S GHOSTLY
HIGHWAYMAN

Out of nowhere, an eerie figure in a three-cornered hat and a flowing cape was seen on horseback to emerge from a mist early one foggy morning in November 1976. He was coming from the direction of Huyton's Twig Lane towards Cotsford Road. A 55-year-old man named David had been on his way to Twig Lane, where a friend named Ron would pick him up in a transit van to give him a lift to his workplace in Prescot. On this morning, David left his home on Cotsford Road a little earlier than usual (6.50am) because he had accidentally set his alarm clock ten minutes fast. The fog gave a ghostly aspect to the road and a ground mist blanketed everything up to knee-level. As David left his home he had heard the distinctive clip-clop of a horse somewhere in the distance and thought that perhaps a mounted policeman was in the area – but then as David walked up the road he saw the silhouette of the horse he'd heard a minute earlier; it was a huge animal, like a shire horse in build, and sitting on it was a very alarming figure in a tricorn hat and a long cloak of some sort – and this outdated figure was pointing a gun at David as it stood there stock-still. David halted and wondered what to do. He decided to turn and run in a confused state, and as he ran off he thought he heard the man on horseback shout something that sounded like: 'Come back!'

David never had a telephone landline – and in those days, mobile phones of the type we use now were unheard of – and so he decided to go to a phone box to alert the police to the nutter in fancy dress, but then he wondered if the person was just demented, or possibly someone perpetrating a hoax, and as David walked towards the phone box, he saw his mate Ron passing in the transit van, so he ran towards him and flagged the vehicle down. Before he could say a word, Ron suddenly said to him: 'There's a fellah up there dressed as a highwayman.' Ron pointed towards the Liverpool Road end of twig Lane. David then told him how he'd seen the very same figure minutes ago and how the lunatic had aimed a gun at him. The two men then drove up Twig Lane to look for the outlandish man on horseback, but he was nowhere to be seen. David never reported the incident and Ron dropped him off at his Prescot workplace before driving to his own workplace in the Whiston area. David never mentioned the "highwayman" to anyone else, but that day during lunchtime at his work canteen, a 30-year-old man named Stan said his sister had been coming back from her boyfriend's house on Dinas Lane a few nights ago, and as she was walking up Lincombe Road when she heard a horse galloping behind her. She turned to see a man in a black cloak and "funny old-fashioned hat" on, tearing down the road on a huge horse. The man shouted something to her as he rode past, and then, as he passed Jubilee Park, he vanished into thin air, but the sound of the horse's hooves could be heard for a about half a minute until they faded away.

When David heard of this encounter with the

highwayman, he told Stan about his own meeting with what must have been a ghost. About a week after this, David was again going to work of a morning, only this time there wasn't a trace of any fog about and it was a bright clear sunny morning. As David reached the junction of Twig Lane, he heard the distant sounds of a horse galloping along, but could not see any horse or the ghostly highwayman anywhere.

I have received many reports of the so-called Huyton Highwayman over the years, and from what I can gather, he and his spectral steed have been at large in the Huyton, Page Moss and Whiston areas for many decades. Huyton is, of course, an ancient place, and its name is probably derived from the Anglo-Saxon words "heah" and "tun" meaning an elevated enclosure. Huyton is referred as Hitune in the Domesday Book, but the spelling we know today appeared in the 13th century. Huyton in the 18th century was, like many other rural towns, frequented by highwaymen, including the infamous Black Jack, who terrorised both stagecoaches and lone travellers on the roads between Huyton and Liverpool. For many years a rumour has persisted that a highwayman's treasure lies buried somewhere near Huyton Quarry Station. In 1933, 10 silver coins dating from around 1708 where found near the station and since then, many amateur archaeologists and budding treasure hunters have gone in search of the fabled highwayman's treasure. One rainy evening in 1910, several drinkers leaving the Rose and Crown pub in Huyton are said to have encountered the ghost of a highwayman and his horse. On that occasion the highwayman rode towards the Parish Church of St Michael, and was seen to fade away before it reached the walls of the cemetery. In December of that same year, just before Christmas, the apparition of the highwayman was seen – this time without his horse – standing inside the snow-covered cemetery, and on this occasion, a hooded figure which looked like a monk, was standing next to the highwayman, apparently in conversation. A group of children and two elderly men were the witnesses to this intriguing incident. During excavations around St Michael's Church in 1873, as a wall was being repaired, a stone column (thought to be of Saxon origin) carved with four helmeted heads, was unearthed in the grounds of the church as well as a sandstone font, both dating from the 9th century. When these discoveries were made, the hooded ghost was seen in the vicinity, and this is often the case when hallowed ground is disturbed; it often triggers paranormal activity. When a Mr H. E . Smith mentioned the sightings of the ghostly monk to the Historic Society at their meeting at the Royal Institution in Colquitt Street on November 27, 1873, there were sneers and sniggers all round. Over 130 years later, some still laugh at the idea of ghosts.

In the 1890s, a figure on horseback that looked exactly like the archetypal Dick Turpin type of highwayman was seen riding along on a heavy draft horse on the railway tracks near the level-crossing of Huyton Station. On this occasion, the ghost and his horse were seen in broad daylight, and were also seen to dissolve into thin air as many looked on. A few oldsters claimed that this same apparition had been seen back in 1852, minutes before a fatal accident involving one Thomas Sparkes took place in October of that year. Sparkes, of Liverpool, was getting into the carriage as the train was in motion, when he slipped and received such injuries on the feet and ankles, that amputation of both legs below the knees 'was obliged immediately to be made' as the reporter in *The Times* put it. Sparkes died a fortnight afterwards. The identity of the ghostly highwayman – if indeed all the reports are of the same character – remains unknown.

Postscript: The story of the Huyton Highwayman reminds me of a similar story that was related to me by a man named Stephen who I met after a talk on ghosts at St George's Hall in 2003. In the 1960s, Stephen was, by his very own admission, a tearaway, and one day the 16-year-old Everton hooligan unscrewed the petrol cap of a car in the city centre and threw a lighted match into it. He was lucky to escape with his life, for the car almost immediately exploded into a fireball. A policeman gave chase and during the pursuit, the constable suddenly dived forward and grabbed Stephen's legs, bringing him down. Crowds cheered as the policeman then marched the young pyromaniac to the police station. Stephen was sentenced to a borstal on the outskirts of Merseyside, but managed to escape and go on the run. He met another yob – a 19-year-old skinhead named Mark (wanted in connection with a series of thefts from a warehouse in Widnes) – and the two youths set out for London in a dilapidated Ford Anglia Mark had stolen from Edge Lane a fortnight before. The London police were soon notified and Mark had a feeling the cops in the capital would be lying in wait, and so he went with his intuition and drove towards north-east Greater London, where the

114

car broke down. Stephen and Mark abandoned the steaming vehicle around 10pm and headed blindly into what they saw as an ideal cover – Epping Forest. This ancient forest is the remnant of an extensive 60,000 acre hunting ground, used by the chieftains and kings of Neolithic, Saxon, Norman and Tudor Britain. Although there are roads which enable the motorist, horse rider and cyclist to explore Epping Forest, the ancient woodland is only truly appreciated by the rambler on foot, and the young Liverpudlian city-dwellers soon realised just how big the forest was, and how spooky the woodland was at night, with owls hooting and foxes and other nocturnal creatures darting about. Moonlight streamed into the forest on this frosty night, and Stephen was complaining about how hungry he was as Mark selfishly finished off a packet of cheese and onion crisps. All Stephen had eaten since they entered the forest an hour ago was two digestive biscuits, and the 16-year-old's stomach was making loud rumbling sounds which Mark seemed to find funny. Young Stephen was also parched. All of a sudden, as the two young men approached a glade, their noses caught a whiff of something very appetising – as if someone was cooking in the vicinity. And then they both noticed a tiny silverfish-glimmer of light in the distance. Stephen and Mark crept towards the light, and saw it was a fire with three figures sitting around it. Mark whispered to Stephen, telling him that the men were probably tramps, but they were cooking something on a spit, and whatever it was, 'is ours for the taking,' he boasted. Stephen had a bad feeling about the silhouetted men around the fire, and he thought he and Mark should go the long way around them and get out of the godforsaken forest and find a shop to rob food from. Mark started saying he wasn't afraid of anyone and produced a flick-knife, and then he slowly walked towards the fire and hid behind a tree which gave him a better view of the 'vagrants'.

They were not vagrants at all. They were three very odd-looking men wearing clothes that would have been worn perhaps two hundred years ago. One wore a three-cornered hat and a long coat with pale coloured trousers and leather boots to his knees. He sat cross-legged, gazing into the flames of the fire, over which some skinned animal roasted on a spit with a crackling sound. Another man, possibly in his thirties, was lying nearby on some folded garments, and his hair was scraped back and he sported a ponytail. He wore the same type of long coat, trousers and boots as his colleague, as well as a white shirt. As he lay on his back, he was fiddling with a long firearm that Stephen and Mark had only seen in films depicting the 18th century – it was a flintlock. The third man wore a three-pointed tricorn had and a long black coat, but he was sitting facing the fire with his back to the nervous observers. He had a bottle by his side which he swigged from as the teenagers looked on. About twenty to thirty feet behind the outdated men, three horses stood in the row, tethered to the trees, and the rightmost horse was clearly visible because the moonlight was catching the light-coloured marking – or 'blaze' as it is known – on its nose. This horse seemed to sense the presence of Stephen and Mark, and became restless.

'We'd better go,' Mark suddenly whispered, and Stephen didn't have to be told twice. The two young tearaways turned and began to run, and when they had covered about fifty yards, both heard a gruff voice cry out. Stephen thought this was one of the men shouting: 'Who goes there?'

The youths then heard a loud crack and something whistled between their heads and struck the trunk of a tree in front of them, blowing fragments of bark everywhere. Stephen really picked up speed when he realised he was being shot at and ran off at a tangent, away from Mark. The young outlaws eventually found one another back at the place where they had entered the forest, and they wandered back to civilization, wondering who the three old-fashioned men had been in Epping Forest. That night, Stephen and Mark were captured by the police, and when they were in custody, they were separately questioned as to where they had been earlier, and to different interviewers, both young men gave an identical account of the three men sitting round the fire. A sergeant later told Stephen that in the 18th century, the highwayman Dick Turpin and some fellow criminals had a hideout in Epping Forest. The sergeant said he and several other people had seen the ghosts of various people in the forest over the years. Epping Forest is notorious as a place where many a London murderer has buried his victims, and no doubt there are still many bodies awaiting discovery there.

MIMIC

One pleasant summer evening in August 2010, a 52-year-old man named Howard left his house on Aigburth's Sandhurst Street and walked about a hundred yards down that street to the red post office pillar box on the corner of his street and Bryanston Road. As Howard posted the letter into the box, he saw old Mrs Graves, a former neighbour from Errol Street, which runs parallel to Sandhurst Street.

'Hello there,' Howard said to the old woman, who was in her mid-seventies, and Mrs Graves smiled and nodded to Howard, then walked on towards Bryanston Road. Howard thought that it was odd how the old woman had not stopped to talk to him as she usually did, but then he surmised that Mrs Graves wasn't well or perhaps was in a hurry to get home rather than stand about talking. As Howard walked back towards his house, he saw Mrs Graves walking towards him, which was, of course, quite impossible, as he had just seen her walking down Bryanston Road, about eighty yards behind him. How on earth then, was the old woman now passing his house? Mrs Graves stopped and said to Howard: 'Isn't it a lovely evening?'

Howard nodded, but was so dumbfounded by the apparent 'transportation' of Mrs Graves from around the corner, he was stuck for words. Later that evening, around 11.30pm, Howard's partner Sandra came home from the local fish and chips shop, where she worked part-time, and she said something that made the hairs on the back of Howard's neck stand on end.

'Hey, do you know if old Mrs Graves has a twin sister?' Sandra asked.

Howard shot a look of surprise at his partner.

Sandra then told him: 'She came into the chippy around half-six and got her usual portion of chips and a carton of curry, and then she left, and about ten seconds after she had gone out the shop, her exact double came up to the front of the chippy and just stood there looking in at me through the window.'

Howard then told him what he'd witnessed earlier in the evening when he had gone to post a letter, and Sandra said: 'You're not just saying this to spook me are you?'

'No, I swear,' Howard told her, 'it was like she'd been teleported from around the corner. It was well weird.'

'That's really creeped me out,' Sandra told him, and she hugged her boyfriend as they sat on the sofa watching the telly, which had been muted. Sandra then recalled something. 'The Mrs Graves who looked in at me had a brooch in her lapel, with like rubies in, and I don't think the Mrs Graves who came in for the curry and chips had any brooch on.'

'There's got to be a rational explanation,' Howard reasoned, stroking Sandra's head as he recalled what seemed to have been the doppelganger of Mrs Graves by the post office pillar box.

Two days later, Mrs Graves came into the chippy and Sandra asked her if she had an identical twin. Mrs Graves said she didn't and asked Sandra why she had posed such an odd question. 'Oh, I just saw your double the other day,' Sandra told the old pensioner, who simply raised here eyebrows and shrugged, stuck for words.

A few days later Howard and Sandra went into the back parlour of their home after the Sunday dinner to watch the new huge plasma TV Howard had set up in there. Sandra then took the curtains down and started to clean the windows with a bottle of Windolene. Howard read a book on his Kindle and enjoyed a cigarette as he put his feet up. He had spent a fortune on the new TV and unbelievably there was nothing which really interested him on any of the cable channels at the moment, just gardening programmes, cookery shows, repeats of old films and boring documentaries. After about twenty minutes of reading had elapsed, Howard happened to look up from the Kindle at the cleaned windows, and through them he saw the backs of the other houses and his own backyard wall, and there, sat upon the wall was Kubrick, the tortoise-shell cat belonging to next door's neighbours. Kubrick sat there with his usual expressionless face, and his green eyes gazed through the windows at Howard. Howard read a few more pages, then went to see Sandra, who was cleaning up in the kitchen. The couple were talking in the kitchen, in front of the sink, when Sandra also noticed Kubrick – who was now sitting further along the wall, gazing through the kitchen window at her. She smiled and waved at Kubrick, who knew Sandra well and often slunk in from the backyard when the kitchen door was ajar. Sandra would feed him tiny pieces of boiled ham, which the cat loved (as long as they were not too big, as the cat was a fussy eater). Sandra opened the kitchen door and waited. Kubrick came into the kitchen, and when Sandra took some boiled ham out the fridge, the cat didn't sit looking up at her as he normally would, but instead went into the back parlour where Howard was now flipping through the TV channels.

Sandra went into the parlour, and began to talk to Kubrick, uttering the nonsensical phrases some people do when they address cats and babies. 'Aw, he's just a ickle baby isn't he?' Sandra said to the neighbours' cat, when suddenly, she went quiet. Howard looked at his girlfriend because he noticed the silence when she suddenly shut up. He saw goosebumps on her forearms and a scared look in her eyes. 'What's up?' Howard asked, knowing instinctively something was wrong.

'That isn't Kubrick,' Sandra suddenly said, backing away from the cat.

The feline looked at her.

'What do you mean?' Howard muted the TV.

'Howard, look at his eyes,' Sandra said.

The cat's eyes were now of a very dark blue – ultramarine blue in fact – and not the usual yellowish green eyes Kubrick had. Howard felt a cold shudder when this discrepancy was pointed out to him, and then he also noticed that the cat seemed longer than the neighbour's cat, and its neck also seemed longer.

'Oh God, look!' Sandra pointed to the window, and there on the backyard wall, was Kubrick taking swipes at a tiny fly that was too little to be seen by Howard or Sandra.

The couple then turned to look back at the other cat – and its face seemed to have almost human expressions upon it that really unsettled Howard and Sandra. The cat then hurried out the room and ran into the kitchen, where it shot off towards the open door. When Sandra looked into the yard, she saw only the real Kubrick, who came running to greet her.

Almost an hour went past before Howard said something which made Sandra really think. He said it was odd how he and Sandra had seen someone imitating an old woman not so long ago, and now something was impersonating the neighbour's cat. Sandra said it was just coincidence. Someone had looked like Mrs Graves, and some cat with the same tortoise-shell markings had come on the scene. But deep down, Sandra suspected that something supernatural *was* going on, and Howard definitely believed that this was so. But the biggest shock was yet to come.

Three days later, on the Wednesday of that week, Howard went out with three male colleagues he worked with at a garage off Aigburth Road. Sandra said she'd be okay staying in that night with a few female friends she'd known since her schooldays. Howard and his mates went on a pub crawl around the city centre and ended up in the Philharmonic public house on Hope Street, where they finally all went their separate ways around 11.30pm. As Howard flagged down a hackney cab to take him home to Aigburth, his mobile rang. It was Sandra, and she asked him how his 'blokes night out' had gone. Howard said it had gone okay, but he was now on his way home. He also asked Sandra if she wanted him to stop off anywhere to get her and her mates a kebab or pizza. 'Nah, we're all stuffed love,' Sandra told him, 'you just get back as soon as you can. I missed you tonight.'

Howard began to feel a little peckish as he rode

home in the cab, and so he asked the taxi driver to go to a kebab house. The cabby said he knew a real good one nearby, and Howard asked the cabby if he wanted anything to eat. The cabby declined and thanked him anyway. Howard got his kebab and was soon home – but Sandra wasn't there. Howard went into the kitchen, and then the back parlour, but Sandra was nowhere to be seen. He went upstairs to his bedroom to find his girlfriend asleep in bed. When he woke her up she told him that the husband of one of her mates – a woman named Jenny - had come round to the house around 9pm in a drunken state, and accused Jenny of cheating on him. Jenny's husband became so violent, Sandra had called the police and they had taken him away. Jenny then had to be taken home after admitting she'd had an affair with someone. And so by 9.30pm, Sandra's two other friends had decided to call it a day. Sandra then went to bed.

'But you called me about half an hour ago,' Howard said, recalling the phone call.

'I didn't,' Sandra told him with a baffled look. 'I've been in bed since around ten.'

'I asked you if you wanted anything bringing in and you said you were stuffed,' Howard remembered the conversation on his mobile clearly.

'I'm starving actually,' Sandra told him, looking at the wrapped up kebab carton that was still in Howard's hand. 'Maybe you misdialled and called someone else?'

'No, listen,' Howard told his girlfriend, 'you phoned me – it was you – ' his voice trailed off as he suddenly recalled the strange incidents concerning Mrs Graves and the neighbour's cat. He felt cold all of a sudden.

Sandra knew exactly what he was thinking, and looked into his eyes with a knowing look.

'What are they playing at?' Howard murmured. 'What's going on?'

'Let's see your phone,' Sandra asked, and Howard took out the Samsung model and handed it to her. Sandra navigated through the menu and saw her number time-stamped on the 'calls received' page. When she checked her own mobile, it plainly showed that no calls had been made from that mobile to Howard's mobile since yesterday. That morning, at around 4am, Howard awoke to hear Sandra calling to him from downstairs. He went to get up – when he realised that Sandra was lying next to him, asleep. Still the voice, which was distinctively Sandra's, called out from somewhere downstairs. 'Howard!' shouted the impostor downstairs. 'Howard, here!'

Howard woke up Sandra and she also heard the familiar voice calling Howard. Then, after about five minutes, the voice ceased calling Howard's name, and an uneasy silence descended on the house which was suddenly pierced by an eerie sound from outside. A cat began to meow loudly, and suddenly that cat began to call out Howard's name as clear as if a human was reciting it. Howard softly broke off the nervous embrace of his girlfriend and walked towards the blinds.

Sandra tried to call him back. 'No! Howard, don't look out! Please, if you love me, don't look out!'

But Howard's curiosity won, and he went to the window and peered out through the gaps in the Venetian blinds. At first he could see nothing, but then, when his eyes adjusted to that faintly illuminated alleyway below, he saw what looked like the striking pitch-black silhouette of a woman, crouched in an unnatural stance on the top of the backyard wall. Howard swore softly under his breath in shock, and Sandra said, 'What? Who is it?'

'Come and have a look, hurry up,' Howard urged his partner, but when Sandra reached the blinds, she only saw slight movement outside. Howard said the thing had jumped off the wall and had run off down the alleyway. It looked like a woman's outline and yet it moved like an animal – like a cat.

Sandra refused to sleep with the light on for the remainder of that morning, and even when the pale blue light of predawn filtered into the room through the blinds, she was still awake, listening out for the "mimic" – something supernatural which she suspected of playing games with her and her boyfriend. The couple finally fell asleep around 6am, and never woke till eleven. They decided that perhaps they should stay away from the house for a few days, and they went to stay in Sandra's parent's house for four days. When they returned to the house on Sandhurst Road, they were naturally very edgy, and feared the mimic would soon be playing its warped games with them, but thankfully, Howard and Sandra have had no further strange encounters with the thing which seems to have masqueraded as a cat and two humans. Such supernatural mimics undoubtedly exist, and I clearly remember interviewing a woman who said she went upstairs to her little daughter one day, after hearing the child call her name. When she went into the child's bedroom, the little daughter was sitting on the bed, but facing the wall, and as the mother was about to approach her, she happened to glance through the bedroom window and noticed her 'real' daughter playing outside. Only then did the mother sense that the thing sitting on the bed was some eerie impersonator of her child, and she turned and ran out the room as the sinister sham child laughed in a deep voice. I also once interviewed a policewoman named Penny who told me how, when she was twelve, she saw a boy dangling from the branch of a tree as he sobbed. The tree was in Birkenhead Park, and the boy – Charles – was well known to Penny. He was five years of age and always dressed in a distinctive orange and black striped teeshirt. On this afternoon, Charles screamed as he hung from a branch, probably after climbing the tree and losing his nerve. Penny shinned up the tree and shouted 'It's okay, Charlie! I'll get you, hang on!'

But when Penny climbed along the branch and offered her hand to Charles, she saw, to her utmost horror, that the face of the boy was old and wizened, and wore an evil grin. Penny let out a scream and crawled back along the branch and fell, winding herself as she landed. Penny ran off, unable to shout out because she couldn't breath with the impact of the fall. As she ran off through the park, she almost collided with the real Charles, who was, as usual, wearing his distinctive striped teeshirt. Just what the thing was that imitated the little boy remains unknown.

SILHOUETTES

Back in the long-gone summer of 1985 - in June to be a bit more precise - a rather shy 20-year-old man named Matthew Wirke decided to go and stay with his Auntie Ruth, a very spiritual and well, a little odd woman, in her late sixties, who seemed to be shunned by her family most of the time. She lived in an old Victorian house close to Sefton Park, on Ullet Road. Her husband Stan had recently died and she had inherited the contents of his bank account – an account he had never shared with his wife while he was alive. Matthew really got on with Ruth, and found her a fascinating person, a born storyteller, and her apple and cinnamon pies were the most delicious things he had ever tasted. Now that Ruth was widowed and lone, Matthew volunteered to stay with her for a while, even though his father – who was Ruth's youngest brother – had warned him against it. On the first day he visited his Auntie Ruth, she told him to accompany her in a taxi to Boots in the city centre, where she wanted to buy a newfangled contraption called a microwave oven, which could miraculously cook food in minutes. Matthew eagerly went with her, and for the princely sum of £269.95, Ruth purchased the Russell Hobbs microwave. The man at Boots boasted that this big microwave was 'commodious enough to cook a fifteen-pound turkey' – and so Ruth went and purchased a turkey of that weight to put the claim to the test – and the salesman at Boots had been right. For two days, Ruth and Matthew had turkey roast, turkey sandwiches, until the third day, when Ruth gave the half-eaten carcass to the foxes of Sefton Park.

On the following day, Matthew woke up in the 'guest bedroom' just after noon. He had gone to bed late the night before and had read a football magazine called *Shoot!* until about 2am as he listened to the radio. There was a rapping on his door, followed by the faint but distinctive voice of his aunt. 'Can I come in Matthew?' she asked.

'Yeah,' Matthew replied, and sat up in the old bed, wondering what this was about.

Aunt Ruth came into the room with portable television with a loop aerial on the top of it, and the logo on the front had interlocking red green and blue discs – which obviously meant this TV was a colour one. Matthew was excited.

'A little something for you,' Ruth said with a lovely smirk, and she put the new telly on the dresser, then said, 'Put it wherever you like, but I think there are only two plug points in here.'

'Ah, you shouldn't have auntie,' Matthew told her, not meaning a word of it of course, and he got out the bed in nothing but his maroon Y fronts and went to have a look at the portable TV.

On the following day, Matthew went home, but when his father, Terry, saw the colour portable he said: 'You're not having that in this house,' and Matthew and his two older sisters looked at one another with baffled expressions before gazing back at their father's reddening face.

'Why not?' Matthew wanted to know.

'Well if you want that thing in here you can pay the colour telly licence!' Matthew's father told him, with bulging eyes.

'Oh, no one will know – ' Matthew was replying when his father began to shout and bawl.

'Oh and you won't be the one going to prison or getting a big fine if the telly man happens to call here, will you, eh?' he yelled at his son. 'There are thousands of people prosecuted every year and they all thought the telly man would never call on them!'

'You'll have to watch it in your auntie's, Matthew,' said Ada, Matthew's mother, from the doorway of the living room. She had just returned from the shops and couldn't help hearing the conversation from the hallway.

'Oh I'd be better off just living with me Auntie Ruth, I would!' Matthew told his father, and stormed out of the room in a huff, almost colliding with his mum in the hallway.

'Go and stay with her then!' Matthew's father shouted after his sulking son, and as Matthew hurried up the stairs to his room clutching the portable television, his dad gripped the rail of the stairs and shouted: 'Let her pay the licence fee!'

'She already does!' Matthew shouted down the stairs, 'She's got a colour telly of her own!'

'Dad, we must be the only house in Liverpool that still has a black and white telly,' said Tracy, Matthew's 22-year-old sister.

'Well if you could get a proper well-paid job we'd

have one wouldn't we?' her father replied, and he put his newspaper under his arm and walked through the kitchen to the open door which led to the garden. Terry grumpily said: 'God, this bleedin' door's wide open! They've probably heard everything next door. He'll be here tomorrow, just wait and see!'

'Who'll be here Terry? Who?' Ada asked, attempting a grin.

Terry rolled his eyes. 'The telly man! The telly man! You think it's all a joke with that stupid grin on your face –'

'You've got this bleedin' bee in your bonnet about the telly man, ever since – ' Ada suddenly realised she was going to say something she was not supposed to divulge.

'Go on! Tell them you stupid mare!' Terry barked.

'Tell us what?' Pauline, the eldest daughter asked with curiosity in her eyes.

Terry answered them. 'I got done by the telly man, many years ago, when you two were at school. Nearly got sent down, and it was only a black and white telly!'

'Oh,' said Pauline.

'Tell that to your divvy brother up there,' Terry prodded his daughter's chest with the end of the rolled up tabloid.

'Alright, alright, Dad, stop overreacting will you?' Pauline pushed the newspaper away, ' You can get telly stamps, it's no big deal! I'll get them if you want!'

'I'll help you get them as well!' Tracy chipped in.

The front door of the house slammed hard. Ada looked through the narrow window at the side of that front door, and through the net curtain she saw Matthew hurrying down the path with his portable in a

130

huge purple hold-all, no doubt bound for Aunt Ruth's.

Auntie Ruth offered to pay for a colour TV licence to cover Matthew's house, but her nephew shook his head and said, 'Nah, you've done enough auntie.'

But of course, Ruth was a very generous woman, and now she had some money behind her, she went out the next day and bought the colour TV licence for Matthew. That evening, Matthew lay on the bed in the guest bedroom of his aunt's home on Ullet Road, thinking about all the arguments he and his sisters were always having with their father. Terry seemed to be getting more grumpy and crotchety as he got older, whereas just five years ago, he would go to the park and play football with Matthew, and would often take the family out to Blackpool and sometimes down to London. As Matthew thought about those happier times, he thought he heard two people – a man and a woman – arguing somewhere close by. He turned down the volume on the portable telly and now he could hear nothing at all. Matthew had been watching a comedy film - *Carry On Up the Jungle* – and so he assumed the voices had been from the TV, or perhaps from some interference on the set. In those days, radio transmissions from the police and even taxi radio broadcasts occasionally came through on TV sets. However, later that night, Matthew heard the same voices of the distant couple. He turned down the volume on the TV and listened. The voices were still there, and whoever they were they were having a slanging match. Matthew went onto the landing, and listened intently, but now he could hear nothing. He then heard Ruth coming up the stairs on her way to bed. 'Goodnight aunty,' Matthew said, and Ruth smiled and replied, 'Night Matthew. Don't stay up too late.'

Matthew went back into the room, and watched a boring television programme called *Database*, which was about personal computers and their use. He changed channels, switching from Granada to catch a quarter of an hour of *Wimbledon 85*, and finding Desmond Lynam's commentary rather soporific, Matthew dozed off. When he awoke about half an hour later, Matthew saw the last few minutes of *International Athletics* before the weather forecast came on, followed by the closedown of BBC 1. He switched to BBC 2, and seeing it featured nothing but some coverage of the highlights of the first day's play at Lords between England and Australia, he switched off the portable colour TV, turned off the light, and went to bed. Matthew's head had only rested upon the pillow for about twenty seconds when he distinctly heard the man and woman arguing again. He sat up, more annoyed than baffled, and looked towards the window. Was the sound of the argument coming from the street? He wondered. He dragged himself out the bed and went to the window. He parted the lace curtains and saw nothing but Ullet Road, bathed in amber light from the sodium streetlamps. The occasional car rolled past below, and a solitary morose-looking young man walked along with his face to the pavement.

'*I'll kill you...*' said the male voice of the bickering couple, and this sound definitely came from behind Matthew. He turned on his bedside lamp, and sat on the bed. His eyes looked at the portable television, then rose up the wall until they settled on two oval-framed pictures, each about 8 or ten inches in length. The pictures featured silhouettes of a man and a woman – just their heads and shoulders – with their heads seen side-on, so their profiles were prominent. The female had her hair tied up in a bun, and she sported a cute turned-up nose and a thin delicate-looking neck. Her Silhouette was looking at the other frame's shadow-head – that of a man with collar-length hair and a big aquiline nose. His framed silhouette was about six inches away from his female counterpart, and he was looking towards the latter.

As Matthew Wirke looked at the framed silhouettes, he noticed something that immediately made him think he might be dreaming. The head of the male silhouette was clearly moving. The lips of the silhouette were faintly opening and closing, and he was moving his head backwards and forwards slightly as he talked. The same eerie phenomenon was evident in the female silhouette, only her mouth was opening much wider as she shouted something.

Matthew slowly rose from his bed with his heart pounding in his chest. The voices from the animated pictures were growing in intensity.

'*Needles and pins, needles and pins, when a young man marries his trouble begins!*' shouted the male silhouette.

'*I should never have married you!*' screamed the silhouette of the lady. Her voice sounded young, as if she was just out of her teens.

'*Eve, I will have none of your rotten apple!*' the man bawled.

'Matthew! Can you turn the TV down please?' Aunt Ruth's voice came through the bedroom wall. She had heard the quarrelling silhouetted entities from next door; that's how loud they sounded.

Matthew was about to shout back that it wasn't the television that was making this racket, but before he could open his mouth, something surreal but terrifying took place. The male silhouette reached out of the oval frame with two long spindly arms, and the wiry-looking hands seized the little neck of the silhouetted lady and began to throttle her. The shadow man shook the little female head vigorously and the mouth of the lady opened wide as she was steadily throttled.

'*Needles and pins, needles and pins, when a young man is married his trouble begins!*' yelled the sinister two-dimensional strangler, and he shook the female in the other frame with such force, her bun of hair became undone. She made a ghastly rasping, choking sound, and her head became limp in the crushing, strangling hands of the killer. Matthew ran out of the room and flew along the landing towards his Auntie Ruth's door. He rapped hard and then barged in to see his aunt getting out of her bed in her negligee. 'Matthew! I told you to turn the sound down!' she sternly told her nephew.

'It isn't the telly, Aunt Ruth, come and see!' Matthew beckoned her out onto the dark landing, and Ruth followed him. 'You won't believe this!' he shouted, and led Ruth into his bedroom, and she saw the same scary spectacle that her nephew had just witnessed.

'Oh God,' Ruth threw her left hand over her mouth and the other hand clutched Matthew's upper arm. She then dragged him from the room as Matthew looked in horror as the silhouetted strangler shook his floppy-headed victim. As aunt and nephew went down the stairs of the house, they could both hear the faint words coming from the guest bedroom: '*Needles and pins, needles and pins…*'

Ruth and Matthew stood in the kitchen in a right state. Ruth was shaking and Matthew was trying to pretend he wasn't scared but the look of fear was clearly in his eyes. 'Maybe I should go and stay over with your father,' Ruth suggested, and she wondered how she'd be able to muster enough courage to go upstairs to get her clothes from her wardrobe.

'He was strangling her,' Matthew murmured, and now his fear was giving way to confusion. 'Whose silhouettes are they, auntie?'

'They belonged to my husband Stan – I think they were the actual silhouettes of his grandparents. It's so strange.'

They heard a movement on the stairs, and they both froze. Ruth went to the door of the kitchen and looked out across the half-lit hallway – and gasped in shock.

'What is it, auntie?' Matthew, asked, and then he went to the doorway and peered over his aunt's shoulder. For a few moments he could not see what she was staring at – and then he saw it. On the top step of the bottom flight of steps leading to the ground floor was a pair of jet-black legs, visible only from the knees to the shoes. They were as black as the heads of those silhouettes.

'*Needles and pins, needles and pins…*' came a voice from the stairs, and those legs began to descend the stairs ever so slowly. Ruth and Matthew ran across the hallway and Ruth screamed as she heard footsteps closing in on her and her nephew. She undid the catch on the Yale lock, opened the door and she and Matthew stepped outside. Matthew looked back, and then slammed the front door shut with one powerful pull. He and Ruth then walked in a daze along Ullet Road, where Ruth flagged down a taxi cab. She and her nephew rode the cab to Matthew's home in Edge Hill. Just before the taxi reached Matthew's home, Ruth asked her nephew what he had seen when he looked back into the hallways before he closed the door. Matthew said he had seen the flat-looking shadow of a man, but that walking silhouette had a pair of evil-looking blue eyes which had glared at him.

Ruth's brother Terry thought the story about the haunted pictures was hysterical nonsense, and he went over to Ruth's house in the morning to get her clothes. Luckily for Ruth, Terry had kept a spare set of her house keys for a few years. Terry took a look in the guest room of the house and saw the supposedly haunted silhouettes on the wall. Terry could see nothing untoward about them, and he decided to bring them over to his house. Upon his return home, Ruth asked him if he brought her clothes, and Terry smiled and said he had, and after Ruth had dressed and had settled down to breakfast, Terry said, 'Are these the so-called haunted pictures then?' And he took the oval framed silhouettes from a burlap bag and clunked them down on the dining room table.

Ruth recoiled in horror and asked her brother how he could be so insensitive to bring over the very objects that had struck fear into the hearts of her and Matthew. She seized the oval white portraits featuring the stark silhouettes and went into the back garden to hurl them into the bin. By 4pm that day, Ruth decided she'd go back home, and Matthew accompanied her.

On the following morning at 11am, there was a

frantic knocking at the door of Ruth's Ullet Road house. Ruth answered and saw it was her nieces – Matthew's sisters Tracy and Pauline – and they looked very pale. Before they had even set foot in the house the two sisters began to babble about strange goings-on at their house, and Ruth ushered them into the kitchen and gave them a cuppa and biscuits as she listened. Around this time, Matthew, always the late riser, was coming down the stairs, and he heard the familiar voices in the kitchen. He said hello to his sisters but they were too busy talking over one another as they related the strange events of last night. Tracy had heard a couple arguing and screaming around half-past eleven. Then around half-past one in the morning, they had heard terrible screams from the back garden, and Pauline had gone into the upstairs toilet to open the window, which looked onto the garden – and she had seen the silhouettes of a man and a woman, dressed in what seemed like old fashioned clothes, striking one another. Pauline went and fetched Tracy, and she saw the weird-looking couple as well. The girls went to tell their father, and he was already getting up from his bed because he had also heard the arguers and was going to give them a piece of his mind. He went into the toilet and looked out the window to see the couple fighting, and he could only make them out as shadows with no features; like animated life-size figures cut out of black card. This really unnerved Terry, as he recalled what Ruth and Matthew had told him about the strange silhouettes that came out of those oval pictures – and then, with a shiver, Terry remembered that those framed silhouettes had been thrown into the bin in the back garden by Ruth.

For this reason, Terry closed the window and told his daughters to get back to bed. Pauline and Tracy asked him if he was going to tell the couple in the garden to shut up so everyone could sleep and Terry just ignored his daughters' questions and went back to bed. The next morning Terry and the rest of the family seemed relieved when the binmen turned up and emptied the bin containing the accursed oval portraits into the refuse wagon.

After that day, Ruth was never troubled by the silhouettes, and there were no further paranormal goings-on at Matthew's house in Edge Hill. Ruth sadly passed away in the early 1990s, but Matthew asked me to research her husband's grandparents to see if I could possibly throw any light on the haunted picture frames. I discovered a few things that Matthew preferred me not to publish, but he would allow me to print the following. Stan's grandfather most probably strangled his first wife - named Eve - in the early 1870s in Liverpool, and claimed it was a cousin who was later tried and saved by the noose because the relative was believed to be already suffering from a form of insanity before the alleged murder took place. A few years later in the summer of 1875, Stan's grandfather was living in the Walton area of Liverpool with his second wife, who he also attacked on several occasions, and in June of that year, he was briefly interviewed by police after the body of 13-year-old Edward Howell was found hidden beneath shrubbery and brushwood in Anfield Cemetery. The boy had been strangled elsewhere and dumped in the cemetery by his murderer. At the time, Stan's grandfather was seeing a woman who lived in Bidston View, off

Walton Road, in Kirkdale – the very same street where a widow named Margaret Howell - the mother of the dead boy - had lived. The murderer of Edward Howell was never brought to justice, despite a reward being offered, and there were other strange murders in that part of Liverpool in the years after the 1875 strangling case – and Stan's grandfather was always living within a stone's throw of each murder scene. When Matthew was presented with all of this evidence he was very shocked to say the least, and asked me to refrain from naming his distant ancestor. I assured him I'd use false names in the story, and told him that most families would uncover a skeleton or two in their cupboard if they dug deep enough through the layers of generations into the murky past. I cannot explain the phenomenon regarding the silhouettes, and wonder if they now lie in some landfill site in south Liverpool – or whether some curious binman in the 1980s spotted them in that bin and took them home...

A GRIM PREMONITION

Unless you have a strong stomach, you might do well to skip this chapter.

In May 1846, a 50-year-old Liverpool woman named Margaret Davies moved to Ireland to live in Collooney, County Sligo with her husband George, a fisherman who had been born in that county 55 years before. Margaret hadn't settled down long in her little cottage with George when she began to have a series of terrifying, vivid dreams in which she was subjected to the most gruesome sights. All of the dreams involved some violent tragedy that unfolded on a ship, and were so graphic, Margaret would sometimes throw up after waking from the grisly nightmares. He husband George feared for the mental health of his wife and was ready to seek the advice of the parish priest when the dreams thankfully stopped. But then something strange and disturbing took place. George's niece, Mary, who lived about twenty miles away from him in Sligo, wrote to George to tell him how she and her husband and baby son were about to go to Liverpool to make a new life for themselves. George proudly read how Mary and her husband and baby were due to board a new steam ship called *The Rambler* this coming Saturday. Straight away, Margaret Davies told her husband that one of the ships in her nightmare had been called *The Rambler*. Margaret urged George to visit his niece to talk her out of going to Liverpool, but George thought his wife's weird dreams were just the products of indigestion, of eating before bed, something which Margaret was fond of doing. And so Mary boarded *The Rambler* with her husband and child, and the ship, and that vessel, commanded by one Captain McCallister, left Sligo on Saturday 23 May, 1846, and headed out into the waters of Donegal Bay, bound for Liverpool. Because of a technical problem involving a shortage of water for the ship's steam engine, *The Rambler* was forced to drop anchor until the problem was addressed, and the delay resulted in the vessel raising anchor on the Sunday afternoon. She resumed her journey to Liverpool heavily laden. In addition to her goods cargo, *The Rambler* was carrying 700 pigs and 20 head of cattle, and the shortage of room on board the ship forced the stevedores to put some of the animals on the deck. There were also around 450 men, women and children onboard the steamer, as well as the crew of course. By Monday night, at 10.45pm, *The Rambler* had reached the mouth of the Mersey, and as she passed the Perch Rock Lighthouse off New Brighton, the steamer's captain looked in horror at the ship coming towards it. The ship on a collision course with *The Rambler* was the *Sea Nymph*, which had just left Liverpool's Clarence Dock, bound for Cork, commanded by Captain Joseph Thomson. This ship was also packed with passengers. The helms of the two ships were spun to port, but it was no use, and witnesses on both side of the river said that when *The Rambler* and the *Sea Nymph* impacted, there was a sound like a loud clap of thunder – followed by stomach-churning agonised screams and wails of the passengers - as well as the squeals and shrieks of the pigs and cattle - on both ships. The pointed stem of the *Sea Nymph* rammed into the bows of *The Rambler*, cutting the inward-bound vessel in two as far as the waterline, severing the deck halfway across and shaking the entire frame of the vessel, rendering every water-tight compartment of the vessel perfectly useless. So much for the damage to the iron and wood of the ship, but what of the gruesome toll on the human and animal on deck and in the hold of the doomed ship? Consider that the bow of the vessel – the point of cataclysmic impact – was packed with men, women and children – as well as pigs and cattle – and the stench down there had been almost unbearable throughout the passage from Sligo. The victims who had not been horrifically mutilated and injured by the collision stampeded in panic like the animals among them, and many people were trampled to death, including one poor woman who was seen almost naked on the deck, a bloody flattened mess of crushed skull and broken bones, trampled by the cattle, pigs and human feet as the ship started to sink and a terrible frenzy spread amongst the passengers. Another trampled victim, that of a young girl, had her mouth open wide, and her front teeth were embedded in the wooden boards of the deck, and the pressure upon her by the panicking hordes had popped out one of her eyes and burst her little torso. Over a dozen passengers jumped into one of the lifeboats, and instead of waiting for one of the crew to lower the boat into the sea, someone cut the ropes and the lifeboat fell, capsized, and everyone on board drowned. A woman named Mary Connolly, who survived the tragedy, told newspaper reporters in the Northern Hospital (where she made a remarkable recovery) how she saw one of her children kneeling with clasped hands as if in prayer when she came to after the collision, but when she tried to grab at him, his arm came out of the socket of his shoulder, and she realised he was dead. Mary tried to rescue another child among the carnage and saw his face come away with a gush of blood. One passenger stripped naked and jumped off *The Rambler*, intending to swim to the Wirral shore, but the current pulled him under, and he would have drowned if he hadn't been saved by a boy and a fireman who dived in after him from the sinking ship. Blue signal rockets were fired from *The Rambler* to alert the *Magazine* lifeboat, and many heroic rescues took place that traumatic night. Fifty to sixty souls were picked up by the Magazine lifeboat on the first trip, and on the second return trip, to the bows of The Rambler, the rescue team saw the most sickening sights that would haunt them for the rest of their lives. The wreckage was drenched with mingled human and animal blood, and the most sickening spectacles were to be seen. A little boy gazed at the rescuers with a look of utter terror on his face, and his body below his navel was described as 'crushed mincemeat'. The child began to cry then passed away in the arms of one sobbing rescuer. The Magazine life boatmen then came upon a lady whose legs were pinned down by an iron beam, and the bones of the mangled legs were horrifically broken and crushed to powder by the ankles, and they did all they could to rescue her from the entangled mass of twisted metal frames and splintered wood. With her face contorted in agony, the unfortunate young woman cried: 'I have four pounds in my pocket, and if you'll get me out I'll give you all that! Please get me out!' By some miracle, as the ship went steadily down, the rescuers managed to free the lady, who looked down at the gruesome remains of what were once shapely legs, now dangling from her kneecaps. Below this lady, the lifeboat men came upon the heart-wrenching sight of a dead mother in her twenties, with her crushed baby still in her arms, and the dead infant's mouth was still at its mother's nipple. Two of the boatmen, accustomed to even the most gruesome aspects of shipwreck and disaster, began to silently cry at the sight of the dead mother and child. A boat called the *Elizabeth*, moored over by the Perch Rock Lighthouse, soon arrived to rescue more of the victims from both ships. Hundreds were saved as a result. The Reverend Lennon of Liscard was sent for, and he soon arrived to administer spiritual consolation to the survivors, many of whom sustained terrible injuries and mutilations in the disaster. Many Wirral people opened the doors of their houses to the victims on that terrible night, and gave them food, beds and of course, human comfort. Several little boys – who had become separated from the parents in the tragic collision – were welcomed into a house by a Miss Waistell, and at one point, one of these children, a 2-year-od boy named Paddy Connolly, was thought to be an orphan, as no one claimed him for weeks, but he was later reunited with his parents, who had been recovering from severe injuries at the Northern Hospital in Liverpool. Unfortunately, Paddy's brothers and sisters had perished in the accident. No one ever came to claim another little boy who had been put in the care of Miss Waistell, so the young lady adopted him as one of her own.

The remains of thirteen dead bodies, shipped from

The Rambler, were placed in the Magazine lifeboat house, pending identification, and presented a most ghastly sight to those who came to view them. Many came to look at them out of plain morbid curiosity. The stretched, maimed, fractured and mutilated bodies lay there, side by side. Thirteen individuals who, a matter of hours before, had been in the full possession of life, vigour and enthusiasm, many of them looking forward to landing at Liverpool. Now they were the blackened remains of mothers, fathers, brothers, sisters, most of them covered in gore. Some had obviously died an agonising death, by the looks of their clenched teeth, clenched fists, and twisted faces. The arm of a child lay next to his little body. The man in his thirties laying next to him had his foot torn off. The body of a seven-year-old child lay without a face, and on closer inspection, that missing face was to be seen lying folded next to his head like the skin of a cooked chicken. The woman next to him was mangled and lying disjointed like a broken doll. When a police superintendent examined the pockets of the dead, not a single coin was found in any of them. The wreckage of *The Rambler*, which remained buoyant, was towed across the river and eventually repaired at the Clarence Dock, as was the *Sea Nymph*. It was later discovered that the captain and mate of the *Sea Nymph* had 'been in liquor' before the ship set out for Cork.

Over in Collooney, Sligo, the Liverpool woman Margaret Davies almost fainted when the news of the terrible collision reached her ears. She had dreamt of the tragedy in appalling detail, and unfortunately, Mary, the niece of Margaret and George who had boarded *The Rambler*, perished in the disaster. 'I should have heeded you,' Margaret's husband admitted, weeping in his wife's arms when he learned of the dreadful news. As far as I know, Margaret Davies had no further premonitions after that day.

THE TROJAN SOFA

This very strange story unfolded many years ago in the late 1970s. Around July 1979, a 14-year-old house-robber named Kevin bumped into a 13-year-old scallywag named Chris. They met whilst robbing the same youth club somewhere in south Liverpool, each unaware of the other's existence until they bumped into one another in the kitchen of the club, where they ransacked the fridge, removing blocks of ice cream and cans of soft drink. That night, they removed the record player and hi-fi system, loudspeakers, amplifier and microphones, a classical guitar, and a little metal box containing money collected by the students who ran the club for the hire of a coach to take the local underprivileged kids to Blackpool. That money was squandered in the video-game arcades of Lime Street, as were the proceeds accrued from the sale of the stolen items to fences.

Then one day, Kevin and Chris visited a second-hand furniture store to see if there was anything they could rob, but most of the items were simply too big to run off with. This second-hand store was housed in a disused church, and the elderly man who ran it was very trusting. He never dreamt the angel-faced teens roaming the store were opportunistic criminals. Chris suddenly hit on an idea. 'Hey, you know what we could do?' he asked Kevin in an excited tone. 'I've got a cracker idea, listen.'

And Chris told Kevin his idea in a careful whisper close to his ear. 'I could use my Stanley knife to slit that sofa open over there, under the cushions like, along like a seam, and then get in it, and then just lay there. And when the arl fellah locks up this place I'll come out the sofa and unlock the door.'

Kevin thought about the strange proposition. 'Yeah, but he locks the place up with a padlock, so how can you let me in?'

'No, there's a door he goes out of over there look,' Chris whispered, nodding to the doorway at the side of the church. And he was right, it was a reinforced door, and it had a simple Yale lock on it. Outside, there was only one way to open it – with a Yale key, but inside, all Chris would have to do was turn the brass knob to open it to his friend.

'Go 'head then,' Kevin said, and emitted a rasping quiet laugh. 'I'll keep dixie.'

'Unless you wanna do it?' Chris asked him, looking a little flushed in his face.

Kevin shook his head vigorously. 'No, you do it; you suggested it, go 'head!'

'It's too early yet, he doesn't lock up till five, and its only twenty-five to,' Chris replied, eyeing the old grandfather clock that had a sign on it saying 'Not for Sale'.

Kevin had a suggestion. 'Let's go and have a look at the sofa first and see if we could even cut an opening in it where you could be skied away.'

As luck would have it, the old man's attention was drawn to an old woman who came into the premises on a zimmer frame. She asked him if he had an old sideboard. 'Yes, the sideboards are over here madam,' said the well-spoken old man, and he led his aged customer to the other side of the cold room.

The young crooks hurried to the huge sofa - which bore a SOLD sign upon it - and began to remove the four cushions. It felt a bit hollow and saggy anyway. Chris got his Stanley knife out and quickly created a long slit about four feet in length in the material, then began to scoop out some brown straw-like stuffing as Kevin made an odd chortling sound. Chris swore as he pushed a few old springs back and then he said to Kevin: 'You're smaller than me; you'd easily fit in there.'

Both lads kept taking turns to look over at the old man who was just visible through the clutter of furniture. Chairs on tables, floor lampstands, bureaux, chests of drawers, wardrobes, Welsh dressers, and assorted junk all conspired to give excellent cover to the two young scoundrels as they created the Trojan Sofa. All of the stuffing removed from the sofa was placed in the drawers of cabinets and sideboards, and then, just before the old woman on the zimmer frame left the furniture store empty handed, Chris laid in the hollow of the sofa. Kevin sniggered as he covered him up with the lining fabric before placing the four cushions on top of him.

'What are you doing over there?' the old man peeped from behind a mahogany breakfront bookcase.

'Nothin', just lookin' at the sofa, mate,' Kevin replied.

'Well. I'm closing in a minute,' the old man told him, then vanished back among the furniture.

Kevin left the defunct church and walked around the local shop, where he stole a few packets of sweets. When he came out, there was a crimson transit van outside the church, and a white curly-haired man, aged about fifty-five, and a much younger man in his twenties (possibly the fifty-something's son) were carrying *that* sofa out the church – and walking towards the van.

Kevin went cold. He had to do something to distract the men so that Chris could escape from the sofa. He approached the men and shouted to the older one: 'Hey mate! Some kids letting your front tyres down!'

The older man halted for a moment, and then he stretched his neck out and looked around the open back doors of the transit van and said: 'Where? I can't see anyone?'

'There! He's letting them down!' Kevin claimed, pointing at the front right tyre of the van.

The old man swore and said, 'Go on, beat it!'

And the men took the sofa into the van and slammed the doors shut on it. Kevin wondered whether he should try and open the doors and get poor Chris out of there – but decided it wasn't worth the risk. It'd be too bad if Chris was caught, but Kevin didn't think his 'hoppo' was worth getting into trouble for, and so he walked on, eating the Star Bar he had stolen.

Chris, meanwhile, was lying inside the sofa, listening to the transit van's engine rev into life. He felt the van move off, and wondered whether anyone was standing by the sofa in the back of the van or lorry (Chris wasn't sure what type of vehicle he was in). He wanted to peep out from behind a cushion but was scared in case someone saw him. He lay there in the sweltering heat, cursing Kevin for not carrying out this job. The van started to accelerate, and then it swerved as it rounded a corner, and then, just when Chris decided he'd get out of the sofa, the van came to a halt. It had arrived at its destination by the sounds of it, as the engine had stopped.

The sounds of the van doors being opened could be clearly heard by the hidden robber, and then Chris felt the sensation of two men jumping into the van. The floor of the van shook. Boots thumped near.

'Shall I take the cushions off or carry this with them on?' asked a rough voice.

Oh, please leave them on! Chris thought.

'Nah, leave them, you get the other end and back out,' said the older, deeper voice.

The sofa rocked as the men's four hands grappled with it.

'This weighs a bleedin' ton,' complained the younger voice. 'Sure there's no murder victim stuck in here?'

'You're out of shape lad,' said the older voice, 'I could hear you wheezing before when you took this into the van.'

'Wheezing?'

'Yeah, first signs you're out of shape.'

And the men carried the long sofa into the house and placed it down somewhere. A man with an effeminate-sounding voice could then be heard, and he said: 'Ah, thanks boys. Wait there, I have a little something for you,' and Chris heard his shoes walking away with a gentle tapping sound. In his absence, the younger man said, 'He sounds like a pufter. He's dead tall as well isn't he?'

The older man said: 'Hey, shut up, he's alright him. He's a bit eccentric but he's alright. Just talks funny, yeah, he is too tall like; get your ball off the roof he would.'

The gentle tapping of feet returned, and the camp-sounding man said, 'There's your money and here's a cake I baked just for you two.'

'Ah, you shouldn't have bothered Mr Kearns,' said the older-sounding voice.

The two van drivers left, and then Mr Kearns began to sing a song that had been in the charts a few years before; *Seasons in the Sun* by Terry Jacks. And then he must have sat down on the sofa, because Chris felt the cushion above press down violently hard on his face, and for a few moments he could hardly breathe in the suffocating confines of the sofa, but, just before the teenager could attempt to push upwards at the smothering cushion, Mr Kearns got his backside off the sofa to answer a ringing telephone. Enough was enough. Chris felt his right-front jean pocket for the Stanley knife, and then he decided to cut a small piece out the back of the sofa to create a peephole. He saw nothing but blue and silver patterned wallpaper about five inches away. He guessed he was in the hallway of the house, and thought he could perhaps just leap out of the sofa and get out of the house as quickly as possible. If Mr Kearns tried to stop him, Chris would have to use the knife on him. He listened first, and he heard Mr Kearns say: 'Okay, well I tell you what then, I'll go and collect it now if that's okay. Yes. See you in a mo.'

Chris listened to the sounds of the telephone receiver being placed back in its cradle. He then heard Kearns singing that Terry Jacks song again. About two minute later, he heard the front door slam shut, followed by the sounds of keys rattling about in locks.

Then Chris could make out the distant thuds of what

sounded like Kearns walking away from the house down his garden path. Now the opportunity had arisen at last to get out of the accursed second-hand sofa and rob a few things in the house before making a getaway. Chris ripped back the coarse jute lining fabric, and then he pushed the cushions up from him. He sat up and looked about. The bright sunlight shining into the window in the front door stung his eyes after lying in the dark for what seemed like a very long time. He got up off the sofa and had a look about. He was in the long hallway of a house. What if there was someone else in the place? Chris peeped around the doorway of a parlour. Not a soul was about, not even a pet to be seen. Where should he start? Chris went through the cupboards of the kitchen as fast as he could. Nothing of any value. He went into the living room and in the drawer of a sideboard he discovered a biscuit tin, and it contained various documents. A pale blue rent book, a driving licence. An old car tax disc – and two rolls of ten pound notes that came to £210 pound, bound with elastic bands, as well as a little plastic Barclays bank coin bag full of fifty-pence pieces. 'Very very nice,' Chris found himself whispering with glee. He wasn't sure whether he should go upstairs now and have another root, but then he thought he might just be pushing his luck. He decided to take the lovely little two-hundred-odd quid and get clean away before Kearns got back. He went to the kitchen door leading to the backyard, and saw something strange. There was a keyhole about five inches from the floor, and there was another keyhole about five inches from the top of the door. This meant you'd have to unlock the top and then the bottom lock – if you could find the keys –

and there were no keys to be found. And so, reluctantly, Chris hurried out the living room and down the hallway, past the sofa and its scattered cushions – and there he found the same set-up. A lock at the bottom of the door and another at the top. 'What the Hell…' Chris complained, and looked about desperately for the keys, for the door had been locked by Kearns before he had set off on his journey. Chris swore under his breath and went to the kitchen. There, on the wall, was a little funny plaque, about 8 inches wide and four inches tall, and the four words on it read: 'We'll watch your keys.' Above it was two little comical models of women in headscarves leaning over a fence with little cigarettes in their mouths. Chris snatched the two separate keys from the hooks on the plaque and went to the kitchen. He inserted one of the keys into the bottom keyhole and turned it. It clicked. He then tried to open the door. It wouldn't budge. He pulled a chair out from under the kitchen table. It had a spindle-filled backing and a seat made of intertwined rushes. It looked very old – antique even. Christ scraped the legs of the chair across the tiled floor to the door which led to the backyard. He stood on the chair and inserted one of the keys into the keyhole at the top of the door. It turned and clicked. 'Very nice,' the robber said with nerves, and he stepped down from the chair – and he turned the handle, but the damned door refused to open. 'How the Hell are you supposed to open this?' he said to himself. It was as if the keys had to be inserted *simultaneously* into the top and bottom keyholes and turned at the same time, but to do that, Chris's arms would have to be freakishly long. He took the chair to the front door and tried inserting the key in the top lock. It turned and something clicked, but still the door wouldn't open. He tried the other key in the bottom keyhole and it turned as easily as the key had in the top lock – but still the door refused to open. Through the frosted half-moon window of the front door, Chris heard the gate handle being pressed. He heard the hinge of the gate squeak as it was pushed open, and the footfalls. He picked up the chair and ran down the hallway with it to place it under the kitchen table. He looked back down the hallway and heard the locks clicking on the front door. Chris ran to the heavy thick purple curtains that went right down to the floor in the living room and hid behind them.

Moments later he heard Kearns come into the hallway. The front door was still open, and remained open for a while because Chris could hear an ice cream van's jingling theme nearby and the white-noise rush of traffic passing by. The teenaged housebreaker guessed that Kearns was looking at the scattered sofa cushions in the hallway and the ripped fabric. He'd probably already found the hollow Chris had excavated in the sofa. Now was the time for Chris to run out from the curtains and down the hallways and out of the house – but Kearns slammed the door. He didn't come into the living room; he went upstairs. Chris heard the thump-thump-thump of the householder on the carpeted stairway. Was he going to call the police? Chris had not seen a telephone up there. The only telephone was on that crescent table in the hallway. Why then, had Kearns gone upstairs? Chris decided he would have to smash one of the windows soon and then just make a break out the house that way. He hated glass though, because he had cut his wrist breaking into a house via a window when he was just ten, and had needed a blood transfusion. Time dragged on. Chris took the Stanley knife out of his pocket and slid the triangular blade out of the black sleek body. He peeped out from behind the curtain, and at first he didn't see Kearns, because clouds had slid over the sun outside now, casting greyness over the area. The room was darker than before, and suddenly, Chris saw something that literally put the fear of God into him. A man, at least seven feet in height, with abnormally long arms and freakishly long narrow legs, was sitting in the armchair of the living room, and on his head he wore a black mantilla veil of the type a widow might wear at a funeral. He wore a black blouse of some sort, and a short matte black skirt and black tights. His pointed black shiny shoes were huge, size 14 at least. He was sitting ther with his legs obscenely wide apart so Chris could see the man's black knickers. And in his left hand, this freak of nature held a long carving knife with the blade tip pointing to the ceiling and its black handle resting on the vinyl padded arm of the chair. The eerie transvestite had a deathly pale face with heavy black make-up encircling each eye, and those eyes were fixed on Chris, and seemed full of mockery. The lips were coated with dark red lipstick and curved up in a ghastly grin of discoloured teeth.

'Hello,' the figure said, and Chris immediately recognised the camp tone of the voice. It was indeed Mr Kearns. 'I'm going to cut you up into little bits and I'm going to put you in a pie with some cranberry sauce,' he said.

156

Chris felt faint. He suddenly lifted the Stanley knife up in a threatening manner, but the abnormally tall transvestite let out a shriek of laughter, and said, 'That doesn't scare me! Look!' he said, and lifted up his long thing hand and pressed the tip of the massive carving knife into the centre of his palm, drawing blood. 'Doesn't even hurt! Ha! Ha!'

Chris found himself trying to run past this terrifying figure, but his legs seemed to be moving in slow motion. The man dressed as a woman got up in a flash from the chair and had to duck as he passed through the doorway into the hallway. Chris knew he couldn't get out of the house through that double-locked front door, so he ran up the stairs to one of the rooms, and when he looked back, he saw the 'woman' in black coming awkwardly up the stairs, impeded by his huge long feet, which were too big to take each step on the staircase. 'You won't get away! You're going to be dead soon!' he shouted after Chris. Chris pushed open the door to one of the rooms and ran inside, and he saw the walls of the room were plastered with various female models of the day, and someone had scribbled zig-zag lines on every face of the beauties with a red marker. There was a white plaster bust of some woman on a sideboard, and her nose had been hacked off. Chris picked up the bust and hurled it at the window, smashing the pane in completely. He looked out the window and saw the top of the backyard wall about fifteen feet below. He would have to jump out onto it, even if it meant risking a broken neck. He saw the door of the room open, and the sinister veiled head of the giant psychopath peeped in. 'Come back and I promise you I won't lay a finger on you!' Kearns said in a very insincere voice.

Chris swore at him at the top of his voice, and Kearns let out a spine-chilling scream and rushed into the room. The hand that held the carving knife was raised and ready to strike. Chris stepped onto the bottom of the window frame, crouched, and threw himself out, intending to land on the top of the wall. His feet landed on the top of the wall, but the moss that coated the bricks caused him to slip and fall into the entry. Chris landed on his feet with such a force, he felt as if the top of his legs had gone through to his chest, and he found himself staggering down the entry, unable to breathe in or out, and unable to speak. He finally emerged from the entry near Aigburth Road and from there he walked three miles home in a dreadful state. He suffered from realistic recurring nightmares about the weird knife-wielding transvestite for many years until his death in 1986.

MORE LIVERPOOL TIMESLIPS

I have covered the concept of timewarps and slippages in time in many of my books and it was I who first mentioned the Bold Street timeslips which are now even mentioned on Wikipedia and other internet websites, although some web 'authors' maintain that these incidents are all 'urban myths' (and these nameless, faceless individuals ignorantly insult the integrity and bravery of the many people from all walks of life who came forward to tell me of their experiences). My numerous accounts of the Bold Street timewarps were presented to the public in the hope that other people who had experienced time loss or displacement would come forward to describe what had happened to them, and I was not disappointed. I estimate that well in excess of four hundred people have written to me by email and postal mail, or called me at radio stations, to tell me of their timeslip experiences, and rarely a week goes by without a reader contacting me to tell me of yet another timewarp incident which happened to them or someone they know. What follows is just a small selection of these fascinating timeslip accounts. In the 1960s, a reader named Cathy - who was nineteen when the following incident happened, was a typical teen who loved clothes, and, well, I'll let Cathy tell the story: 'It was the Swinging Sixties and I loved buying clothes and wore a wild array of coloured dresses and mini skirts, mostly in clashing colours like orange and pink and purple; usually worn with boots up to the knees or chunky-heeled shoes. To fund my wardrobe I worked in the city. Jobs were easy to find then, you would give up one job on a Friday, and find another by the following Monday. I went to work for a firm of Chartered Accountants called Charles E. Dolby who had offices in old chambers in Dale Street. This was an ancient decrepit building which would have been perfect for a film set of a Dickens drama. I guess nothing had changed since the eighteenth century. A few other businesses occupied this building. I worked on the ground floor in a tiny office with two other girls. About six article clerks had the next office, and they were paid buttons because they were training to be accountants, but actually did most of the work. The office toilets were located on the top floor, up four flights of stairs and were housed inside a very large room; a room that was definitely not originally made with toilet facilities in mind; it was all such a waste of space, especially as most of the offices were tiny pokey little rooms. This huge room at the top of the building had about eight toilets in cubicles in a line opposite the only door. They were on a higher level, you had to climb up a step. The whole floor area was old wooden boards, not polished but in a dry dusty untreated condition. All the offices had their own key to this room and the door was a very heavy old fashioned solid oak, with a new Yale lock fitted so when you closed it, it locked behind you. Outside the steps leading up to this door were made of concrete, obviously a later addition to this building, no wood in sight. Now, I've been in many haunted places such as Dean Hall, supposedly the most haunted house in England, and many old pubs and halls with ghosts, and I have never felt a thing - not the slightest vibe, so it is really amazing that whenever I entered this room at the top of the offices I could feel an atmosphere immediately – so much so – that I would only use these toilets if I was absolutely desperate. The minute I entered there was a total quietness, it was freezing, I could feel I was being watched. It was absolutely, terrifyingly scary. I never mentioned this to anyone. I don't know why, perhaps they would think me odd. No-one else seemed to be bothered about it and all the staff used the toilets whenever they needed to with no comment about them. One morning I decided to get in early, I had stacks of work to do, all the end of year accounts had to be typed and I wanted to get a head start, so I caught an earlier train from my home in Rock Ferry to James Street Station. I picked up the mail on the way into the building and instead of opening up our office, I needed the loo so without thinking, got the key off the hook in the outer office and ran up all the flights of stairs, opened the big old door and dropping the mail onto a sink went into our office's loo. As soon as I locked the door, the whole room erupted into bedlam. I went into a state of total shock, and was so petrified I couldn't move a muscle. The room outside my cubicle was filled with the sound of wooden clogs running and jumping on the bare boarded floor. Outside the room, the floor and stairs were concrete, so this was all happening inside on the wooden floorboards. Voices - raised and high pitched - were making sounds so terrible I felt if I opened the door I would be faced with mad lunatics all in an uncontrollable frenzy. This went on for ages – and I really mean ages. I stood behind that door unable to move for fifteen to twenty minutes, and all the while pandemonium was on the other side of a thin wooden door with gaps above and below. Even as I recall this my heart is racing; I have never known fear like it. Somehow I managed to get my brain to work. I realised I had to get out of there; I had to pluck up the courage to make a run for it, through a crowd of crazed ghosts. How do you get up the courage to do that? I was well aware that whatever was making all that noise was not of this earth. They were not human. They were spirits of some sort and definitely not friendly. Even to this day the memory of this is so sharp I will never forget it. I planned to open the door and run, and after a few false starts and shaking with fear I managed to do just that – I opened the door. Silence hit me - total and absolute silence; an empty room, freezing temperature, almost humming with silence. It was as if someone just flicked a switch and turned off a blaring radio. I ran for the door, forgetting the post and in a fumbling panic got out of there. I was shaking, almost hysterical when I got back to my office, so much time had passed that everyone were at their desks working. I never went into that room again; nothing would induce me to enter it. If ever I needed the loo, I would leave the office and use the facilities of Exchange Station. Soon after I left that company and went to live in Portugal. Years later I found myself in Liverpool and discovered that the old chambers had gone – been pulled down making way for the new. And I wonder if the ghosts went with it, or have they somehow found their way into the new building?'

Strange goings-on at the buildings Cathy refers to have indeed been reported to me quite a few times over the years. A phantom bell and a pair of faint male voices arguing over something that just can't be made out have been heard in the newer buildings built next to the chambers Cathy mentioned, but that is nothing compared to a man named Graham, who worked at 11 Dale Street – the very offices of the same Charles E Dolby Cathy mentioned in her chilling recollection. This incident took place in the early 1970s, and Graham was just seventeen, and employed as an office boy at the firm who ran errands, made the tea and posted bundles of letters. Graham had only been with the firm for three days when something quite bizarre took place. It was a wintry morning and the teenager turned up for work around half-past eight, and found himself lost. He went up several flights of stairs and found himself in a dark warren of old offices he had never seen before. In one of these offices, the flames of two candles could be seen flickering through the pane of frosted glass in a door, and Graham rapped on the door, deciding he'd ask whoever was in the office if he could direct him to his proper workplace. A voice answered: 'Enter!' and Graham turned the doorknob and went into the room to see a portly round faced man dressed in a black jacket, a white high-collar and an odd-looking tie. He was hunched over the green leather writing surface of a huge oaken desk that was covered with stacks of books, scrolls tied with coloured ribbon, inkpots, and the two candles which Graham had seen through the frosted pane in the door. In his hand, the stranger at the desk held an antiquated feathered quill. He looked over the top of a pair of wire-framed spectacles and smiled at Graham. 'I've never seen you before, what's your name boy?' he asked.

Graham believed the man was a ghost, that the dusty

old-fashioned office was some phantasmagorical illusion from long ago, and so he never answered the chubby elder's question, but instead, backed out of the room. He noticed the sound of horse's hooves clip-clopping outside, and the trundling of the cart or carriage the unseen animals were pulling, and that really unnerved the office boy. Graham closed the door and turned to hurry down the dark stairway, and eventually heard the welcoming sound of an electric typewriter clattering away in the offices back in the 20th century. When I asked Graham to describe the man seated at the desk with the quill, he said he was the spitting image of the actor who played the senior menswear salesman Mr Grainger in the old BBC comedy, *Are You Being Served?* I obtained a photograph of Arthur Brough, who played Mr Grainger until his death in 1978, and Graham said he was the double of the man he had seen, sitting at the outdated desk back in the early 1970s. Graham and two workmates searched the corridors of the building but never found that old man or his office. Another person named Steve Gibbon, who in the 1980s worked in an office in that building where Graham was employed, said he was astonished one day to see the name 'Pioneer Assurance Building' in gold letters on a frosted pane of glass in the vestibule door. He went to fetch his boss, but when he came back, the vestibule door was gone. In the 1890s, that office was indeed called the Pioneer Assurance Building.This whole area of Dale Street is steeped in ghosts and, it comes as no surprise to me at all, for Hackins Hey, which runs alongside the haunted building where Cathy and Graham had supernatural experiences, is a very old and narrow lane where you will find Liverpool's oldest pub, Ye Hole in the Wall, as well as the Saddle Inn, which fronts onto Dale Street. Both of these pubs have their fair share of ghosts.

Staying on Dale Street, we come next to another series of fascinating timeslips which occurred in one of the city's most well-known and oldest pubs – Rigby's, which Horatio Nelson allegedly visited on several occasions in the 1790s. Rigby's - named after a former owner and spirit and wine wholesaler named Thomas Rigby (1815-1886), is said to date back to 1726, according to a date on its façade, but this date in all probability, refers to the earlier incarnation of the pub when the premises were the Cross Keys. Nevertheless, Rigby's is an old and very atmospheric pub and has been the scene of many strange goings-on of a paranormal nature over the years. In the 1980s, Ann and Katy, two women in their early forties, called into Rigby's one day at noon on their lunch hour. Both women worked as secretaries at different local legal firms, and on this particular day, ghosts and the supernatural were the furthest things from the mind of these ladies. All they wanted was a sandwich, a smoke and of course a little light liquid refreshment. The secretaries had only been seated for about ten minutes when Ann went to the toilet. The minutes dragged by, and Katy noticed her friend was taking longer than she usually did when she powdered her nose, and so she went to the ladies' toilet and became very suspicious when she discovered that Ann was not in there. She asked two people she knew if they had seen Ann come out of the toilet, and the two people – who were female friends Katy had known for years – said they had definitely seen her go into the toilet, but neither of them recalled her coming out. As Katy and these two people discussed where Ann could have gone to, the missing secretary came out of the toilet Katy had just visited. Ann looked pale and distant. Katy asked her where she had been, and Ann told her something very strange had taken place a few minutes ago. She had walked into the toilet and experienced some sort of dizzy spell. Everything had gone pale grey, and Ann had found herself in what she could only describe as some 'void of just nothingness'. There was no sensation of up or down, and no floor or ceiling or walls to be seen. It was as if she had just been floating in a grey fog in some type of Limbo. And then, about a minute later, Ann heard the toilet door squeaking open, and the sounds of people chatting in the pub. The greyness faded and Ann found herself standing in the toilet, looking at the wall. The experience had been more baffling than frightening, although it was some time before Ann would venture into that toilet on her own again. A few years afterwards, in the same pub, something took place which also defied explanation. Like the last incident, this one took place during the day, again around lunchtime. A man in his fifties named Harry, who ran a newsagent in the city centre, went into Rigby's one rainy March day around one in the afternoon. He had been serving in his shop since 6am and was now having a short break while his friend Tony served behind the counter for him. Harry would then return to the shop around 4pm and serve till just after teatime. He usually had lunch at Rigby's or the Trial's pub. On this day, Harry took an early copy of the *Liverpool Echo* into Rigby's and ordered a pint of bitter while he decided what he would eat. He wasn't feeling that hungry on this inclement day, and thought he might just have a packet of cheese and onion crisps instead of a substantial meal. He finished his pint, went to the toilet, and then, just before he came out of the gents, he washed his hands, and thought he heard a roar of loud laughter coming from the bar. He opened the door of the pub, and a strong smell of cigarettes reminiscent of the old Senior Service brand his father smoked wafted into his face. Now sunlight was streaming through the windows of the pub as if summer had suddenly arrived in the middle of March. Then Harry noticed something much stranger than the drastic change in the weather: the bar was full of military men; Royal Air Force men in blue-grey uniforms, army men and their officers, and all of the women were dressed in the style of the 1940s. The men who were not wearing caps or hats had their hair cropped short and slicked back with oil or Brylcreem, and the women had their hair styled as the women did back in the dark days of World War Two. Harry slowly made his way through the backdated drinkers and tried to find his seat and the *Liverpool Echo* he had been reading, and he soon saw that the layout, furnishings and seats were all different now. The barmaid who had served Harry minutes ago was nowhere to be seen, and he knew no one in the place. Harry began to doubt his own sanity at first, but then felt his stomach turn over when he realised he had somehow gone back in time over forty years by the looks of things. He looked out a window and saw trams, and sandbags piled up against a wall further down the road, and an ARP warden crossing Dale Street. All of the people out

167

there in the street were dressed in the style of the 1940s. Harry took a deep breath, and a tall broad-shouldered man in an RAF uniform gently patted his shoulder as he squeezed past him to go and talk to a group of men who were seated around a table. Harry thought he could hear a piano start to play at this point, and he decided to go outside. Outside, the sun quickly faded in the sky, and the warmth faded with it. Rain patted against Harry's face, and he looked about to see a modern double-decker bus rolling past the pub, followed by a white transit van. All of the people on Dale Street were now dressed in the style of the 1980s. Harry went back into Rigby's to see a man sitting in his seat, reading his copy of the *Echo*. There was no sign of the military men or the 1940s barmaid. Harry went back to his shop immediately and told his friend Tony what had just happened. A customer overheard the conversation and said he too had experienced a similar timeslip in Rigby's in the 1970s, and had seen Teddy Boys come into the pub and attack a man who was dressed like something out of a black and white gangster film. When several customers went to the aid of the man who was being attacked, they saw him and the teds vanish into thin air.

One mild afternoon in February 2012, I was walking along Woolton Road with a friend, near to Our Lady's Bishop Eton school, when I happened to hear an unusual droning sound above and to the left. My friend and I looked up and agreed that the plane looked like an old WWII Messerschmitt. This plane flew into an unusual low cloud which had a faint yellowish tint compared to the other higher clouds. As soon as the antique plane flew into this cloud, the sound from its engine stopped immediately. I later received many emails from readers in Woolton, Wavertree, Old Swan, Childwall, Huyton, Mossley Hill, Aintree, Fazakerley, Anfield and Netherton, all reporting sightings of outdated planes flying over the skies of Liverpool. One man was driving along near the Fiveways Roundabout in Childwall when he spotted what looked like a Lancaster flying low over the rooftops. A man in his eighties named George, heard the unmistakable whine of a well-tuned Merlin engine as he left the allotment on Thingwall Road in February 2012, and looked up to see a Spitfire flying overhead. George's nephew also saw the outdated plane as it headed towards the south-east. George had seen and heard Spitfires when he was in the army, and knew without a doubt that one of those legendary planes had flown over Wavertree, even though the last operational Spitfire had flown in the 1950s. I immediately checked the newspapers and the net to see if there were any air displays involving World War Two aircraft in the region; there weren't any such displays being held anywhere in the North West. A few years before this widespread aerial timeslip, I was contacted by a retired pilot who told me how, in the 1990s, he was flying a passenger jet high over Liverpool, bound for the Continent, when he almost collided with a Lancaster bomber. The pilot, co-pilot, and most of the aircrew saw the Wellington at such close quarters, they could actually see airmen sitting in the gun turrets. The pilot of the jet took extreme evasive action, which shook the passengers up a little, and he, the co-pilot and crew agreed to say nothing about the chilling encounter and had to tell the ruffled passengers that the plane had encountered some 'air turbulence'. Had the captain of the airliner informed air traffic control of the encounter, he felt he would have been hauled before a psychiatrist and deemed mentally unfit to fly a plane. The encounter took place in the late afternoon with excellent visibility, and the Lancaster looked solid as it crossed the flight-path of the jet, slanting down out of the clear blue sky, bound perhaps for the airbase at Burtonwood, in a bygone age.

We know, or think we know, that time is real, but what is it? If you happen to look at the clock and see the time is 9pm, then look again twenty minutes later and see it is 10pm, chances are, you will believe the clock and will not immediately suspect someone of turning the clock forward while your attention was elsewhere. Likewise, if you went into a coma and were unconscious for a month, you would believe a doctor if he told you that you'd only been asleep for a few hours. Time only seems to exist where there is consciousness, and I truly believe that the time is near when someone will make a breakthrough in our understanding of the time-space continuum and this discovery will probably result in physical time travel or a way of viewing the past through a television camera which can pear through a manmade rip in time or perhaps a 'wormhole' of the type now being discussed by physicists specialising in quantum mechanics, and when this technology comes to pass, the past will be opened, and not just the distant past we look to in history book, but the recent past, and that could mean that one day, the police will be able to check anyone's alibi by peering into the past to see if a murder suspect was really where he or she said she was at a given time. I imagine politicians will not be too keen on such a prying device...

THE MAN WHO WASN'T THERE

The following strange story took place in the winter of
1997 on Allerton Road, not too far from the legendary
'shelter in the middle of the roundabout' referred to in
the world-famous Beatles song *Penny Lane*. Allerton
Road has its fair share of noble charity shops, staffed
by volunteers from all walks of life, and it was in one
of these shops one bitterly cold and grey afternoon in
January 1997, when a woman in her sixties named
Patricia left her house on Dovedale Road and went to
shop for a few items at Woolworths. By 3pm she
decided she'd call into a certain charity shop for a
browse. This shop had a little bookcase section full of
hardbacks and paperbacks featuring all the well-told
adult and children's tales from the writers most of us
know – including a few we have never heard from.
There was also a single cubicle with a swish curtain
were Patricia liked to try on a second-hand dress or
even a pair of donated slacks or pristine jeans given to
the shop by some lady whose waistline or taste in
fashion had undergone some change. There were
children's toys in the shop too, everything from
archaic board games from the pre-computer-console
era to the Rubik's cube. Patricia still had a record
player, and this shop always had a good stock of vinyl
forty-fives, thirty-three-and-a-thirds, plus even the odd
seventy-eight – which will be all gobbledygook to
listeners of iPods and their digital music. Ornaments,
shoes, racks of coats, cassette tapes of old ballad
singers, nostalgic comic books, alphabetical telephone

address books, brass wall plates and bronze plaques, pop-art prints on mirrors, Guinness brand ashtrays, polka dot umbrellas, Welsh dolls with their cropped 'witch's hat', tiny piggy banks with the words 'My Rolls Royce Fund' on their glazed hides, lost teddy bears, accordion handbags, pocket solitaire, Crying Boy pictures, Newtons Cradles, hanging mats, Tuscany orange floor lamps, ye olde maps of the world printed on brass-finished pictures, Dinky cars, and – the thing that had attracted the attention of Patricia: a Francie doll – with hair that grows – in the original orange and pink box. A long time ago, around 1966, Patricia's daughter, Samantha, who was then 5-years-old, loved that doll Francie. The two had become inseparable until Sam accidentally left the doll on a bus during an outing to town one day. The little girl cried her eyes out and would never accept a replacement. Sam was thirty-six now with two daughters of her own. Patricia had to get this Francie doll for her. It was just £2, and as Patricia waited at the counter to buy the doll, a man behind her said, 'You buying it back?'

Patricia turned and saw a man, aged about seventy-something, about five-feet three inches or less, standing there with a trilby, a brownish-yellow overcoat, baggy beige trousers, and a pair of shiny brown brogues. He had the brightest blue eyes Patricia had ever seen, and they were smiling eyes.

'Oh, no, this was never mine, ha!' Patricia said, and she grinned and looked at the boxed doll in her hand.

'People do that you see,' explained the old man in a soft voice, 'they bring things in here and then they get all sentimental and buy them back.'

'No, this is for my daughter. She had a doll just like

this when she was just a little girl,' Patricia began to explain, when the man interrupted her as he pointed to the window of the charity shop. 'You're probably too young to remember the trams,' he said.

'Oh no, I remember them well,' Patricia said, flattered at the man thinking she was too young to recall those antiquated green gleaming hulks.

'The terminus was over there, and there was a clock on the top of that shelter. Do you remember the barber Bioletti over there?' the old man asked, and now his pale blue eyes sparkled into life. Hailstones clattered on the window of the charity shop and the noise from the shower almost drowned out his words.

Patricia paid for the Francie doll and Sarah, the young lady behind the counter smiled and wrapped it in a plastic carrier bag, then looked to the left of Patricia with a puzzled stare. Patricia turned to see what Sarah was looking at. The old man in the trilby had turned to walk towards the cubicle – but there was a woman in there trying on a skirt, so Sarah shouted out: 'Er, sir! There's someone in there! Don't go in - ' and before she could finish the sentence, Sarah let out a sort of yelp of exclamation, because the old man collapsed – into a heap of clothes. Patricia witnessed this surreal and eerie incident. She and Sarah looked down at the floor, and saw just the toe of a shiny brown brogue shoe peeping out from a crumpled brownish-yellow overcoat. Beneath the coat the women could see the pair of beige trousers, and on top of this pile of empty clothes was the trilby the old man had worn. Of the old man who had existed seconds ago between the hat and the brogues, there was no trace. It was some time before Sarah dared to pick up

174

the trilby, and she lifted it with a shaking hand as if she expected the old man's head to be under it. 'You saw it, didn't you?' Sarah kept saying to Patricia, who nodded unconsciously. Sarah left the shop that afternoon after phoning her sister in-law and asking her to come and fill in for her, just for an hour before the shop closed. It transpired, I believe, that the clothes the ghost had worn had been donated by his wife after he had suddenly dropped dead, from heart failure, on Smithdown Place, just a stone's throw from the charity shop. I have also heard that, every now and then, the nostalgic and solid-looking ghost performs his same vanishing trick at the charity shop, only he wears other people's cast offs, which makes the trick seem all the more sinister.

THE UNEXPLAINABLES

It's very satisfying to learn of a haunting, to look into the history of the house or place where the ghost was seen, and to resolve the matter by identifying the apparition through extensive research into censuses, old newspaper records, street directories, public records and so on, but there are so many reports that come my way which cannot be easily resolved and explained, no matter how much research is undertaken, and the following stories are of this kind – the unexplainables I call them, and they are filed away under that name in my private records.

One rainy night in November 2010, a man in his fifties we shall call Bill, from Bagnall Street, Anfield, left his house and went round the corner of the street to the off-licence on Walton Breck Road, which, incidentally, is rather unimaginatively named "The Offy". Walton Breck Road was unusually quiet at 10pm, with just two cars passing down it in an easterly direction. As Bill was crossing the road he saw something large and dark to his right on a large square of wasteland between Venice Street and Varthen Street, where houses and shops once stood. At first, the Bagnall Street resident assumed the dark object walking in his direction was a large dog, but when he turned to face the thing, he saw it was not a dog at all, but a huge silhouetted bird, like a giant raven, walking silently towards him on its four-toed feet with a waddling gait. Bill stopped in his tracks as he reached the other side of the road. This bird, in his estimation, about four feet in height. May I point out at this juncture that Bill had not been drinking. He had been painting his mother's living room walls all day and had been looking forward to a relaxing night with a bottle of wine, a big packet of Maltesers and a DVD. Bill swore under his breath, more out of fear than astonishment, and he turned and walked back across Walton Breck Road and hurried to his mother's house. He looked back at one point, expecting the giant sinister winged creature to be following him, but thankfully it wasn't, and Bill's mother Mary knew her son was not lying when he told her what he had seen because nothing got in the way of her son and his bottle of wine, and Bill refused to go back out the door that night, and kept looking out the window to see if he could see the oversized bird. He called a friend named David on Spellow Lane and told him what he had seen, and David, who loved mysteries of this sort, drove round to Bill's house, deliberately going slow when he passed the piece of wasteland off Walton Breck Road where Bill had allegedly seen the huge unearthly black bird. David didn't see anything out the ordinary there at all, and as much as he tried, he could not persuade Bill to go out looking for the bird. A few days later, Bill was in his local newsagents, Anfield News, when he overheard two women talking as they waited in a small queue. One of the women said her daughter had seen a huge bird walking up the middle of Baltic Street – and this street is the one next to Bagnall Street. Bill tapped the woman on the shoulder and said, 'Excuse me love, I saw that bird,' and he told the woman and her friend about his encounter with the raven-like giant. 'Ooh, I wonder what it is?' said the old woman, and her friend shrugged and smiled, then said, 'There's no bird that big surely? Only Emu!'

Bill emailed me to see if I had heard about any such bird. I told him that a month before, I had received an email from a 22-year-old student named Kimberley who had seen a massive black bird fly over Stanley Park. This was in early October and around 6.45pm. Kimberley and her friend tried to video the bird on their phone but it was too quick, and the student's boyfriend, a young man from Chester named Matt, tried to follow the bird on his mountain bike. According to Mike, quite a few people saw the enormous creature actually roost on top of Everton's Goodison Park stadium before it flew off into the gathering twilight – towards nearby Anfield Cemetery. It may be a black coincidence, but shortly after this, Bill, the man who first saw the mysterious bird, lost his brother, who suffered a heart attack and died, at the age of forty-three – and the mother of Kimberley, the student who saw the bird flying over Stanley Park, was diagnosed with cervical cancer, but thankfully, she made a full recovery after undergoing treatment. The enigmatic giant bird was compared to a raven by all who saw it, and the raven has always been regarded as a death omen. Of course, all black birds, as well as night birds such as rooks, owls, ravens and crows have always been regarded as omens of ill-luck, and on the subject of portents of death, I must include the following strange story among this baffling collection of inexplicable curiosities.

In August 1973, a number of people living in the streets surrounding Calderstones Park saw a white fox on the prowl after dark, and many of these witnesses subsequently died within days of seeing the albino-like animal. A woman walking her dog at 10pm thought a stray white dog was walking along the pavement on the other side of Harthill Road, until she saw its bushy tail and the tell-tale profile formed by its pointed muzzle and distinctive ears. The woman's poodle tugged hard on its leash and barked furiously at the white fox, which stopped and looked across the road with a pair of penetrating ruby red eyes. The woman later told her husband that the creature seemed to wear an uncanny grin as it looked at her. It then ran off into the distance and crossed the road, heading for the gates to Calderstones Park, where it jumped up onto a five-foot wall to gain entry to the park. Three days after this encounter, the woman who had seen the white fox on Harthill Road died in her sleep. Her husband was a superstitious man who believed the white fox had been some omen of death. Other people began to see the snowy-coated animal; it was encountered by a milkman near Menlove Avenue, but he seems to have lived to tell the tale, and is still alive at the time of writing, but a 32-year-old man named Leigh – an amateur photographer from Woolton Hill – may have succumbed to the curse of the White Fox, and he had one of the strangest encounters of all with the creature. He was in Calderstones Park just before dawn one September morning that year, waiting to capture a shot of the sunrise over the trees, when he saw a troop of at least fifteen foxes, all sitting peacefully in a row, beneath the extensive spreading boughs of the oldest tree in the north west – the park's Allerton Oak, reputed to be around 1,000 years old. The fox sitting in the middle of the skulk of foxes was white. This was before the era of digital cameras, and so Leigh tried to fit his flashgun to his SLR camera but the foxes ran off. Within a fortnight, Leigh died after coming down with a cold which turned into full-blown pneumonia. Hours before he died, he suffered a number of nightmares about the White Fox and then slipped into unconsciousness.

The White Fox was seen again for a while in 1977, but not one person who saw it seems to have suffered any bad luck, and another fox with an ivory coat was seen in Calderstones Park several times in the 1990s. I heard rumours that those who had seen it had died in car crashes and all manner of gruesome circumstances, but, despite intensive research, could not validate any of these claims. Foxes only live for a few years, so it seems unlikely that the white fox encountered in 1973 was the same one seen in the 1990s – unless of course, the White Fox is some form of supernatural manifestation.

Calderstones Park is the place to see the enigmatic Calder Stones, Liverpool 's most important archaeological relics – and where are they kept? In a greenhouse in the park! The six surviving stone slabs are thought to be about 4,000 years old and the tallest stone is about 8 feet tall and three feet wide. They originally stood on nearby Calderstones Road as part of an ancient burial mound. One of the first references to the stones is in the summer of 1568, when they were alluded to as the Calldway stones. Around 1765 the burial mound and the stones were disturbed and there were rumours amongst the locals that some malevolent force had been released when the ashes of the cremated people interred in the mound had been used as fertiliser by the desecrators. The local ale went sour, a child was stillborn, and an oxen fell dead for no apparent reason. Some believe the mysterious markings on the Calder Stones are star maps, whilst others believe the graven symbols were inscribed by ancient priests not unlike the archetypal druid. On 15 March 2012, a number of people in Allerton saw a tall eerie hooded figure wearing what looked like some monk's cowl, standing (and some accounts say hovering) by the so-called "Robin Hood's Stone", an upright slab of sandstone which stands at the junction of Booker Avenue and Archerfield Road, Mossley Hill. The stone is said to be one of the Calder Stones – and is around 8 feet tall. The long scored lines which run longitudinally down the monolith have, over the years, been seen to give off an orange luminescence – possibly generated by piezoelectricity. In the time of Henry VIII some thought the long score marks on the standing stone had been made by archers dragging the heads of arrows down the grooves to sharpen them, but the marks are in fact, thousands of years old. The stone should rightfully be placed back among the other stones, and those stones should ideally be put back in their original position. Muriel Jones was visiting a relative in Mossley Hill on the evening of 15 March 2012, and when she was returning to her home in Allerton, at around 10.35pm, she was walking down Booker Avenue when she noticed a tall figure with a pointed hood and a long robe which went down to the pavement, standing about three feet away from the Robin Hood's Stone. Sensing this outlandish figure was sinister, Mrs Jones crossed the road and met a woman she had known for years named Mary, who was walking her dog. Mary said she had seen the figure earlier on around 10.10pm, and as both women looked on, the abnormally tall 'monk' faded away into nothingness before their eyes. Mrs Jones hurried home, believing she'd seen a ghost, but Mary went home and fetched her sceptical husband to see the weird figure, and they saw the monk was back in the same spot. This was around 11.40pm. Mary's husband Ken walked across the road but kept at a distance from the figure, sensing it was unearthly, and he quickly returned to Mary, saying he had seen the 'thing's face'. Ken said the monk's face inside the hood was mostly in shadow, but the nose and lower face looked grey. The couple went home as the monk stood stock still. Mary and Ken said they could not sleep that night because their dog kept barking downstairs, and the couple also heard their gate squeak five times, between two and four in the morning, as if someone – or something – was opening it. Ken and Mary, being mindful of the apparition they had seen less than 300 yards away, were too scared to look out the window to see what was opening the gate.

There are other unexplainables in my files, and we go back in time forty years from the last one to confront a creature I have written about many times before in my books. I'll tell you the story first.

When a man of the cloth tells you a story, you tend to give the narrative more credence than if it came from a regular member of the public, and the following story was related to me many years ago by a Catholic priest who is now retired, and we'll call him Father Connolly. In March 1972 a 10-year-old golden-haired girl named Claire was supposed to attend a charity talent show put on by her school on the outskirts of Liverpool, but her brother was unable to give her a lift because he came down with mumps of all things, and so the 35-year-old local priest Father Connolly turned up at Claire's house in the Paddington area of Liverpool at teatime, and patiently waited as the girl watched the last few minutes of her favourite telly cartoon, *Touché Turtle*, and then he put the girl in his old Volkswagen Beetle before going back into the house to get Claire's beautiful dress for the show from her mum. When he returned to the car the priest found Claire was all giggly for some reason, and asked her why. The girl cupped her hand round her mouth and shook her head. 'All nerves I suppose,' the priest decided, and drove off from North View and headed for Edge Lane. 'What song are you going to be singing Claire?', Father Connolly enquired.

'*All Kinds of Everything*, the song Dana sung Father,' Claire replied, and the priest lifted his eyebrows and smiled as he nodded, 'Good choice. And you have a fine voice, and a beautiful dress, so you'll be on *Opportunity Knocks* next, I can foresee it.'

As the car passed the Botanic Park, Claire started giggling again and the priest said, all tongue in cheek: 'Laughing at nothing's the first sign of madness you know?' But then he heard a sniggering sound behind him too. 'Claire, is someone else in this car?'

Claire burst out laughing and nodded, and said: 'Sorry father, my friend Brian wants to come to the show as well.' And as she said this the priest got the shock of his life, because a weird round green face rose from the back seat into full view. The face had large square prominent teeth in a huge grinning mouth, a turned up sharp nose, small blue eyes, pointed ears and a burgundy-coloured beard. On his head, "Brian" wore a black pointed cap. "Ah, I'm sorry I gave you a start father,' said Brian, 'it's quite a mask isn't it?'

The shocked priest almost went through a red light. Open-mouthed, he gazed at the weird goblin-faced child in the rear view mirror, and said: 'Does your mother know you're going to the show? Why did you hide in my car?"

Brian let out a belly laugh, and Father Connolly could see that the supposed "mask" Brian wore was too realistic, and he went cold. 'That's no mask, you – devil!' the priest shouted, and Brian roared with laughter, as did Claire too. The priest stopped the car, took his rosary from the glove compartment and turned to thrust it in the thing's face, but by then the entity had left the car. The priest heard the back left passenger door close gently, and he gingerly got out the vehicle to see where the 'thing' had run off too, but could see nothing of it in the darkness.

Claire burst into tears, and said Brian would never be able to find his way back home now. She asked the priest if they could go and look for him. The priest was too stunned to answer at first, and then he shouted, 'No, we are not going to look for that abomination!'

Claire begged him to go and look for her 'friend' but Father Connolly drove off – and he turned the car 180 degrees and headed back to Claire's house. The priest quizzed the girl about Brian all the way home but Claire remained as tight-lipped as her mother, who also said nothing when the priest told her what had happened. Father Connolly stood on the doorstep of the house and blessed the residence – and Claire's mother slammed the door in his face. Mother and daughter still attended church but avoided eye contact whenever Father Connolly was in the pulpit.

The priest never fathomed just what the thing was in his backseat that night. Claire's house, incidentally, was close to that part of Kensington where *leprechauns* were reported back in 1964, and this latter incident has been featured many times in my books, including *Strange Liverpool*, in which I dedicated a whole section to the Little People sightings, called *The Summer of the Leprechaun*.

ENCOUNTER WITH A ZOMBIE

There are so many mysteries surrounding World War Two, but one in particular always haunts my imagination. There were many veterans of the conflict who recalled some very strange incidents in the latter days of the war as the Third Reich disintegrated. Russian, British, American and Canadian troops converging on Berlin encountered Hitler Youth and SS men who seemed impervious to machine gun fire. When some of these soldiers (many of them were boys who had been brainwashed and enlisted into the Hitler Youth Movement) were seen at close quarters, some had bullet holes in their torsos and limbs, and horrific injuries to their faces, and yet they were trying their utmost to defend Berlin from the might of the Red Army, as well as the British, Canadian and other armies of the alliance against the Nazis. After the war, some of the G.I.s and other soldiers of the alliance swore that they fought zombies. One American spoke of seeing bullet wounds in a boy's face that had taken off his nose and blasted out his left cheek, revealing his molars and jawbone, and yet he did not seem to be in any pain, and appeared very calm and professional as he reloaded his rifle – until he was finally cut down by a carbine. More of these weird stories circulated after the war, of Nazi scientists injecting drugs into the boy soldiers of Hitler Youth and soldiers of the SS to make them mindless obeying automatons who could not be stopped by bullets unless they were decapitated or blown to bits by bombs – a zombie army in effect.

It is known that Nazi scientists froze victims from the concentration camps until they died and then attempted to resuscitate them – always unsuccessfully. These were just some of the gruesome experiments carried out on the inmates of Auschwitz; other victims were submerged and once they had drowned, attempts were made to bring the victims back to life. It was claimed that if some method could be discovered to reanimate the drowned bodies, it could obviously be put to use where prized Nazi pilots had drowned after ditching their planes in the sea.

Since the days of Hitler, the conspiracy theories have raged over whether fluoridation of a nation's drinking water would make the average citizen slavishly devoted to those in power, and with or without mind control drugs in the water supply, we are all manipulated by the media and the internet to a certain degree, but true 'zombification' of the masses is still a few years away. What of real zombies of the types we see in such tongue-in-cheek films such as *Day of the Dead* and *Night of the Living Dead*? Well, I have written about a local zombie case in the Haunted Liverpool series before. In *Haunted Liverpool 7* I documented the strange case of the resurrected Victorian Walter Slim, alleged to have taken place in 1971, and in *Haunted Liverpool 13* I related the creepy tale of a bona fide zombie created by a Haitian gentleman named Josué Beauchamp in the 1930s. The following true story unfolded many years ago in the 1990s, when two lads in their twenties named Ryan and Neil, went to the Cabin Club, which is located on the corner of Wood Street and Berry Street, just across the road from St Luke's, the 'bombed-out Church'. Ryan and Neil went there to meet members of the opposite sex, but instead became rather drunk, and at one point in the drinking spree, Neil tried to climb the big rocking horse that was a feature of the club, but fell on top of his friend. The two men, both from the Smithdown Road area of Liverpool, then got talking to a young black man who was of similar age, and his name was Colly – but whether this was his first name or some nickname derived from his surname was never established. Colly, Neil and Ryan ended up leaving the club and went to another one in the area where the music was mellower and they could hear themselves talk, and it was in this other club, which was on Seel Street, where the subject somehow turned to the supernatural. Colly claimed that there was a weird underground flat under Paradise Street where an old Jamaican man practised all sorts of real magic. This subterranean residence was stashed with marijuana and all sorts of psychedelic drugs, but was said to be guarded by a real-life zombie. Ryan and Neil laughed when Colly told them this. Colly said he could validate his weird tale by showing Ryan and Neil how to get into the magician's place. 'Show us then, go on,' Neil challenged Colly, who took them that very morning at 2.30 am to an alleyway behind a crumbling warehouse near Duke Street. He climbed over a backyard wall and pointed to the window of a derelict house. 'You go in there and you go down to the cellar, and then there's a passage which leads straight to the magician's place,' Colly said, all matter of fact, and his eyes rolled with his drunkenness.

'Look Colly lad, we're all too bevvied to go and find this underground place,' Ryan reasoned, 'so why don't we go down tomorrow when we are all sober, and I'll bring a torch as well?'

Colly reluctantly agreed, as he wanted to prove he was not making the story of the magician up, and he went home to Toxteth after promising he'd meet Ryan and Neil on the following evening at 8pm. He didn't show, but Ryan and Neil went into the derelict house Colly had pointed out at 10pm, determined to prove that the Toxteth storyteller was just fibbing. Instead, they did find a long tunnel which ran, according to their estimations, somewhere under Paradise Street, and as they explored it, Neil kept urging his friend to go back. 'This tunnel could cave in and no one would even know we were down here,' Neil warned Ryan, but his friend's curiosity was getting the better of him and he walked on down the tunnel for about eighty feet, sweeping the feeble beam of a tiny pen-sized torch until he saw an old wooden maroon door at the end of the passage. There was about five inches of water on the floor here. Ryan took careful steps through the muddied puddles in case they concealed a hole, and upon reaching the door, he reached for the round brass knob in the maroon door and turned it. To his surprise, and to Neil's horror, the door opened. Straight away the two men were greeted by the waft of strong incense of some sort, and a dim orange light shining from a small solitary bulb was hanging from the ceiling of a long corridor with bare sandstone walls. 'I'm going,' Neil whispered, and went to turn around but Ryan grabbed his arm and under his breath, he said: 'Shut up. Come on.'

Ryan led the way as they crept down the corridor which led to another passage which ran at right angles across the corridor. 'Left or right?' Ryan murmured, deciding what way to go. He went left, and there was another door about twenty feet away, and this one was black, with a black handle on it. Ryan turned it, but the door wouldn't budge, so he went back up the passage and tried the other door, which was a white one with a black handle. He tried that handle, and the door opened. A sweet-smelling fragrance mingled with warm air assaulted Ryan's nose, and he peeped in to see a large vault with sandstone walls some twelve feet in height, and upon those walls were symbols and circles, scrawled in chalk and paint, and both men felt these symbols had something to do with the occult. There was a dining table in the middle of the high-ceilinged room, covered with a fine white linen tablecloth, and in the centre of the table there were bowls of fruit and unused, unlit candles set in expensive-looking candelabra. There were two black-wooded chairs at the table. To the left of the table was a fireplace of some sort, bordered with black marble and a fire surround, and above the mantelpiece there was an arched purple-tinted mirror in an ebonised and gilded frame, with floral cresting and a strange little horned head as the centrepiece at the top of the frame. 'Look, that fire's still lit, let's go!' Neil told Ryan with a very earnest expression, but Ryan was fascinated by the subterranean lair, and he suddenly opened his jacket and pointed to the air pistol tucked into his trousers. 'What's that supposed to do?' Neil asked with a nervous smirk.

'It fires two-two bollies, that's what it does,' Ryan answered in all seriousness.

'Oh, well we'll be okay now, Ry, we're up against a black magician but we can fire ball bearings at him,'

Neil said, shaking his head. 'I'm going – I've seen enough.'

There were footsteps outside.

The two men froze and looked at the door. Ryan switched off the pathetic weak-beamed torch and drew the air pistol from his belt. Neil was visibly shaking, and his eyes were fixed on the door with a look of utter terror in them.

'Get under there, quick!' Ryan pointed to the dining table, and Neil got under the large table and watched the door from under the fall of the cloth as Neil joined him. The door opened, and feet in Doc Marten boots walked into the room. The door closed, and the feet went towards the fire. The two explorers peeped out from under the tablecloth at the strange-looking man standing before the purple mirror. He was well over six feet in height, wore faded jeans, was stripped to the waist, and had large hairy-backed hands. His head was shaved, and his face was reflected in the mirror. The reflection of the face was chilling. The eyes were just like the black eye-sockets of a skull, and the nose was non-existent – just a triangular hole. The cheeks were sunken, and Ryan and Neil could clearly see a stitched-up 5-inch wound in the front of the neck as if someone had cut the stranger's throat just under the Adam's apple.

Ryan and Neil were just going to make a dash for it when they saw the mirror change. The stranger's reflection vanished to be replaced by a weird scene. It looked like the viewpoint you'd see if you could look into someone's room via their mirror over the mantelpiece. Ryan and Neil could see the back of a clock, candlesticks on either side of the clock, which was resting on an unseen mantelpiece. The room reflected in the mirror bore no resemblance to the sandstone-walled vault; instead, the room in the mirror was decorated with cheap-looking woodchip wallpaper, and there was a rather scuffed sofa with a dated floral pattern to it. A woman walked into view, and came right up to the mirror and looked into it, obviously oblivious to the man on the other side of her mirror with the skeletal face. The woman was beautiful, and aged about twenty to twenty-five. She leaned forward and began to squeeze a spot on her chin. There was a tiny spurt of pus that went onto her mirror, and her beautiful face now grimaced as he stared at the yellowish-white spot before wiping it off her side of the mirror with her index finger.

Neil tapped Ryan on the arm and whispered, 'I'm going.'

Ryan nodded, and the two men crawled out from under the table on the side nearest the door. As Ryan pulled open the door, the grotesque-face of the thing standing before the mirror turned to the men, and then it ran towards them. 'Shit!' Neil exclaimed and pushed past Ryan and ran out into the corridor. Ryan lifted the air pistol – and saw the silver ball-bearing roll out the end of the barrel and fall onto the floor. He threw the air pistol at the face of the tall ghoulish man, and the pistol glanced off him and landed on the table. The face of the tall fiend now had a crack running from the inside corner of the left eye, down to the chin. Ryan turned and ran down the corridor, and as he turned the corner, he saw Neil already opening the door at the end of the dimly-lit passage. The heavy footfalls of the skeleton-faced pursuer were gaining on

Ryan, and he ran as fast as he could. He an up the flight of stone steps and out into the yard, and here the two men saw a very strange sight. A small black man, about five feet tall, was sitting on top of the yard wall. He had a maroon-coloured fez on his head, and wore some sort of dark green and black cloak. The odd-looking man sat there, smiling, and when he saw Ryan leap up the wall to get away from the ghoul, he shouted: 'Babylon!' And at that moment, Ryan felt as if some powerful invisible hands were pushing against his buttocks, and he was thrown clean over the top of the wall and landed amongst the rubble and bricks in the entry with so much force, he was winded, and found it difficult to run, but somehow he managed to get away. As Ryan and Neil reached the safety of a well-lit Duke Street, they both heard the diminutive black man howling with laughter. Days after this, Colly, the man who had first told Ryan and Neil about the underground room, was found dead in his bed from a suspected drug overdose.

Ryan and Neil never dared go anywhere near that derelict house which gave access to the underground lair of the 'magician' and whenever they told anyone about their encounter with what seemed to be some sort of zombie, no one took them serious. However, many years later, when the massive Grosvenor Project got under way, entire streets were demolished to make way for the Liverpool One shopping complex, and during the excavations made by workmen to dig the footings for the new buildings, many finds of archaeological interest were made, including the uncovering of plague pits, parts of the old dock wall – and also the uncovering of a strange vault under

Paradise Street. The walls of the vault, believed to be some forgotten storage cellar, were covered with all sorts of unintelligible symbols. The vault was filled in, and all of the other things that were discovered in the excavations. The grave of Joseph Williamson, the so-called Mole of Edge Hill, was even found in that part of Liverpool years before, after being lost for decades. Lord knows what else is buried under the streets of Liverpool – perhaps even the lair of a magician and his zombie sentinel.

THE FAMILY OF SOULS

On the last day of September 2009 at 6am, a girl with green, scarlet and black spiky hair buried someone who had been very close to her in the grounds of St James's Cemetery, a sunken churchyard dating from Victorian times which I have written so much about in my books. Over fifty thousand people lay buried there, a hundred feet below street level, most of them without a headstone, because the heathen city council moved their grave markers, monuments and memorial stones years ago. The girl with the tri-coloured hair was 17-year-old Madison, and the someone she was burying was Rosy, her beloved cat. Madison had found her dying under the garden hedge after some low-life in a car had deliberately swerved to run Rosy over as the frightened cat fled across the road. The grave digger was Charles, Madison's 14-year-old brother. She called him Charlie; he usually called her Maddie.

They both had a good cry after Maddie stroked Rosy's head for the last time. The cat looked as if she was just asleep, and Maddie thought of those summer days when the dust floated about on the shafts of sunlight as Rosy slept in her very own high-backed chair in the bedroom, often making funny little noises as she had a troubled dream. Maddie thought about the last time she had seen Rosy, going down the path under a starry sky, a few nights ago. The cat had looked back, and Maddie could see her best friend's beautiful eyes gazing back at her and never dreamt in a million years that she'd soon meet a slow and agonising death. Tears flowed through the teen's thick black eyeliner as she whispered, 'Bye, Rosy,' before covering her head with the little end of the wide tartan scarf that had become the cat's shroud.

Maddie knelt there for a while, then looked up at Charlie, and his eyes were pink and watery, and he began to gently shovel the earth into the hole. Maddie got up from her bended knee and walked away into falling leaves. She listened to the usual songs on her iPod as she walked away from her brother. She felt numb with the sadness. Her mother had talked about buying a new cat, but no one could ever take Rosy's place. Boyfriends came and went, crushes too, but no one had ever been as close to Maddie as Rosy, not even Charlie, and he was close.

'*All that falls shall rise again. It's never over, Maddie,*' said a male voice out the blue.

Maddie paused her iPod and then took out one of the earphones from her busby hairstyle. She turned to see that Charlie had been too far away to have said anything. He'd have had to shout from that distance, and anyhow it wasn't even his type of squeaky voice. This voice was low, and much more mature. A falling brown oak leaf bounced of the tip of Maddie's pierced bottom lip and spiralled to the floor. There was an eerie stillness in the cemetery Maddie felt such affection for. A tranquil silence had crystallised around her. She coughed to prove she hadn't gone deaf.

In the distance, Charlie was patting down the earth with the spade, and had the brains to put back the clods of grassy earth on the grave so the ground didn't look too disturbed there. Sick people would probably take great delight in exhuming the grave of a beloved pet, hence the earliness of the burial, while the late-rising degenerates were still in bed.

'*Maddie...*' said that voice again, and this time the iPod wasn't even playing. Maddie turned around, and felt herself drawn to one particular blue-black gravestone among a row that lined the bottom of the grassy wooded slope which rises up to the cathedral. She walked ever so slowly towards the gravestone, until she could read the name on it. His first name had been Thomas, and he had died in the late Victorian period, but it didn't say how he had died, whether it was from a fever or if he had been murdered, or died in battle; it just said: 'who fell asleep on...' followed by the date of his passing.

'*Yes, that's where they laid me...*' said the invisible, unknown man. Maddie was speechless, and heard the sound of running. She turned to her right and saw Charlie hurrying through the morning mist wit the shovel now wrapped in two black polythene bin-liner bags. 'You okay?' he asked.

Maddie said nothing, because she didn't want to scare her younger brother by telling him about the disembodied voice. She walked with him out of the cemetery, the two of them kicking their way through the yellow and brown drift of fallen leaves, and the mystery of the voice somehow relieved the heartache of losing Rosy. For the rest of that Wednesday morning, she thought about Thomas as she lay on her bed, listening to songs by one of her favourite bands, My Chemical Romance. Maddie's mother came up to her room and asked her if she wanted breakfast but the girl shook her head and lay back on her bed. Her eyes settled on the poster of Hayley Williams, lead vocalist of the band Paramore, and after a while, Maddie dozed off into one of those states of consciousness between sleeping and waking. All of a sudden, she found herself in some dark room, with a candle flame swaying before her. Beyond that flame she saw a pale face. She knew it was Thomas, the young man who had been buried in St James's Cemetery well over a century ago. Maddie had a lot of dreams like this where she knew people and places she had never set eyes on before. This time she knew it was her boyfriend Thomas, and that they were in her other bedroom – the one in that other house before she had been Maddie, when she had lived in the 1960s. They had just come back from the Cavern club on Mathew Street, and had just made love, and now they were sitting round a table, dabbling in the occult. 'Look into the flame, Denise, Thomas was saying. Yes, that was my name then, Maddie recalled with a sweet nostalgic feeling – Denise.

'Stare into that flame and look down the centuries,' Thomas said softly, 'and see how we have always been together, soulmates from the Dawn of Time. We can never be apart; even death cannot keep us apart.'

'Thomas, I remember now, you and me forever and ever, and the Family of Souls!' Maddie said excitedly; it was all coming back now.

'Yes, the Family of Souls, my love,' Thomas replied, moving in to kiss her. 'Charlie and Alex – and the elemental spirit Kar.'

Maddie recalled her cat. 'Oh, yes, Kar! She was Rosy this time, and last time – who was she last time Thomas?'

'She was the dog we had – Kelly,' Thomas told her,

'so don't be sad because you lost Rosy – she always comes back to the Family of Souls – '

'Maddie!' said a young sharp voice.

Maddie woke from the dream, and she could have throttled Charlie for waking her from the exhilarating dream. She swore at her younger brother and asked him what he wanted. He wanted to know where his Call of Duty Play Station game was. 'I don't know! You had it last! Get out my room!' Maddie yelled at him.

'Emo!' Charlie shouted, and hurried from the room. He heard something his sister had hurled at him hit the door behind him with a loud bang.

That afternoon, Maddie went to Grand Central on Renshaw Street, and there she met her friend Claudia, who she had gone to school with before Maddie had dropped out because of a long bout of depression. Claudia and Maddie went to a café called the Egg on nearby Newington, and over coffee and chocolate cake they caught up on each other's lives, and eventually, Maddie told Claudia about the voice in the cemetery coming from the grave of a Victorian named Thomas, and of the strange dream about the 'Family of Souls'. Claudia didn't disbelieve her former school friend; instead she seemed very intrigued, and asked Maddie a strange question: 'Is it okay if I try and hypnotise you?'

'What?' Maddie was rather taken aback by the odd request.

Claudia said she had been teaching herself hypnosis and had recently managed to put her mother into a light trance so she could remember where she put the housekeys she had mislaid. Now Claudia wanted to probe Maddie's mind to see if she could get to the bottom of the mystery of Thomas and the supposed previous lives he had shared with Maddie.

'I'm not sure,' Maddie told her friend, 'I'm worried I might go into some trance and you won't be able to get me back out of it again.'

'Don't be daft Maddie,' Claudia replied, ' It's easy getting you out of the trance. Just give it a try, it's no big deal.'

So Maddie agreed to be hypnotised and the session took place in the attic 'den' of Claudia's home over in Birkenhead. 'That's one beautiful couch,' Maddie remarked upon the expensive long brown Vladimir Kagan sofa Claudia's father had bought for his daughter. Maddie was told to lie on the sofa, and she did. Claudia pulled the roller blind down over a window and then began to induce the trance by asking Maddie to count from ten to one, after telling her that each spoken number would make her more relaxed than the previous one. Then Claudia deepened the trance with her well-rehearsed lines from her book on hypnosis. Within minutes, Maddie was well and truly under the spell of hypnosis. Some people just can't be hypnotised, but a small percentage seem particularly susceptible to hypnotic suggestion, and Maddie obviously belonged to this latter group. Claudia took her friend back through the years, and asked Maddie what she could see, and Maddie described her life seen through the eyes of a person of different ages. At last, Claudia guided her to the year 1992 – the year Maddie was born – and Maddie startled her friend by describing her entry into the world; leaving the warmth and safety of the womb, and the blinding light of the room she was born into as she left her mother's body.

Claudia told Maddie to go back further, and Maddie became silent for a while, then began to talk in a slightly different accent and at a faster rate than normal. 'What's your name now?' Claudia asked, and Maddie said it was Denise, and gave a surname too. 'What year is it?' Claudia asked, and straight away, Maddie replied: 'It's nineteen sixty-four.'

'Do you know what day it is, Denise?' Claudia queried, 'and the day if possible?'

'I think it's a Friday – Friday the ninth of October,' 'Denise' replied.

Claudia asked her friend where she was and who she was with, and Maddie smiled, and her eyes flickered and exhibited what sleep-researchers term as R.E.M. – rapid eye movement – caused by the eyeballs swivelling side to side as the brain dreams. Maddie said: 'I'm with Tom, and Alex, and the dog Kelly. I'm in a good mood because we are going to the Cavern tonight. Tom likes John Lee Hooker and Alex likes the Bluesicians, and they're all at the Cavern tonight. We're in Tom's house in Everton.'

Claudia took her friend even further back, and she discovered that Maddie was in Nazi-occupied France during World War Two, and Tom – now referred to as Thomas, had been arrested by the Nazi's because he was part of the French Resistance. Maddie was talking in French, and Claudia could just about understand her, as her own knowledge of the language was very average. Claudia took Maddie further back, and in Victorian times, it transpired that Thomas was dying of consumption, and during his funeral, Maddie – who had been married to him - had tried to overdose on laudanum but a doctor had saved her. Claudia took

Maddie back through further reincarnations until her hypnotised friend spoke in a language she could not understand - and so, Claudia gently took Maddie forwards through time, and all the time, during this intriguing journey through some eleven lives, Claudia had been scribbling notes on a lined pad with a pen. When Maddie was taken out of the hypnotic state, she burst into tears, and said she wanted to kill herself so she could be with Thomas and her friend throughout the ages, Alex, as well as her beloved pet, Kar. Claudia had to drag Maddie away from the attic window as the girl tried to throw herself to her death, and things got that bad, the police had to be called for, and an ambulance. Maddie was sedated and almost sectioned by a psychiatrist, who severely reprimanded Claudia for dabbling with hypnotism. The psychiatrist said Maddie had dreamt up the whole 'Thomas and the family of souls' scenario. Maddie had merely exhibited the extraordinary mental power of mythopoeia – an ability of the unconscious mind to fabricate stories which had no basis in reality. Maddie was put on all sorts of medication, and one evening in the psychiatric hospital, the girl was astounded to hear footsteps approaching after a nurse had just left the room. A tall man in a long black coat, carrying a top hat, approached her bed and knelt beside it. It was her eternal lover – her constant soulmate Thomas, and his pale hands clasped Maddie's hands. He looked into her eyes, and his green eyes seemed to glow with some sort of preternatural luminosity. He kissed Maddie's knuckle and told her not to make any further suicide attempts. Where he and Alex and Kar existed there was no time, and so they were all prepared to wait for her - and Charlie too - until they all moved on to the next incarnation. Maddie sobbed and sat up in the bed and hugged Thomas, and he said he had only been allowed several minutes to 'come through' to be with her, and hinted that he had begged some higher force to grant him this visit. The precious seconds soon passed, and when it was time to leave, Thomas promised Maddie he would always be looking down on her, always near, and then he said: 'I have always loved you, I love you now, and I always will love you, my eternal love,' and then he bid Maddie goodbye, and as he walked off, towards the closed door, he looked round one more time, and seemed to be in tears. He turned away and walked through the solid door to the private ward, and seconds later, that door flew open, and two nurses came into the room. They wanted to know who had just visited Maddie, because the two of them had heard the taps of someone walking into the ward. Maddie just smiled now, convinced that she had not hallucinated Thomas and the family of souls, and she just said, 'Ah, you're hearing things – you should be in this ward, not me.'

Maddie quickly recovered from her 'illness' and later returned to a life of relative normality. She still visits one of the graves of Thomas – the one down in St James's Cemetery – and she always leaves a single rose, to represent her undying love, on his grave.

Can I just tell you another story about the 'soulmate' phenomenon? Read on.

One late April afternoon in 1967, Greg Flint, aged 40, sat down with his broadsheet copy of the *Liverpool Echo*; a cuppa at his side, and a Woodbine cigarette to smoke, and the television on and turned down low in the background – pure bliss after working at an estate agent's office in Allerton all day. The time was 4.55pm, and one of Greg's favourite performers, Joe Brown, was due to come on the telly any minute in a weekly programme called *Joe and Co.* Greg's dry lips never even touched the rim of his cuppa when something, which has never been explained to this day, took place. The disembodied head of Betty, Greg's ex, appeared in mid air, about five feet in front of him, and the strange apparition was surrounded by a bluish halo of light. Greg swore in shock at the ghostly vision. Betty looked as if she was in great pain – and then, as mysteriously as it appeared, the spectral form vanished into thin air. Greg was definitely not the sort who believed in ghosts, but he had a gut feeling that this was some sort of sign that Betty was either dead or in trouble, and reluctantly, Greg left his house in Fazakerley and drove nearly ten miles to the house of his ex-wife on Hunts Cross Avenue. Greg knocked on the door, and wondered if Betty's husband Gareth – a huge Welsh brute of a man – would come to the door on the bounce, as he hated Greg having anything to do with Betty, but there was no answer. Greg was now wondering if he was losing his marbles. He had been overworking recently – volunteering for Saturdays at the estate agents and helping out with his brother's business on Sundays. He walked down the path, then stopped in his tracks when he heard Betty cry out. He turned and looked through the letterbox – and saw his former wife crumpled on the floor at the bottom of the stairs. 'Hang on sweetheart!' Greg shouted. He hadn't used that term of endearment for years. He backed up, then kicked the front door hard. It flew open, and Greg immediately went to Betty's aid. She had foolishly put her hands in the pockets of her coat as she walked down the stairs, and stumbled. She had broken her arm and injured her back. When Gareth came home late from work, a neighbour directed him to the hospital, where Greg stood toe to toe with him and warned him not to read anything into the situation. 'How did you know she'd fallen down the stairs?' Gareth asked, gritting his teeth, 'We're not even on the phone! Just passing by were you?'

A fight almost broke out until a nurse and a doctor intervened, and Gareth blamed Greg for making a scene, calling him a 'jealous ex' – and Greg was escorted from the hospital by the matron. Almost a year to the day after this, Greg was in the bath, having a relaxing soak – when he suddenly heard screams downstairs. There was no mistaking it – it was Betty, and she was screaming at the top of her voice. Greg got out the bath, dried off as quickly as possible and within thirty-five minutes he was pulling into Betty's house – just in time to save her, for she was being beat-up by a drunken Gareth. Greg booted the front door open, flew across the hall, and knocked out the wife-beater with one upper-cut. Betty divorced Gareth and remarried Greg, a soulmate who was definitely on her 'wavelength'.

STRANGERS IN THE NIGHT

One night in August 2010, 19-year-old Kelly Louise Jordain of West Derby was invited to a party at the house of her friend Sophie in St Helens. The party was going well until about 1.30am, when the copious amounts of consumed drink began to make a few of the guests a bit argumentative. There was a remark made by a girl named Emma about Kelly's false eyelashes, and Kelly retorted by criticising the 'plummy' coloured hair of Emma and this in turn led to Emma's boyfriend criticising Kelly's 'dated' ringtone. It all ended at 1.40 am with Kelly Louise throwing her drink in Emma's face. Sophie told her to get out, and then, after Kelly stormed out of the house, she saw her phone's battery indicator was 2 per cent full, and about to die. She tried to find the number for the taxis in her contacts, but she couldn't and as she was halfway through asking the woman on the 118 118 service for a number to a taxi company in the St Helen's area, the phone died. Kelly wondered how she'd get back to her home in West Derby, and by 2am she was wandering along the East Lancs Road by the Rainford Bypass, trying to flag down a taxi. After about five minutes, a petite lady of around Kelly's age came walking towards her from Rainford Road, from the direction of St Helen's Cemetery. The girl was dressed in a white dress that went to her knees, and was barefooted. In her hands she held a pair of light shoes, Keds in fact. The girl's face was pale and her hair was reddish and shoulder length. She smiled at Kelly and then she said, 'Are you trying to get home as well?'

Kelly thought there was something odd about the girl, but smiled back and nodded, before replying: 'Yeah – why, what's happened to you?'

'I had a bad row with my fellah,' the girl said, and looked at the pavement as she stood next to Kelly. 'I'm going home, I've had enough.'

'Where do you live?' Kelly asked, keeping her eyes on the few cars on the road at this time in case one of them was a private cab.

'Kensington,' the girl told her. At closer quarters now, Kelly could see she only looked young – probably younger than her, and she had freckles that were just showing through the foundation.

'Oh, Kenny,' said Kelly, 'that's miles away. If I find a cab you can get in with me and I'll get out at West Derby and you can just pay from there to Kenny if you want?'

'I'm skint,' the girl admitted, and seemed quite ashamed of it.

'How old are you?' Kelly asked.

'Seventeen, why? Do I look it?'

'Nah, you look about sixteen – you sure you're seventeen?' Kelly asked with a look of suspicion in her dark eyes.

'Yeah, turned seventeen in June,' the girl told her and looked up at last into Kelly's eyes.

'What's your name?'

'Brittany,' was the reply, and Brittany smiled and seemed almost embarrassed by her name, and asked Kelly what her name was.

'Kelly. Yay! Is that a cab?' Kelly shouted and waved

and jumped up and down at the private hire cab passing by but it drove on into the night down the East Lancs, so Kelly gave it the single finger gesture. All of a sudden, a white lorry with the word 'Unigate' emblazoned on its side pulled up, and a bald-headed man peered out the side window of the cab and looked at Kelly and Brittany.

He said nothing for half a minute, but just stared at the teenagers as his engine ticked over.

'What are you looking at?' Kelly asked him, with an expression which lay somewhere between amusement and disgust.

'Do you two want a lift?' the lorry driver asked.

Kelly just wanted to go home. Her feet were killing her, and she felt tired. She also wanted to see Brittany going home safely as well. She naturally didn't trust the lorry driver, but as she looked at him, she started to get the feeling he was alright. He certainly didn't look menacing.

'I haven't got all night,' he said impatiently, checking his mirrors. 'You two want a lift or not?'

'I'm trying to get to West Derby and she needs to get to Kensington,' Kelly told him at last.

The driver nodded and told the girls: 'Okay, get in – and mind the traffic as you do.'

The teens climbed into the cab of the vehicle and then the lorry moved off down the East Lancs.

The driver looked straight ahead through the windshield and said: 'What are you two doing out at this hour in the morning? There are some maniacs about nowadays you know?'

'I've been to a crap party, and this girl's had an argument with her boyfriend,' Kelly Louise explained.

Then she asked: 'Are you going to West Derby?'

'Near parts of it,' the driver replied, 'what part are you from?'

'Do you know Meadow Lane?' Kelly asked.

Without turning to look at her, the driver said: 'Meadow Lane…is that off Muirhead Avenue?'

'Yes,' Kelly nodded vigorously, 'yeah, by the avenue.' And then Kelly posed a question to the driver. 'Where are you going anyway?'

'Miles away over to the Wirral,' the driver replied, and then he turned to Brittany and asked, 'You're a bit quiet aren't you?'

Brittany just smiled and said nothing. She looked out beyond the side passenger window at the nightscape scrolling by.

'She gave me the creeps when she walked towards me earlier on,' Kelly said with a sidelong smirk towards her young associate. 'She was walking from the cemetery. Thought she was a ghost.'

The driver slowed the vehicle and shot a strange look at Kelly, then asked: 'She was coming from the cemetery?'

Kelly nodded. It was as if he knew something odd about Brittany.

The driver turned to Brittany and kept taking alternate glances between her and the ribbon of tarmac that stretched into the distance. 'Where exactly have you come from tonight?' he asked the pallid-faced girl.

'Bleak Hill Road – why?' Brittany told the lorry driver.

At this precise moment, for some unaccountable reason, Kelly felt goosebumps rise up on her forearms, and she also felt the hairs on the back of her neck prickle up. A very eerie mood was filling the cab, and it was now deadly quiet. Just the faint hum of the lorry's engine and the faint light from the green and orange luminous dials lit up the three faces in the cab.

'Bleak Hill Road; quite a distance from Kensington isn't it?' the driver asked Brittany, with great suspicion in his voice.

Brittany remained silent, as if she didn't know what to say in reply.

'See this stretch of road here?' the driver said, gazing through the windshield at the section of the East Lancs near the Blindfoot Road junction. There was a ground mist rolling into the path of the lorry from the black unlit fields of vastness on either side of the motorway. 'On many occasions, at this time in the morning, a couple – a man and a woman, both in their twenties by the looks of them, have been seen, arm in arm, skipping out into the road here. I hit them one morning, round three.'

Kelly went cold. 'Hit them? Did they die like?'

'I hit them and I heard their bodies hit the bodywork,' said the driver, and he slapped his hand on the steering wheel to emphasise the talk of impact with the couple. 'And I pulled over, and I saw his head jammed between the two front wheels. I nearly collapsed, as you can imagine. And then I looked, and there was nothing there.'

'How?' Kelly was baffled by the driver's account.

'Spirits,' the driver told her. 'Spirits of a couple who had died on this road. They made a suicide pact for some reason, and got drunk, and then jumped out into the road in front of a juggernaut. Years ago. They're still doing it, but I don't know why. I do not know why they still do it. I think its like when something really bad happens to you and you are that traumatised, you dream about it, have recurring nightmares about it. The dead couple might be doing that. They might be reliving their deaths because of the shock. I don't know.'

Then the driver slowed the lorry, and cruised to a halt.

Brittany and Kelly looked at one another, perplexed.

'Why have you stopped?' Kelly asked the driver.

The driver was looking through the windscreen of the vehicle with wide eyes and a wide-open mouth, as if he had just seen something terrifying on the road ahead. Kelly and Brittany tried to follow the line of his gaze to see what he was looking at, but could see nothing down the motorway that could instil such fear as there was on his face.

'You okay?' Kelly asked the driver, but he seemed rigid with fear, and the look of terror in his face was so disquieting, the two teenagers decided to get out of that lorry. Kelly suspected the driver was deranged, and when she and Brittany climbed down out of the cab, they clung to one another and hurried down the grass verge alongside the motorway. They walked and then looked back, and saw the headlights of the Unigate lorry slowly fade away – and the vehicle faded away with the dwindling headlamps. Only then did the girls realise they had been riding in a ghostly lorry, and they shuddered. They walked and walked until they were lucky to spot a Hackney cab near the junction of Moorgate Road. Kelly told the cab driver what had happened, and after the taxi-driver had heard her story, he said: 'Was this white lorry a milk lorry? Did it have Unigate written on the side of it?'

'Yeah!' said Brittany and Kelly simultaneously.

'That lorry has been seen by people, and motorists, a few times over the years. I think the driver hit a man and a woman who were running across the motorway. The two of them were blind drunk. He killed them and then the lorry turned over and he died as well.'

Kelly and Brittany went cold when they were told this, because neither of them had mentioned the 'Unigate' logo on the side of the lorry.

I have heard about the phantom Lorry of the East Lancs many times over the years, and of people being picked up by the phantom driver of the unearthly vehicle. He always seems to stop and become terror-stricken when he reaches the spot where he died on that stretch of motorway.

NANNY'S SECRET

During a book-signing in 2006, an elderly, refined-looking woman named Marjorie told me a very interesting story about her grandmother, and I wanted to write about it immediately, but Marjorie asked me to withhold the story – until she had died. She believed she'd be dead within five years of meeting me, and sadly, she was to be proved right. In 2011 her daughter got in touch to tell me of Marjorie's passing, and to remind me of the details of the intriguing account. Around the year 1900, Elizabeth, a lady of substance in the Aigburth area of Liverpool became a widow at the age of twenty-nine, and, and so a nanny was sought to look after her two children, 7-year-old George and 5-year-old Gertie. Quite a few women applied for the job, but one of the applicants, Mrs Margaret Clarke, was quickly hired, for although she was from the working classes, Mrs Clarke seemed to have a very caring nature, but was also a very pragmatic woman. She was a strawberry blonde with threads of grey becoming noticeable, and quite tanned, which, in the Victorian age, was deemed as rather unappealing in the fairer sex. Mrs Clarke said she was normally as white as a lily but had become tanned through hop-picking n the fields of Ormskirk in the previous summer. The nanny's accent could veer onto the coarse side now and then, with some odd colloquialisms; for example, she called young George "Jackaroo" and a "Larrikin", and always referred to the kettle as the "Billy can". All the same, the children loved Nanny, and all of the servants got on quite well with her too. One day, after she had told George and Gertie a marvellous tale about the days when she sold lavender and shamrock outside the theatre in Williamson Square as a 7-year-old girl, George noticed the strange white mark on the side of Nanny's face, and asked her if it was a scar. She said it was indeed a scar from an occasion when a woman tried to disfigure her by throwing vitriol in her face.

'What's vitriol Nanny?' George asked, and he was told it was a very strong acid that burned through skin. 'Who threw it at you?' Gertie wanted to know, and that point, Elizabeth, the mother of the children and the mistress of the household, came into the nursery, and Nanny immediately stopped talking about the vitriol-throwing incident. Elizabeth felt there was something about Margaret Clarke she just couldn't put her finger on. It was plain to see that in her younger days, Nanny had been a beautiful woman, yet it was also obvious that she had been a real character in her day. Sometimes in the evening, the servants would stand at the bottom of the stairs and look up the flights of steps in awe as they heard Nanny's beautiful voice singing lullabies to the children. Elizabeth tried to get the Nanny to open up about her past, but Margaret would always change the subject. And then, one day, there was a visitor to the house who revealed the true identity of the Nanny. He was a retired magistrate, a well-travelled man named Edward, and upon seeing Nanny, his face became very pale, while Nanny's eyes widened with shock. 'Ah, so it is you!' Edward exclaimed upon seeing Mrs Clarke, 'You have come back!'

Nanny went to walk out of the room with her head bowed as tears streamed from her eyes. Edward turned to Elizabeth and said: 'Do you know who she is?' Elizabeth gave a puzzled look at the former magistrate when he referred to her nanny Margaret, who halted with her hand on the handle of the drawing room door. The retired judge gave a sadistic smirk, then projected his plummy stentorian voice - a voice that had condemned many a man to death - across the room at Margaret: 'In the annals of harlotry I doubt there is a name more famous than that of Maggie May!'

There was no gasp of disbelief from Elizabeth, but the face on the mistress of the house was priceless in the eyes of the quondam Justice of the Peace. There was a louring pause while Margaret froze at the door as still and lifeless-looking as a statue. She produced a handkerchief and after dabbing her eyes she turned to the smug snowy-haired man. The nanny warned him: 'You have cast the first stone, and I shall throw a rock back at you now, you old hypocrite!'

'Margaret!' Elizabeth recoiled, throwing her hands to her mouth. Edward, the faded judge of people, clutched the arm rests of the ostentatious fauteuil as a cerise pinkness blossomed in his cheeks. His eyes bulged and he spat froth as he struggled for a reply to the outrageous reply from Mrs Clarke, but before he could compose a sentence, the sharp-tongued nanny began to detail the peculiar quirks of the old man's sexual behaviour.

'Enough!' cried Elizabeth, rushing to Edward to steady him as he lurched forward with his hand on his chest. 'You are dismissed Mrs Clarke!'

'With pleasure!' the Nanny roared, and she turned and stormed out of the drawing room and went to her humble lodgings in the eaves of the mansion to pack her things. As she left the house, she saw the family doctor arrive to treat the old judge's funny turn. The children of the house, George and Gertie, were deeply upset when they learned Margaret – or Maggie as they called her – had been sacked, and Gertie burst into tears. Elizabeth told her little daughter that the nanny had said bad things to Edward, and Gertie asked what type of bad things had been said and if they were true – and Elizabeth had a crisis of conscience. She realised that Margaret had understandably been hurt when Edward had revealed her shameful past and had merely fought back at the hypocritical person pointing the accusing finger. Oh, what to do? Elizabeth immediately left the house to seek the advice of her friend, the Right Reverend Bishop Robert Brindle, at the newly-opened Church of St Charles. Bishop Brindle had been a friend of Elizabeth's late husband when both men served together in the Sudan campaign; Brindle as an army chaplain, and Elizabeth's husband as a captain. When the clergyman had heard of the thorny circumstances leading to the dismissal of Margaret, he grabbed his coat and hat, and left his study with Elizabeth in tow, quoting an old Moorish proverb from his army days: 'Forgiveness from the heart is better than a box of gold.'

And so Elizabeth and the Bishop went in search of Maggie May. They visited Sefton Park, which was often frequented by many down on their luck who had no one to turn to, but Maggie was not there. Just when the Bishop was about to give up, he happened to meet police sergeant Peter Miller, who had started to attend St Charles's Church, and Miller told him that a fair-haired woman had been seen walking into the river from St Michael's shoreline ("the Cast Iron Shore") – and there was no trace of her.

On the banks of the shore, Elizabeth and the Bishop Robert Brindle surveyed the river, dreading the sight of a body, but saw nothing, and then came a familiar sound that lifted Elizabeth's spirits – the beautiful singing voice of Maggie May, drifting on the salty breeze across the shore of St Michael's-in-the-Hamlet – but from where? The Bishop pointed to the ancient fisherman's cottage. The sweet melody led them inside the humble single-storey abode of old Mr Shaw and his sister. Swathed in ragged (but dry) male attire besides the hob sat Maggie drinking rum and carousing. She had walked into the Mersey, intending to end it all – to be rid of her unfortunate past forever, but sixty-year-old Mr Shaw had swum out to save her, and he was very reluctant to let her go when Elizabeth begged Maggie to come back to the mansion, but come back she did, and she was doted on and given the best fireside chair and a bowl of some mustard-concoction to place her feet in as she warmed her bones.

Elizabeth apologised for dismissing her, and Maggie asked if Edward the old magistrate was alright. Elizabeth said he was, and as the flames danced in the coals of the grate, the Bishop listened to the Nanny's potted history of her life.

'For as long as I can remember, I always sang. Used to sing myself asleep when I was a child. I lived with my mother and stepfather off London Road, and when mam died he started to beat me. He used to throw me out onto the streets to make money for him. This was when I must have been six. I sold shamrock and lavender outside the New Star Music Hall (now the Playhouse Theatre) in Williamson Square. I got the best business outside the Walker (Art Gallery) and the Royal Alexandra (now called the Empire), but I got my break outside the New Star on Williamson Square. Dan Saunders owned it, and he heard me singing outside the stage door. He came out and asked me what my name was, and when I told him he said, "Little Maggie May, you're going to be on the top of the bill one day," and he took me in the theatre and gave me lemonade and Eccles cakes, and he sat at a piano and told me to sing a song. I was shy and my face was flushed and my throat dried up. But Dan was lovely, and he told all the actors to go away, and they did, and I started to sing.'

'What did you sing, Maggie,' asked the Bishop and softly smiled. Maggie's reddened eyes, full of nostalgic sorrow, seemed lost in the glowing coals. 'I sang this, Bishop,' the nanny replied, and began a soul-stirring rendition of *Amazing Grace*. Then Maggie continued her narrative. 'I got home late from the music hall, and my stepfather beat me. He was drunk, and threw me out. That night I slept on the steps of St George's Hall, sheltering from the rain. I used to sleep there a lot when he threw me out, and always had this same dream – that mam was alive, and she'd always be cooking in the kitchen, as she used to do, making stew and sometimes pudding. I loved those days when I helped her in the kitchen. Mr Saunders kept giving me lessons and then he put me on the stage as "Little Maggie May" – and something amazing happened…'

Little Maggie May, as the child was billed, was a

natural on the stage of the New Star Music Hall, and the audience adored her. At first the little cherub from the grim streets of Liverpool stood stock-still centre-stage in the limelight, until some critic in the audience began to shout, 'Move about will ye child?' And Maggie began to skip around the stage to hilarious applause. In the wings, professionals such as the high-earning clown William Wallett (known as Queen Victoria's Jester) and the Chantrell Family of Acrobats, recognised new talent when they saw it, and Wallett knew Little Maggie would be a hard act to follow – and he was right. After her ten-minute spot the child received a standing ovation, and the stage was showered with coins. When Wallett came on he was booed and someone pelted him a dead duck that had been smuggled in from the market. Every performer lived in mortal fear of being struck with this feathered symbol of the audience's displeasure. Little Maggie May was instructed to sing *Amazing Grace* and literally pushed back onstage by Dan Saunders, the owner of the music hall. Hats were launched into the air and the crowds cheered. 'Give us *Sweet Molly Malone*!' someone shouted, and Little Maggie May happened to know the old song word for word, for it was a favourite of her late mother's, and so she cried towards the end, thinking of her mammy, and there was not a dry eye in the house when the crowd saw the child shedding real tears. 'Encore!' the audience chanted, and Maggie gave a courtesy bow. The audience surged forward, some clambering over the musicians in the orchestra pit to shake the girl's doll-like hand, and pandemonium broke out. Dan Saunders had to come out onto the stage and with his hand on his heart, solemnly promise the crowds that Little Maggie May would become a regular feature at the New Star Music Hall. 'One more, one more!' the crowd chanted and stomped in time. Saunders bent down to the centre of this Biblical adulation and asked, 'Maggie do you know any more songs? We're in trouble if you don't, girl.' Maggie said she knew *Greensleeves*, and so the orchestra was briefed, and the crowds returned to their seats. In the forests of the printed word, much has been written about the great vocalists from the enchanting Sirens of Ancient Greece to the 20th Century's Maria Callas, but when Little Maggie began to sing *Greensleeves* a cappella – with the full orchestra poised to accompany her after the first verse, time stood still in that Liverpool theatre, and people later swore the performance was a religious experience, as if an angel had been allowed an earthly audience. Little Maggie's May's future was made, or so it was widely thought, but in the wings, standing in the shadows, stood a man known as Flowery Jack, the notorious" King Pimp of Lime Street". He saw a great future for Little Maggie as well, and he bided his time, and when the child's star began to set during her teens - when the management of the music hall changed hands, Flowery Jack moved in and took a blossoming Maggie May to Lime Street's Crown Hotel to launch her career – and a legend was born. At this time, the Queen of the Harlots was Polly Hogan, but then teenager Maggie May, crowned with red roses and a fine scarlet dress, came into the pub - and sparks soon flew.

Sixteen-year-old Maggie May was introduced to the staff and motley drinkers of Lime Street's Crown Hotel pub by the refined pimp Flowery Jack, and many couldn't believe that the tall beauty before them was the same girl who had made them laugh and cry in the New Star Music Hall just a few years ago. Was this really the little girl who now stood before them? What a vision she presented with her golden hair elaborately styled, her flawless pale porcelain skin and those huge expressive eyes and that striking shapely figure. Maggie wore a crown of roses in her hair, and a beautiful blood-red velveteen dress adorned with rose motifs. On her feet she wore scarlet satin ballet shoes. She held half-unwrapped gifts from a multitude of admirers in her arms and the male drinkers swarmed around her. One man named Jackson, who had returned from the United States, presented Maggie with a real gold nugget, which she dutifully handed to her 'promoter' Flowery Jack. Up until this day, 37-year-old Polly Hogan had been the unofficial Queen of the Harlots, and she gritted her ivory dentures when she saw her obvious replacement. To her little 4ft 8 friend Geraldine Faylin, Polly declared: 'Well, Ged, I'll jolly well be hanged if she thinks she's taking over my pub,' and Polly said this in her nasally cocksure style, the product of her long nose and adenoid condition. Little Ged Faylin thinned almond shaped eyes set in a pink round face and looked up at her friend: 'Shall I splash her with something, my dear Polly? Melt that pretty face of hers?'

Polly's huge brown eyes darted left and right, and she slapped her hand over Ged's mouth. 'No, love, you don't have to do that – yet.'

Jealous Ged, as the dwarf Geraldine was known, loved nothing more than buying a penny bottle of vitriol (sulphuric acid) from the chemist to hurl into some beauty's face in a suitably dark alleyway. Polly pushed her way through the crowds of mesmerised men of all ages who were swarming round Maggie, until she came face to face with her perceived Nemesis. 'So you're the famous Maggie May, are you?' she asked, speaking from the back of her nose.

Maggie said nothing, but her faint Mona Lisa smirk and the way her heavy-lidded eyes looked Polly up and down plainly told everyone that Polly was not even considered a threat to such a beautiful young lady; no competition! Maggie turned away and Polly shouted: 'How the bleedin' mighty have fallen! Little Maggie May turned streetwalker!' And the Crown's new owner, Billy Barton, came running from round the bar to tell Polly to 'shut that vile trap' – as Maggie May suddenly turned round and launched a punch that knocked Polly's ivory dentures out. The crowd cheered as Polly fell heavily – onto little Ged Faylin. The poor midget screamed nasty threats of disfigurement at Maggie, and Flowery Jack told four burly men to lift Maggie onto their shoulders – which they did. 'Hip-hip hooray!' Jack yelled thrice, before gleefully announcing, 'Drinks on the house! God save Maggie May, the new Queen of Lime Street! Now let's tell them at the Vines lads!'

And Flowery Jack and a formidable mob (many of them members of the High Rip Gang) carried Maggie out the pub and down Lime Street to the Vines pub to confirm the 'coronation'.

Back at the Crown pub, Ged Faylin told her unconscious friend: 'I'm bled if she thinks you're finished, Polly,' before sneaking out the pub, intending to get the bottle of acid.

Maggie May's coronation was cautiously accepted by the management of the Vines pub – a drinking establishment named after its manager, Joseph Vines, a very shrewd businessman who turned a blind eye to Lime Street's sisterhood of harlots. This was what some of the men came for; the sailors, the labouring men as well as the slummers (toffs disguised as working people) – they came not only for the drink and the conversation and the singalongs, but also for a temptation that stretched back to Genesis – the pleasures of the flesh. Flowery Jack, Liverpool's most famous pimp, was suspiciously absent as everyone gave a toast to Maggie May, and a few minutes into the celebrations he came into the Vines with his 'wide-awake' hat stylishly slanted, adjusting the perfect rose backed with maidenhair fern in his lapel. He went straight up to Maggie and took her behind the bar into the manager's room, where he explained the 'situation': 'There's a very well-to-do man outside in a carriage. He's a good client of mine and he wants you and another girl, so are you all right with that me dear?'

Maggie May looked afraid. This was her first customer. All the bravado had evaporated. 'What do you mean – me and *another* girl?' she asked Flowery, and he put his index fingertip on her lip and said, 'There's nowt queer about that, now let's be going – and none of your swearing; this gent's an educated toff.' Flowery took Maggie to Bolton Street at the back of the Vines and there the silver-tongued procurer was paid in an alleyway by the tall top-hatted gent. He said, 'Come,' and curled his index finger, beckoning Maggie to accompany him into the black lacquered carriage.

Maggie looked back at Flowery, who waved her off:

'Go on, he's a gent! You'll be alright my love.'

Imagine Maggie's face when she stepped up into the luxurious carriage, only to see the top-hatted upper-class gent sitting next to none other than Geraldine "Ged" Faylin – the mad midget who had wanted to throw acid in Maggie's face. 'What's she doing here?' Maggie asked, but the gentleman smiled and reached up to the little hatch in the roof of the compartment. He slid back a small door and gave instructions to the driver, and the carriage moved off. 'She has a fascinating face,' said the well-heeled client in a perfect Queen's English accent, and his long pale fingers stroked Ged Faylin's little cup face. The little thing smiled as he did this. 'What an unusual birth-mark!' the middle-aged man said, inspecting the black mole at the corner of Ged's lip. Maggie asked the man what his name was, and he told her it was Jerome. 'And what is it that you do, Jerome?' Maggie asked. 'I'm a surgeon,' he replied. Nothing more was said throughout the long journey to a mansion off Edge Lane, even though Maggie threw many questions at Jerome. She just wanted to jump out the carriage and go back to singing on a stage. At the mansion, Ged Faylin was taken to another room in the grand abode, and Maggie was taken to a room with the word "Wednesday" printed in gold on its door. 'You shall be Wednesday,' Jerome told her, feeling Maggie's face, 'that is your name from now on.'

Maggie saw the other doors of the deep-carpeted corridor – all named after the other days of the week. 'My name's Maggie, not bleedin' Wednesday!' she protested, unaware of the horrors she would soon witness.

Hours passed in that well-furnished prison of a room in Jerome's Edge Lane mansion, and at last Maggie was summoned to the surgeon's vast master bedroom, where the illustrious client waited naked in his four-poster. Maggie arrived in the dark chamber, and saw Jerome sitting up in bed, puffing on an opium pipe. The sharp smell of the opiate was known to Maggie and made her sick. 'Divest!' Jerome barked, and at this point Maggie noticed a large jar on a cabinet beside the bed. By the dim scarlet lamp, Maggie saw something in that jar – and she felt faint. It was the pickled body of the midget Faylin. The little shaven-headed corpse gazed at Maggie from the jar with a pair of large sad eyes, devoid of all life now. As Maggie backed out of the room, Jerome told her that Faylin had choked to death at supper, and he had merely put her in formaldehyde pending an autopsy, but Maggie didn't believe him, and suspected that this was some sexual fetish of his – to make love with a corpse at the bedside. He must have murdered Faylin, just in the pursuit of sexual gratification, Maggie thought through a haze of panic and she ran off, and somehow escaped from the mansion to walk back (through torrential rain) to Flowery Jack's house on Cumberland Street. Flowery denied the surgeon was a murderer and said he now had no choice but to place Maggie in the care of another pimp in London, or Jerome would come after her for defaming him. Maggie was subsequently placed in an upper-class Mayfair brothel, and mixed with top courtesans of the day such as Liverpool-born Catherine Walters (known as "Skittles"), Cora Pearl, and Marguerite Bellanger (mistress to the Emperor Napoleon III). Maggie became privy to the greatest secrets and hidden scandals of high society – and even of royalty - and one day she told a regular trusted client about the clandestine night-time weddings of the "Uranians" (a secret sect of distinguished men of standing who, by law, had to keep their homosexuality expressly hidden in Victorian times). When this "scandal" broke, Maggie May was forcibly exiled to Australia (but not Van Diemen's Land as the old song says). Here, Maggie's name was changed to Clarke, and she lived in obscurity in Sydney and Adelaide until all of the people involved in the scandals had died, and only then was it safe to return home. People Maggie had known back in Liverpool wondered what had become of her, and soon the famous ballad writers of the town penned a bawdy folk song to explain the famous harlot's absence. Maggie would cry when that cruel song reached the shores of Australia, as she had never robbed anyone. Maggie May returned to Liverpool as a nanny by 1900, and although a retired judge insensitively unmasked her as one of the most famous prostitutes in the world, Maggie's employer, Elizabeth, her friend the Bishop Robert Brindle, and Elizabeth's two children, George and Gertie, all loved her. Maggie often returned to the Crown Hotel, the Vines pub, and Liverpool Playhouse, no doubt to reminisce on her astonishing life. Sometime in the 1930s, Maggie passed away and for many years, people spoke about the incredible funeral cortege - a long train of cars behind the grand looking black carriage that took the legendary lady to her grave – said to be up in Ford Cemetery. Some of the older people who had known Maggie stood solemnly at the roadside, doffing their hats and waving at the hearse. I often wonder if the little ghostly female urchin often seen sleeping against one of the pillars of St George's Hall is the phantom of Maggie May as a child, for she slept there when her stepfather threw her onto the streets at night. I will set out Maggie's full life story in a book one day, to set the record straight and to pay homage to Liverpool's forgotten courtesan.

PET HOLE

As incredible as the following story may seem, it is, as far as I have been able to establish, backed up by the testimony of quite a few people. I have had to change a few names for legal reasons.

Once upon a time, many years ago in the 1970s, there lived a rather lonely 9-year-old child named Colin, and he lived with his mother, grandmother and uncle in a fifteen storey tower block near William Henry Street. This tower block was one of three that were known by the infamous nickname of "The Piggeries" because vandals had destroyed the amenities of the tower block. The degenerate hooligans removed light bulbs from the staircases of the blocks, turning them into treacherous pitch-black death traps for women who had to somehow drag prams up the fifteen storeys, because the lifts rarely worked, and the vandals defecated and urinated in these same lifts. Each of the dystopian blocks housed seventy families, and the flat Colin lived in was on the top floor, fifteen storeys up. Colin was not really aware of the high-rise slum he was living in; children are often insulated from a harsh reality by their childish perception; it's as if they inhabit a separate universe to the seriously-minded adult. Anyway, one day in the early 1970s, just a week before Christmas, Colin was playing with his little toy balsa wood plane, holding it up in the air and steering it across the living room as his grandmother watched the telly. The time was around two in the afternoon. Colin put down the balsa glider with its rubber band operated propeller, and gazed out towards Everton. He wondered where his father had gone. He had just decided to leave earlier in the year, and Colin hoped he'd come home in time for Christmas, not just because he knew his Dad would bring him some toys, but because he also missed his father. Colin's dad used to tell him stories before he went to bed each night, and nowadays when Colin asked his mother to do the same, she'd always say, 'Oh, I don't know any stories, Colin, now get to sleep.'

Colin lifted the net curtains and gazed up at the grey overcast skies over the city – when he noticed something. A tiny green light – just like the twinkling fairy light of the Christmas tree – was coming down out the sky. 'Nan! Look at this!' he shouted to his grandmother, pointing to the descending light. But she was too engrossed by an Abbott and Costello film. The light floated down towards the window next door – the window of Colin's bedroom, so the lad ran out the living room and raced through the hall and into his bedroom to witness the dramatic entry of the "thing" into his life. The bright twinkling light hit the window – and went through it, and went out as it hit the windowsill – and it left a faint grey dot there in the white paint of the sill. Colin hurried across the bedroom to see what it was. It was a pale grey disc, the size of a half-penny piece, and it was moving across the windowsill.

Colin put his hand adjacent to the edge of the windowsill and wiped the grey disc onto his palm.

He got the shock of his life. There was now a hole in

his hand the size of a half-penny coin. He held his hand up to his face and looked straight through the hole in his palm. He could see straight through the hole, which had a red – blood-coloured edge to it. Then this grisly peephole moved across Colin's palm towards his thumb. Colin couldn't understand what he was looking at, but his childish mind accepted that he was holding a hole that could actually move about and had some sort of intelligence behind it. He went to show his Nan, and she squinted through her glasses at the moving hole and said, 'What is it? I can't see what you're showing me, Colin.'

'I've got a pet hole Nan,' Colin told her and laughed.

Nan looked back at the television and began to chuckle at the antics of Abbot and Costello.

At teatime, Colin's mother came in from work and found her son eating all sorts of sweets and bars of chocolate in his room, and she immediately asked him where he had obtained the money to buy these goodies. Colin looked stuck for words, and he gazed wide-eyed for a moment with a mouth ringed with chocolate, caught off guard – then said he had found a five-pound note on the landing outside the flat. 'I don't believe you,' his mother told him. She knew just from his expression and flushed face that he was lying. 'Now where did you get the money for all this? Hey? Have you been stealing it out of your Nan's purse?'

Colin tried to tell her the truth. He had put the 'hole' on the glass cabinet in the sweet shop, and the hole had expanded and let him take whatever he wanted from the cabinet. Colin's mother said, 'Tell the truth or you're going to bed!'

Colin repeated his seemingly far-fetched story, and

so his mother stormed off to Nan and asked her to check her purse, as she thought Colin might have taken some money from it. Nan checked the purse and saw that nothing was amiss. This worried Colin's mother, for now she thought her boy had stolen the money from someone else. Because she couldn't get to the bottom of the mystery, she grounded Colin and he had to stay in his room all day.

The boy played with the grey disc-shaped "pet". He stroked the thing and it felt like glass sometimes, and like jelly at other times. Sometimes it felt as if it was vibrating, a bit like a cat purring with satisfaction perhaps as he stroked it. On one occasion, Colin put the hole on his arm and began to poke it with a pencil tip, and all of a sudden he felt excruciating pain in his arm at that point, and a spurt of blood came out of the hole in his arm and splashed in his face. The boy cried out, but then the hole closed up and there was no sign of injury to the skin, just bloodstains on his arm and splashes of blood on his face. Colin tried to put the hole in a matchbox, but it couldn't be contained by anything, because of its strange topological nature. In the end, the hole crawled through the windowpane, and out on to the window ledge, and here it became a bright green point of light and floated away, up into the sky, until it was lost among the greyness of the low oppressive snow clouds of December. Colin cried his eyes out and told his 'pet' to come back, but he never set eyes on the strange entity after that day. The owner of the local sweetshop later told Colin's mother about a strange hole that had appeared in the cabinet where his chocolate bars and other sweets were on display.

The hole seemed to expand and shrink as he looked

on, which baffled and naturally unnerved him. Colin's mother had also seen the tip of her son's middle finger vanish when he had tried to show her the unearthly creature. Colin's friends also saw the eerie hole in action as it crawled over their hands. We'll probably never know what the "hole" was; perhaps it was some visiting alien life form, or some entity from a higher dimension. As Shakespeare said, 'there are more things in heaven and earth'…

THE ELEMENTAL

In the summer of 1985, a 45-year-old Gateacre man named Paul asked his 9-year-old daughter Christine why she was miserable on such a lovely blisteringly sunny afternoon, right in the middle of the school holidays as well. The child said nothing, but just sat on the end of the sofa, with her right hand supporting her chin as she gazed morosely out the window at the grass verge and the road and field beyond that. 'Come on, what is it? What's up, Chrissy?' Paul asked her.

'I dunno, I just feel glum,' Christine told him, and then after a thoughtful pause, the girl added: 'I think I'm depressed.'

'Depressed?' Paul smiled at the word. He knew all about depression, having suffered from it for years. In this day and age – the mid 1980s, Prozac (or Fluoxetine to give it its technical name) was known but not available to treat depression until 1986 in Belgium and the USA in the following year. Paul had been prescribed the usual antidepressants for his depression but stopped taking them after he suffered from a phenomenon known as REM Rebound – in which the patient suffers from lucid and graphic nightmares after taking the pills. Only the love and patience of his wife Lauren got him through most of the black hell of depression, and in the end, a book on self-hypnosis that Paul had found by chance in Childwall Library proved to be the antidote. The author of the book suggested all sorts of kooky procedures which most psychiatrists would ridicule, but one of them seemed to work in Paul's case. He looked in a mirror, and grabbed the air above his head, imagining he was grabbing hold of the depression. He then threw it out the window – and straight away, he felt as if he had had this massive weight lifted from his head. His mind seemed clearer, and he actually felt good being alive.

'I think I'm depressed because my friend George isn't talking to me dad,' Christine told her father with a frowning mouth.

'Well, if you are depressed, let's get rid of your depression shall we?' Paul said, and he smiled and leaned over Christine. He fixed his spectacled eyes on her right shoulder and said, 'Ah, there it is! Keep still!'

Christine's head turned rapidly to look right; she expected something to be on her shoulder; a bug perhaps.

Paul reached out and grabbed the imaginary depression cloud and went over to the window. He turned the stiff handle of the window frame, smiled as he looked back at an astonished open-mouthed Christine, then opened the window and looked out, and there, to his left, was his wife Lauren, talking to her neighbour over the garden fence. Lauren stopped whispering to her neighbour and turned to look at her husband. 'What are you doing?' she asked, seeing him with his hand sticking out of the open window. Paul smiled and said, 'Catch Christine's depression!' in a jokey manor and hurled the imaginary thing at her.

Lauren shook her head and then turned to resume the gossiping session with her neighbour. Paul closed the window, went back over to Christine and said, 'Now, how do you feel?'

But the child was already watching the telly and

giggling at the energetic antics of Rod Hull and his puppet in *Emu's All-Live Pink Windmill Show*.

'Well, you've picked up all of a sudden!' Paul told the child, but the little girl was too busy laughing at Emu's antics to hear what her father was saying. 'Depression my foot,' Paul muttered, and went into the hallway. It was half-past four, and time to prepare the tea. He was about to go out into the garden to ask Lauren what she wanted for tea when his wife came into the hallway in tears.

'What's the matter?' Paul asked, full of natural concern for his wife, but she pushed his reaching hand away and hurried upstairs to the bedroom. Paul followed hot on her heels, and when he reached the bedroom he found his wife lying face down on the bed, crying her eyes out. Once again he asked her what the matter was but she was so upset she could hardly speak. Paul turned her over to face him, and said, 'Come on, come on, love, tell me what brought all this on.'

'I'm sorry,' Lauren told him, reaching for an empty cardboard tissue box. Paul went into the bathroom and unwound some tissue from a toilet roll then hurried back to his distressed wife. She wiped her tears and said, 'I don't even know why I'm crying, I just felt so worthless before, I'm sorry – ' she began to sob again and Paul held Lauren in his arms and patted her back. At this point he had not yet thought it strange how his daughter had been miserable and near to tears all day, and now, after he had pretended to grab her 'depression' and hurl it out the window – perchance in Lauren's direction – he now had a wife who was in tears yet unable to explain just why she was so deeply upset.

'It just came on me before,' Lauren said between a succession of sobs, 'it's horrible. Maybe I'm going through the change early.'

'You're only thirty-five Lauren,' Paul tried to reassure her with a sham chuckle.

'It can happen, oh, why do I feel so down?' Lauren then started to cry again.

All of a sudden, the penny dropped, and Paul thought about the way he had dealt with Christine's so-called depression. He said to Lauren: 'Listen, I am going to get shut of this depression that's come over you, but you have to believe me! Have you got that?'

Lauren gave a puzzled look in her tearful eyes. She didn't understand.

Paul adjusted his spectacles, pushing them up his nose a little, then gazed intently at his wife's right shoulder. He pretended to grab something there as he said the words: 'There! Got it! I have your depression.' Only this time as he closed his fist around the imaginary depression demon, he felt as if he had grabbed something jelly-like and it squirmed in his hand – yet he couldn't see what it was. He pulled the invisible writhing thing from his wife's shoulder, and it felt as if this unseen 'creature' was holding onto his wife by a tentacle, because he couldn't quite pull it fully clear from her. Then they both heard a snapping sound, and Paul felt the thing become detached from his wife's shoulder.

'Oh my God!' Lauren exclaimed, looking at Paul's clenched fist, 'What is that?'

Paul rushed to the window, and opened it, and he pushed the net curtain aside and looked out onto the sunny street. He looked at his fist, and felt the thing beating like a heart against his tightly curled fingers. He tried to throw it but he could feel it clinging on by some thread or perhaps some spindly limb, and so he dragged it from his hand with his other hand and this time when he threw it, the invisible ghastly entity must have gone sailing through the air. Paul closed the window and turned to see his wife standing close to him. Neither of them said nothing for a while, and then they both hugged one another tightly. Lauren swore and she used profanities Paul had never heard her utter in all their married years together. 'What was it?' she said, over and over. Paul told her about Christine's bout of depression and then he shrugged and said, 'It's as if that thing, whatever it was, made people depressed.'

'Don't tell anyone,' Lauren advised her husband, 'they'd think we were crazy.'

But of course, many years later, Paul wrote to me and was surprised when I told him I had heard of such cases before. In the 1950s, Reggie, a certain bookmaker in the Scotland Road area became so depressed, he decided to end his life. The depression just struck out the blue one beautiful sunny afternoon when he was sitting on his doorstep, reading a newspaper. He actually felt as if something had invaded his body through a point on his neck just below his right ear. He told his wife about the strange feeling of something invading his neck, and how a peculiar sensation had now spread to his head, but she thought he was just suffering from a hangover after the previous night of hard-drinking. The depression got that bad, Reggie put a gun barrel in his mouth one day and pulled the trigger, and for some reason – perhaps it was a mechanical defect – the gun never fired. The bookie went to his doctor and the result of a cursory examination was Reggie being sent for an x-ray of his head and neck. Nothing untoward was found. Reggie's wife told her neighbour about her husband's suicidal attempts because of his strange depression, and this neighbour told the bookmaker's wife that it sounded like some sort of possession, especially the way her husband had described being invaded by something. The neighbour got in touch with someone who in turn contacted an old gypsy woman named Frieda, and Frieda paid a visit to the bookmaker, and made him drink a strange concoction of various items she had obtained in the local chemist. Reggie went into convulsions soon afterwards, and Frieda, the bookie's wife, and her brother, all saw something semi-transparent, which looked like a jellyfish, emerge from Reggie's mouth. Reggie's brother in law belted this thing with a poker as it scuttled across the floor, and it let out a horrible screeching sound, then seemed to disappear. Reggie awoke soon afterwards to find that all of his depression and morbid thoughts of suicide and death had evaporated. The mystery deepened that week when Reggie was visited by his 7-year-old nephew John, who came to stay with the bookmaker for a day. John had not heard of the strange 'exorcism' by the gypsy, but on the day he came to stay, he kept looking at a corner of the room, and the boy crayoned what he saw on a scrap of paper. It looked like a jelly fish with blue spots on and two creepy-looking black domed eyes. Reggie asked the boy what the drawing was supposed to represent, and John said, 'I don't know but it's in that corner over there uncle, and it won't keep still.'

No one could see anything in the corner, but Reggie told everyone to get out the house, and he went and boiled a kettle of water, then poured it in the corner indicated by his nephew, and as he did, he heard a shrieking sound, and afterwards he found a pool of pale blue liquid in that corner. When John saw this pool of blue fluid, he said, 'Ah, you've killed *it* uncle.'

The boy's mother told Reggie that John had the gift of second sight and was able to see ghosts, but the boy was at a loss to explain what the jellyfish-like thing was he had seen in the corner of his uncle's living room.

I have heard of similar cases to this over the years, and these invisible beings that can allegedly cause major depression and suicidal tendencies may be what are known as 'elementals' in the occult world. They are very mysterious creatures that are said to have a symbiotic relationship with their 'host' for a while. Symbiotic creatures live together with the host, usually to their mutual advantage, until they get greedy or there is some reaction, and the host dies, or in this case kills itself, and the elemental then finds another host. I am not saying that any depressive illness is caused by an elemental. 'Infection' by such creatures, if they exist, are apparently extremely rare. If you believe you are depressed, and your depression is affecting your life and the lives of those around you, you must immediately book an appointment with your doctor.

THE WITCH OF
COUNTY ROAD

There are a surprising number of graves beneath the streets of Liverpool where purported witches and alleged vampires are said to lay – and, apparently, none of them are at rest. In my previous books I have written about the 'vampire grave' which lies beneath the junction of Rupert Lane, Breck Road, Heyworth Street and Everton Road, where a man – who was alleged to drink human and animal blood (including the blood of the wife he murdered) – was staked face-down in 1680, but there are other strange graves of this sort which have rarely been alluded to in print. In 2001, Arthur Jones, a man in his early eighties came to one of my booksignings to tell me of a first-hand account of an incident I had heard about before, only from second-hand sources – the finding of the so-called Witch of Walton. Arthur Jones was barely seventeen when the incident happened in the winter of 1937. That year, Arthur was working with his father as a labourer for the council, and one frosty day the two of them were digging a hole on Walton's County Road to reach a water pipe that had burst. During the dig, a strange find was made at the junction of Newark Street by the Harlech Castle public house: the arched-back skeleton of what was presumed to be a woman with long locks of red hair still attached to her skull, with her wrists bound together behind her back with some sort of strong twine, and the bound wrists were in turn tied to the corpse's bound ankles. There was some sort of thick leather gag clenched between the skeleton's teeth, but most startling of all was the thick pointed wooden post – about six inches in diameter and five feet in length, which had been driven through the skeleton, staking the person face down, and, moreover, seven long iron nails had also been driven through the neck and legs. These nails, being of rusted iron, are a clue to the archaic thinking behind the ancient burial ritual, because traditionally, iron nails were always used to prevent witches from rising from their graves. Stakes such as the corpse the County Road skeleton was pierced with were conventionally driven through the bodies of suicides, witches and suspected vampires to stop their troubled spirits from rising. Arthur and his father reported the find, and a van from the council turned up and took the crumbling bones away. Nothing more was heard of the incident. Arthur's father was later told that the skeleton was not the remains of the victim of some sadistic murderer of modern times, but the remains of some executed woman - most probably a young witch (who was youthful enough to have a full head of red hair still attached to her calcified scalp when unearthed) had been staked down after burial hundreds of years ago.

Not long afterwards, after the pipe was fixed and the hole was filled in, strange things began to happen in the area where the witch grave had been unearthed, including the mysterious deaths of five people in a 300-yard radius of the witch-grave. All five people who died within a short span of a nine days, died while screaming out in their sleep, and there were rumours that 'strange crosses' had been scratched into the chests of some of the victims, and these bizarre symbols were even noted by pathologists. Now let us go back to Victorian times to seek further connections with the Walton Witch. In the pub close to the witch grave, the Harlech Castle Hotel, a series of uncanny events unfolded shortly after the Halloween of 1895. The landlord of the pub at this time was a seasoned publican named Edward Gough, who had run other pubs in Bostock Street and other areas of the north end off Great Homer Street. His niece, 13-year-old Jane Godwin, often stayed in one of the rooms over the Harlech Castle, and one November evening, Jane's mother (Edward Gough's sister) began to talk about the strange customs of Halloween (which was known as Duck-Apple Night in those times), which had just taken place. Mrs Godwin talked about the old scrying practice of girls looking into a mirror at midnight by candlelight as they brushed their hair in order to catch a supernatural glimpse of their future husbands. Then, in the course of the conversation about such supernatural matters, Mr Gough mentioned the 'forgotten art of looking-glass-gazing' whereby a person staring intently at his or her own reflection in a mirror at night by candlelight would see the reflection of their face gradually change into that of the Devil. Jane Godwin was a very impressionable child and that very night, she crept out of her bed, just after 1am and lit a candle. She placed it on the mantelpiece of her room, next to an old ornate framed mirror. The girl fixed her gaze on her own reflection so that her eyes met her own reflected eyes. Nothing out of the ordinary happened in the first minute, but after about three minutes, Jane's eyes began to tire, and the candle flame swayed side to side in the draught passing

242

through the room from a loose window pane to the gap under her door. As Jane beheld her own face, she saw it slowly change, and morph into a face that seemed quite strange and unfamiliar. The colour of her face in the mirror drained away until the face reflected was tinged with a strange green cast, and then all of a sudden, the reflection of Jane's raven black hair turned reddish brown, and then the young teenager found herself face to face with a girl she had never set eyes on before. This girl seemed around Jane's age, and she was wearing some sort of old-fashioned looking green dress.

Jane suddenly realised she could not move, and the girl, in a very strange accent, said: 'Do not be afraid Jane, do not be afraid. Thou art to take my place Jane, fall into my eyes. Fall into them Jane.'

The large dark eyes of the green-faced apparition seemed to become huge, and black, like bottomless pits, and in the blackness of the vast pupils, Jane could see and hear crying children. There were about five or six boys and girls – only their little tormented faces were visible, and they seemed to float and bob about. Jane could hear her own heart beating hard in her chest as panic gripped her. The words of the red-haired girl with the pale green face seemed to echo. 'Fall into my eyes Jane, fall into them!'

The room all around Jane darkened and the candle began to shrink as if it was moving further and further away. Jane felt a little ice cold hand grab her right hand, and the child, a male, said: 'I want my mamma!'

Jane couldn't even turn her head to look down at the distressed child in the Limbo of blackness; her neck was paralysed. The green face grinned, and Jane could see that the girl's left front tooth was slightly discoloured.

Jane then realised that she was somehow 'inside' the mirror, and all around was cold enveloping darkness. In her mind, Jane said, 'Jesus Christ, please save me!'

Edward Gough suddenly walked into Jane's bedroom with an oil lamp in his hand, and his entrance seemed to break the terrifying spell. Jane found herself standing on the hearth rug before the fireplace with the candle still burning on the mantelpiece. Now all she saw when she looked at the mirror was her own reflection, and over her left shoulder she saw the startled face of her Uncle Edward. The girl was so afraid of the green-faced girl, she refused to stay in the Harlech Castle for the remainder of that morning and Edward Gough had to take an hysterical Jane and her mother home immediately. The girl refused to step foot in her uncle's pub again. Why had Edward Gough gone to his niece's room that night? He said he had been sleeping soundly when he and his wife were awakened by the sound of an unfamiliar voice – that of a girl – chanting 'Fall into my eyes'. A friend of the family staying in another room in the pub had also heard the unknown girl's voice.

This incident is surely related to the witch grave that was located just a few feet outside the pub, but just who was buried face-down, with a giant stake rammed through her and her wrists and ankles bound together? We'll probably never know. Whoever she was, she must have been greatly feared for so many precautionary measures to be implemented to stop the girl rising from her grave.

Not far from the Harlech Castle, around the same time as the mirror-scrying incident, a couple – a Mr and Mrs Parry, would cling to one another in the bedroom of their lodgings at 91 County Road almost every night as their sleep was disturbed by the singing and dancing of a woman who appeared on the wall next to their bed. The shadow of the long-haired nimble woman would twirl about and kick her legs up as she sung in an eerie voice. The house belonged to a grocer named Richard Smith, who had let the room out to the Parrys, and when they first told him about the ghostly shadow, he thought the couple were just seeing things, but then one night, Mr Parry called his landlord into the room and Smith saw the sinister dancing and singing silhouette himself. Smith's wife had the room blessed and after that the ghost was seen no more.

Coroner's inquests were frequently carried out at the Harlech Castle Hotel on County Road, including the inquest into the infamous baby-farming case in May 1884. In 1881, during an inquest on a three-year-old boy named Percy Christopher, many present, including the coroner and a Dr Ireland, who had a surgery at 71 County Road, heard female laughter, coming from the cellar of the pub. A policeman went down into the cellar and found it empty.

In July 1895, the following advert appeared in the 'Persons Wanted' column of the local newspapers: '*BARMAN (Young Man) Wanted, strong, not afraid of work; good references required - Apply by letter only, 63, County Road, Walton.*'

A 25-year-old former soldier named Blakely was one of the many people who applied for the post of barman, and he was accepted because of his level-headedness and strong muscular frame. However, three days into the job, Blakely had to go down into the cellar for some task, and when he returned, his face looked pale, and his eyes seemed full of fear. The customers and other staff members noticed this change in the ex-serviceman's demeanour and asked him what was wrong. Blakely said he'd seen a woman with long hair and a ghastly pale face, hanging upside down from the low ceiling of the cellar like a bat, sniggering at him. As he turned and ran up the stairs, she had shouted to him, 'You will never reach thirty!'

It's unknown if this chilling prediction came to pass, but Blakely packed in his new job that day.

There are those who believe that the Walton Witch returns now and then to the environs of County Road, perhaps believing she can somehow take revenge on those who executed her centuries ago by cursing and haunting the people of today, some of whom may even be descendants of old those old Waltonians who once staked what they believed to have been an evil young witch.

SATHAN

In the summer of 1994, a rather strange apparition (and quite a bizarre one for that matter) terrorised two children, a teenager and an adult in his forties at a house in Ashbourne Avenue, Netherton, in the County Borough of Bootle. Two girls, Sandy and Julie, both aged 7, were being minded by a 15-year-old girl named Angie, at Julie's house, which was just a stone's throw from Bootle Municipal Golf Course. Julie's parents – Steve and Joanne - had paid Angie £10 to mind their daughter and her best friend Sandy while they went out for the night. Angie had minded the girls five times before, and nothing remotely supernatural had ever happened. On this occasion, Steve and Joanne said they'd be coming home a bit later than usual because they would be going to a club with a couple from nearby Park Lane West. 'We'll be home no later than 2am, Angie,' Steve had promised.

The time was coming up to midnight, and Angie told the girls they would have to go to bed soon. Sandy and Julie begged for another half hour so they could watch a video, and then around a quarter past midnight, Angie sternly told the best friends it was bedtime. The girls went to bed, but at a quarter to one when Angie went to check on them, she heard Sandy and Julie singing a song by German eurodance group Real McCoy called *Another Night*, which had been on a cable channel called The Box at that time. 'get to sleep you two,' Angie said, opening the door. The girls giggled and promised they'd get to sleep.

Angie then went downstairs and read a magazine. About ten minutes later, she heard what she could only describe as a faint clip-clopping sound – like a horse on the stairs, only it sounded too contrived to be real. It reminded her of the crude sound effects of a horse's gallop she'd made in her younger days at the school play – by knocking two halves of a hollowed-out coconut together. Angie went out of the living room and stood at the bottom of the stairs. She could hear the girls crying faintly, and so she went up to see what the matter was. Sandy and Julie were hiding under the duvet, sobbing, holding on to one another, and both children were physically shaking.

'Ah, what's up?' Angie asked, full of concern, and the girls grabbed her and hugged her.

'A horrible horse thing came in the room!' said Sandy in a hysterical high-pitched voice, and her surreal description made Julie burst into tears.

'Calm down now, you two,' Angie said, turning on the bedside light. 'You've had a nightmare. Told you not to eat so late didn't I?'

'It was real,' a red-faced Julie screamed, and her cheeks were slicked with tears. Angie took the girls downstairs and when they reached the staircase they clung hard onto their minder and looked about with petrified expressions.

Downstairs, Angie sat the girls on the sofa and brought them glasses of milk and packets of crisps, and then she sat between the girls with her arms around them. 'Ah, you had a bad dream that's all,' she said, trying to reassure Sandy and Julie, and she looked at the clock, then said to Julie: 'Your mum and dad will be home soon love. You'll be okay.'

And then, all of a sudden, Angie – and Julie and Sandy – heard the clip-clopping sound Angie had heard earlier on. It came down the stairs this time, and the girls became hysterical, and ran to the corner of the living room that was diagonally furthest away from the door to the hall. Angie was scared too, but tried not to show it for the children's sake. The clip-clops stopped by the door, and then that door opened inch by inch.

Julie was so afraid, she fainted, and landed on an armchair, and as Angie ran to her aid, she saw something dark out the corner of her eye, peep around the door. She turned to look at it, and saw what looked like the head of a black horse, only it didn't look real – it looked as if it was carved out of some dark wood which contrasted with its stark white eyes and teeth. The head came a little further into the room on a long curved neck reminiscent of the type of neck the Loch Ness monster is pictured as having in the artists' impressions.

Sandy hid behind Angie, who was now absolutely speechless and struck with fear. The artificial horse made a snorting sound, then opened its mouth wide as it threw back its head and whinnied. Angie let out a yelp, swore at the thing, then picked up a heavy smoked glass ashtray from the coffee table and hurled it at the head.

Before the ashtray hit the door to shatter into a hundred shards, the wooden horse head withdrew in an instant, back behind the door.

Then came the sound of the strange creature going back up the stairs, and Angie and Sandy even heard the thing trip and stumble as it ascended the stairs.

The sound of a diesel engine ticking over outside could suddenly be heard, and Angie realised it was Julie's parents; they'd arrived home in a taxi. Angie knelt at the armchair where Julie was laying unconscious and gently shook her. The girl woke up and large bulging fear-filled eyes gazed at the door where the wooden terror had peeped in minutes before. That door opened now and Julie let out an ear-splitting scream as her parents walked into the room. Steve, her father trod on the glass ashtray fragments, and looked down, puzzled. 'What's been going on here?' he asked.

'Daddy!' Julie screamed, and ran straight towards him. Steve reached down and scooped her up in his huge hands and quickly held her aloft in case she stepped on the glass fragments in her bare feet 'What's wrong love?' he asked as his daughter burst into tears.

'Angie, what's been going on here?' Julie's mother asked, her speech slightly slurred. She also swayed somewhat as she tried to keep still whilst delivering the question.

Angie and Sandy told Julie's intoxicated parents what had happened simultaneously, but the facts of the garbled narrative just couldn't sink in.

'A bleedin' horse looked in on yous,' Steve asked, and hiccupped. He smiled, and then looked at his wife. Her eyelids were looking increasingly heavier as the minutes wore on. 'Have you been smoking something Angie?' Steve asked the child minder, but his wife pulled him up and said, 'Now, Steve, you know very well Angie is a clean-living girl, so take back what you just said.'

'It's alright, I'm going now,' Angie said in a sulky

voice and patted Sandy on the head. 'You'll be okay now, Julie's mum and dad are here,' she told the child.

'I want to go home,' Sandy cried, 'I don't want that horse to get me.'

'Woah! Woah! Wait a minute Angie,' said Steve, raising his palm towards Angie. He put Julie down on the armchair, left the room and went upstairs, and then Joanne said, 'Take no notice of him, he's drunk. He was joking about you smoking stuff, Angie. I'm just going the toilet.'

Joanne hurried to the downstairs toilet as Angie sat on the edge of the sofa, comforting the girls who were now climbing up her in tears.

'Can't you stay with us, please Angie?' little Julie was pleading, gazing into Angie's large sad eyes.

'I don't know, I don't think there's room for me to sleep in your bed, love,' Angie said with an attempt at a smile.

Steve's heavy footsteps came bounding down the stairs as he sang: '*A horse is a horse of course of course…*' And he sounded as if he was out of breath as he sang.

He burst into the living room holding the very wooden horse which had struck terror into the girls and their minder earlier in the night. Julie screamed and wet herself, and Sandy ran to hide behind the sofa. Angie looked in horror at the horse, then saw the curved rockers it was mounted on. It was a huge rocking horse, and it was so big, Steve looked out of breath as he placed it on the floor. When he regained his breath, Steve said: 'You've obviously been rooting about up in the spare room Angie. I had intended to give this to Julie for her birthday next week, but she may as well have it now.'

Julie was standing there, soaked because she had wet herself, and her mouth was wide open, but the poor child could hardly cry out because she was in such shock as she looked at the sinister black rocking horse.

'I have not been rooting round upstairs,' cried Angie, so enraged by the audacity of Steve. 'How dare you accuse me of mooching about! I'm not minding Julie anymore!'

Angie had had enough of drunken Steve, and she ran out the room, and as she passed him he tried to grab her arm but Angie slapped his hand away. She left the house, and her heart broke as she heard Julie and Sandy crying for her to come back.

On the following day, Julie's mother, Joanne, came to Angie's house to apologise, and to also relate a very strange incident. Last night, Sandy had been taken back to her own house because she kept saying she was scared of the horse. Julie slept with her mum and dad, and at four in the morning, Joanne and Julie had been awakened by terrible screams from Steve. When Joanne asked him what was wrong, Steve said he had been attacked in the bed by that horse – the rocking horse. He said he had been woken by something, and when he looked up, he saw the creepy long narrow face of the horse over him as he lay in bed. The horse then bit at him, actually drawing blood. Steve kicked at the thing and it eventually ran off out the room. When Steve switched on the light, Julie saw he had rectangular grazes on his neck and a little blood on the pillow. On the following morning, Steve put the rocking horse in the garage. Steve had purchased that rocking horse from a friend who had found it in the attic of his late auntie's home in Aigburth during a furniture clearance. Steve had now given the rocking horse away to another friend who eventually sold it via the items for sale column in the *Liverpool Echo* for £25. Steve learned from his friend that the mane of the rocking horse had been made of real horse hair, and the leather saddle, pommel and stirrups dated back to the Edwardian era. What's more, on the neck of the horse, the name "Sathan" had been inscribed.

This horse was obviously haunted by something – perhaps even the animal spirit of a long-dead horse, or perhaps by something demonic. It's a real puzzler of a case. The whereabouts of the haunted rocking horse are currently unknown.

FATHER MURPHY

In 1995, a woman in her mid-fifties we shall call Jackie lost her husband to a long illness, and on the day after the funeral, in the afternoon, a priest called at the widow's little terraced home on Tiverton Street in Wavertree. Jackie admitted the priest, who said her daughter had called him out, and Jackie, who called herself a 'lapsed Catholic' – a Catholic who never or rarely attends church – felt a little ashamed at the visitation, and told the priest she would be going to church again soon. Her local church was Our Lady of Good Help on Chestnut Grove at the back of the High Street, Wavertree – but the visiting priest – Father Murphy – did not acknowledge that church when Jackie mentioned it. He said something about 'St Anne's' – probably meaning St Anne's Catholic Church on Overbury Street in Edge Hill, a neighbouring district. Father Murphy sat and held Jackie's hand as he sat next to her on the sofa, and really reassured her that her husband had reached Heaven. He said that time was nothing in Heaven, and that one day, Jackie would see her husband again, and when he did, man and wife would feel as if they had only been separated for a day. There was no one else in the house at this time when Father Murphy called. Jackie's son, who was in his twenties, was at work, and her daughter was attending an interview at Wavertree Job Centre, just up the road near to the Picton Clock. Besides coping with the grief from the loss of her husband, Jackie was also suffering from a bad back, a recurring complaint she'd had since her twenties, and she was in great pain with it. Father Murphy seemed to know about this condition. He said to Jackie: 'Back still troubling you?'

Jackie nodded, dumbfounded at the priest's knowledge of her troublesome ailment.

'Back in Ireland there was a man who had the healing touch, and he showed me this trick,' Father Murphy said, and he put his index finger on one side of Jackie's spine and the middle finger on the other side of the spinal bump, and the priest gently ran his fingers up and down Jackie's back, as far as the small of her back, and gradually the pain there faded.

After about two minutes of the priest's healing treatment, Jackie heard a key rattling in the lock of her front door. 'This'll be my daughter, Suzy,' Jackie told the priest, and she turned – but there was now no one sitting next to her on the sofa. Jackie put her hand to her mouth and trembled. She looked around the room, as if the priest could have even sneaked out or hid anywhere, and he was nowhere to be seen. Suzy barged in and said, 'Well that was a waste of time mam; they said I got the date wrong for the interview, so I had to go through this bleedin' rigmarole...'

Jackie was still in shock, and her face looked deadly pale. Suzy knew something had spooked her and asked what was wrong.

'Did anyone pass you in the hallway when you came in then, Suze?' Jackie asked, with a slight tremor in her voice.

'Like who, mam?' Suzy asked, thinking the bereavement might be affecting her mother's soundness of mind.

'Did a priest pass you?' Jackie looked up, and her

large eyes were full of fear.

'A priest? No mam, why?'

'A priest visited me before – and he said you sent for him – and, and he – he was just there – ' Jackie was stammering with nerves.

'*I* sent for him? What are you on about?' Suzy was puzzled by the odd claim.

Jackie told her daughter about every little detail of the visitation, and Suzy became a bit nervous. If there was one thing she was scared of it was ghosts. Nothing more was said about the matter, because Jackie was very superstitious and thought there was no luck in talking about the supernatural (even though her back never troubled her again after Father Murphy's strange therapy), but about three weeks after this incident, Jackie's son David went to have his hair cut just around the corner from his home at a hairdressers called Millie's, and while he was waiting to get his hair done, an old man sitting next to him asked David if he was related to a man named Robert who had lived on Belmont Road, because he was the spitting image of him. 'Yeah, he was my dad,' David told the old man, and the pensioner realised he was speaking about his father in the past tense, and so, he asked: 'Oh, I'm sorry lad, isn't your father no longer with us?'

'He died just under a month back,' David told him. The old man then offered his condolences, and he got chatting with David, and even when he was in the chair getting an old-fashioned 'short back and sides' he continued to reminisce about David's father Robert – who he had always called Robbo - and the old man recalled little anecdotes about him. One story was very intriguing. The old man said that when David's father lost his mother at a very young age (just 18) he became very depressed, and on the day after the funeral, a strange priest going under the name Father Murphy had visited Robbo one afternoon when everyone else was out of the house on Belmont Road. The priest inspired Robbo to regain his faith, which the young man had lost, seeing his mother die from a horrible illness. 'Father Murphy really turned his life around, but your dad didn't know at the time that this priest fellah had been dead for years.'

David went cold when he realised that this same ghostly priest had visited his mother three weeks back. The old man said, 'They think the priest was based up at St Anne's Church – you know, the one on top of that slope in Edge Hill? And I believe he died in some tragedy, but he started to visit his parishioners after they'd buried him. A lot of priests won't talk about it, which is understandable, but Robbo swore that Father Murphy really turned his life around when he was depressed.'

David told his mother about the old man's story, and Jackie got in touch with me in 2009, and was very surprised when I told her that Father Murphy had visited many other people in their hour of need, including a couple on Wavertree's Grosvenor Road who had lost their little baby. The priest reassured the mother she would have twins in the future - two girls - and she did. Murphy had also been encountered at a house on Rathbone Road one Sunday afternoon when a woman who had lost her husband was contemplating suicide in 2006. No one knows why the priest returns from the next world; is it simply out of concern for those who have lost everything, including their faith?

Or is Father Murphy an angel of some sort? We may know more one day, and perhaps even *you* shall receive a visit from him.

THE BEAST

Back in the days when Kirkby was but a cluster of farmsteads and thatched cottages, when the simple rural folk were still cutting and stacking the rich Kirkby moss, when covered wagons of the local farmers would be seen making a trek into Liverpool with their wares each Saturday, there lived a very strange and enigmatic young man, who, according to the gypsies, was some sort of lycanthrope – a man who could turn into a beast. This man's name was Gordon Hale, and he was quite a handsome young man in the early 1880s with his curly head of black hair, large expressive brown eyes, pearly white teeth and boyish face. At six feet and three inches he stood quite tall for that day and age and was aged about 25. His physique was impressive, for he had not an ounce of surplus fat on his frame, and his muscles were well developed, him being a hard-working farm-hand. Hale talked in a refined accent, but showed no superiority, and conversed with everyone from village fool to country doctor on an equal footing. Some believed Hale to be the runaway son of a Sussex aristocrat, and some fancied he was a pugilist who was lying low from the law after killing an opponent, but there were stranger rumours concerning Hale. A pretty milkmaid named Agnes said he had once changed into a hairy beast before her eyes one night in a barn near Kirkby corn mill. All traditional tales of the werewolf have the victim being transformed against his will, but according to Agnes the milkmaid, Hale derived a sexual pleasure from the transmutation – which he could invoke at will. There was some masochistic satisfaction in the stretching of bones and muscle and the stresses and exertions of the flesh as Hale became a powerful hairy brute. Agnes had remained rooted to the spot, more out of fear than curiosity when she witnessed the sickening metamorphosis of Hale into the creature he called the 'Beast'. The Beast was around seven feet in height, and covered in a coat of bristly black hair. The head of this hybrid monstrosity was apelike, except for the nose, which was not flattened as it is in the primates. The nose of the Beast was long and aquiline, and the eyes bulged and were always pink, tinged so by a web of fine red veins. As the Beast, Hale could still talk, but in a much slower and deeper voice, and his vocabulary was very basic and not as comprehensive as it was in full human form. How was Hale able to transform himself into something which resembled the fabled 'missing link' between mankind and the apes? No one knew, but Hale professed to one woman that his ability was down to some freak of nature inherited from his great grandfather, who had begun to change – at will – into a similar creature when he was fifteen.

One summer's evening in 1881, at around 10pm, two young Irish brothers in their twenties named Tom and Marty Cawley grabbed a 16-year-old girl named Mary O'Hare, who was on an errand on Kirkby's Swell Lane. The brothers tried to drag the girl to a derelict shed, no doubt intending to rape the poor teenager, when Gordon Hale, who was out walking on his own in the area, heard Mary's screams. Mr Anders, the Rector of Kirkby, also heard the screams from almost a mile away that night as he was out walking, perhaps seeking inspiration for one of his controversial sermons. When the reverend reached the scene of the attempted rape, he found Mary O'Hare unconscious in a field, and in the dilapidated shed, he found the unconscious brothers, bruised and blood-spattered. Nearby in the shed, the rector saw the shreds of a shirt and two boots that had been torn apart – probably the ones worn by Hale before he changed. Striding from the direction of the shed, across a field of rye, was the unmistakable silhouette of the giant figure known as the Beast, which the rector certainly had no intention of pursuing. A tramp who had seen everything came out of a hedgerow and told the rector how a man had changed into a bear before running after the Irishmen and after seizing them, had run to the shed with one under each arm. Mary regained consciousness and said she believed she would know the man who had changed into a 'devil' before her very eyes. When the brothers Cawley regained their senses, they contradicted Mary O'Hare's story and said they had been trying to protect her from the Beast, but the tramp corroborated Mary's story, and the Irishmen got on their bended knee before the rector and promised they would never touch 'a drop of the demon drink again' – for it was the liquor that was to blame for their shameful conduct. The rector forgave Tom and Marty Cawley and the brothers even attended church for a while – before they reverted to their old ways. Gordon Hale was hunted for a while by the police, and was given shelter by a lady named Georgina, and nothing is known about her beyond the fact that she was a guest at Waverley House, a grand detached villa which still stands today as the Kirkby Conservative Club. In those days, Waverley House featured three entertaining rooms, seven bedrooms, two kitchens, a large conservatory, an extensive wine and beer cellar, and a beautiful garden. Waverley House, standing in 4,862 square yards of land, was owned by 65-year-old Carolina Jeffreys, an American lady who had lost her English husband Thomas, when he was aged 72, in 1875. The widow Jeffreys was comforted by 35-year-old Georgina, who seems to have been a one-time nurse to the late Mr Jeffreys. Gordon Hale fell passionately in love with Georgina, and when he first revealed his terrible secret to her, she almost fainted, but the bonds of true love are strong, and Georgina came to accept Gordon for what he was. Gordon Hale had to do a moonlight flit with Georgina around 1883 when Waverley House was visited by burglars around four o'clock one morning. Gordon Hale turned himself into his atavistic bestial form, and the giant hairy throwback almost killed the two burglars, who somehow managed to escape and inform the police via a lackey. The police cautiously visited the chatelaine Mrs Jeffreys, who denied any burglary attempt had taken place, but one of the policemen noticed a broken downstairs window and also found traces of blood on the carpet of one of the bedrooms of Waverley House. Georgina could not bear to let her lover hit the road without her, and so she fled with him, riding pillion on horseback with Gordon Hale to Heaven knows where. There were rumours that Georgina had twins not long afterwards, a boy and a girl, and the boy allegedly inherited the strange 'talent' of transformation from his father.

On 3 January 1892, Mrs Jeffreys died, aged 76, but not long afterwards, her ghost was seen in and around Waverley House as a rather eerie apparition, dressed all in black, the clothes she had always worn since the death of her beloved husband. This woman in black is said to still haunt the Grade II listed residence today, and I have received many emails and letters from people who have seen the ghost at the Conservative Club on South Park Road.

GHOSTLY SMELLS

At a house in Broadgreen, there is a family of five; mother, father, a 13-year-old son and his sisters, aged 15 and 18. None of them smoke. None of the kids take any drugs nor do they smoke marijuana, and yet, without fail, every time bad news is ready to rear its ugly head, the aroma of pipe tobacco – St Bruno by the smell of it – infiltrates the household. At the time of writing, this phenomenon has occurred five times. The first time it happened, the family were involved in a serious car crash on the following day. Weeks later, at seven in the morning, the aromatic odour invaded the master bedroom of the mother and father, and was so overpowering, the smell woke the couple up – and the father of the family was stung by two wasps that had flown into the room via the bedroom window that had been left a few inches open. The father almost died from an allergic reaction to the stings and had to be taken to hospital. On the third occasion, the 13-year-old son smelt it just before he set out for school, and that day he was knocked down in a hit and run incident and was lucky to escape with just a few bruises and a graze. Then it was the turn of his 15-year-old sister, Kerry. She smelt it as she lay in the bath, and began to cough because the tang of the invisible tobacco fumes were that sharp. Minutes later, Kerry got shampoo in her eye as she sat in the bath, lathering her hair, so she stood up, reached for the towel on the wall-mounted holder, and slipped, falling out of the bath and smashing her head against a radiator. She had to have four stitches in her forehead. A week after that, the tobacco smell manifested itself in the bedroom of Kerry's older sister, Jade, as she was surfing the net on her laptop as she lay on her bed. Mindful of the bad luck which the aroma had brought to the other members of her family, Jade actually said out loud: 'Okay, do your best, go on!'

The tall wardrobe to the right of the bed suddenly tipped over – and fell towards Jade, who yelped and tried to get off the bed, but the wardrobe's edge smashed into her shoulder, dislocating it. Jade's father said she had piled too many of her shoeboxes on top of the wardrobe, but Jade knew, as anyone with common sense did, that piling boxes on top of any wardrobe that is weighed down because it is crammed with outfits and coats, could not make it topple.

I receive many emails and letters about these supernatural aromas, and how they seem to accompany either bad news, good news or some sort of supernatural activity. The most common aromas reported to me, are the scent of violets or lilacs. I have detected these aromas myself at many haunted places over the years, and its strange how they can come into rooms where doors and windows are closed. Scent of violets and lavender seem to be associated with feminine ghosts, whereas smells of turpentine, tobacco, and even decay, seem to be connected with male entities. A woman named Margaret once bumped into me in the old branch of WH Smith on Liverpool's Church Street many years ago and told me how much she liked reading my books, even though some of the stories scared her. She then asked me if I knew anything about strange aromas of ghosts, and I told her the little I knew. 'Whenever my husband is near, I smell Old Spice aftershave,' Margaret told me, and explained how her husband had passed away nearly ten years before. As I stood there talking to Margaret, we both got this powerful whiff of what was unmistakably Old Spice, and we just looked at one another. As this occurred, we were standing by a magazine rack, and the woman said, 'Can you smell what I can smell, Tom?'

I nodded, and said, 'Old Spice.'

Margaret then turned and looked at a copy of *Boxing News* in the vast magazine rack, and she poignantly remarked how her late husband had always read that publication, and as we both looked at the magazine, it lifted up a few inches out of the rack, and then fell onto the floor. I have witnessed poltergeist activity many times and am rather used to the sight of things moving without a rational cause, but Margaret went white with shock.

It's amazing how an aroma can transport you back in time to your childhood. If I smell hot tar, I think of days spent on Melville Place off Myrtle Street, when I would burst the tar bubbles in the road on a sweltering summer's day, or perhaps use the sun-softened tar to stick two ice-lolly sticks together into a cross which I would throw into the air. I'm sure many of you reading this associate certain perfumes, or even the aroma of freshly-baked bread, the smell of newly-cut grass, the distinctive smell of Mr Sheen or Mansion Polish, and even the oily scent of plasticine with past times from your life. Odours and scents are very evocative, and I believe that is why certain spirits generate them. A scent of Evening in Paris can often be smelt at a house in Kensington where a woman who often wore that perfume lived until her death in 1970. The woman's daughter now lives at the house, and whenever she is facing a crisis or some bleak predicament, she always detects the reassuring scent of her mother's favourite perfume.

In 2008, two students in their early twenties named Hailee and Bronwen moved into a ground floor flat in a certain house on Arundel Avenue, off Smithdown Road. The rent was affordable to the girls, and initially they found the atmosphere in the two-bedroomed flat in the red-brick terraced house quite pleasant, but as soon as darkness fell, a very strange ambience infiltrated the dwelling. Both girls had the feeling they were being watched by someone or something, and without fail, always around 9pm, the smell of cigar smoke would creep into the living room and this aroma would follow the girls about. At first, Simon, a boyfriend of Bronwen, said the cigar smoke was just drifting out of a neighbours house and into their flat via the windows, but the smell arrived around 9pm even when all the windows and doors were shut. Hailee bought perfumed candles and put them in the living room to cloak the acrid smell, but instead of masking the odour, it seemed to provoke the unseen smoker. Blue smoke began to fill up the living room, making the girls and their boyfriends cough, and then, one morning at 3.10 am, Hailee was lying in bed, when something woke her up. The only light shining into the room was from a lamp post outside on the other side of Arundel Avenue, but by this light, the student saw something very eerie. A faint shadow was standing to the left of the curtains, and from the head of this vague outline, rings of smoke were being blown. Then Hailee saw a dim orange light – the lit tip of the semi-transparent cigar – being lifted by the ghost to its mouth. The student rolled left across the mattress and ran to the door. She yanked the door open and ran into Bronwen's room, where her friend was fast asleep with Simon. Hailee woke the couple up and told them what she had seen, and Simon rushed from the bed and went into Hailee's bedroom. He could smell the cigar smoke, and the three young people stood at the entrance to the bedroom, listening to the gentle pad of footsteps.

'Oh my God, can you hear it?' Bronwen said, listening to the invisible walker.

Simon let out a scream and grabbed his bare left shoulder with his right hand, and the girls yelped with fright. Simon swore and looked at his shoulder, saying: 'It burnt me! It burnt me!'

The girls saw the red scar left by the glowing tip of the ghostly cigar. Then all three saw the glowing tip tracing a figure of eight in the air before their eyes, and they all backed out of the room and closed the door. After that night, the students went to look for another place to stay. When Hailee told me about this incident, I shocked her by telling her what the number of the house was. The house in question has been haunted by one of the most durable ghosts in Liverpool. Time after time, I have heard of the shadowy figure who haunts the house on Arundel Avenue, and without a doubt, the ghost is of a man who lived at the house in the late Victorian period. He once tried to push a student into the bath she was taking, and almost drowned her. The student ran naked out of the house trying to escape from the entity. In the 1950s the entity was probably the same ghost who used to bang out the 'Death March' on an upright piano belonging to a resident, at all hours in the morning. When a body was left in an open coffin during a wake in the front parlour of this house, the body was found with its each of its arms dangling out the side of the coffin with one of the flowers from a wreath placed between its teeth. I have researched the censuses in an effort to find whose ghost is haunting the house on Arundel Avenue, but so far I have been unsuccessful.

Not all ghostly odours signal the manifestation of menace; many smells from the spirit world bring comfort too. A man in Anfield named James lost his dad Ronnie in 2004, and in 2005, James and his wife were talking about Ronnie, when they suddenly detected the unmistakable smell of Golden Virginia – the tobacco Ronnie always smoked in his roll-ups. James and his wife did not smoke, and no one in the family did, so the odour of tobacco really made them wonder if it was Ronnie telling them that he was still around. On every occasion when James is feeling low, that reassuring smell of his late father's tobacco seems to pick him up again somehow, and whoever's in the house with James at the time will always smell the Golden Virginia aroma as well. A man named Walter in his eighties lives in a beautifully kept house in Aigburth, and he tells me that whenever he detects a beautiful sweet scent not unlike lilac, he hears good news. The smell reminds him of a perfume his late wife Gladys often wore until her death in 1999. On

269

one occasion Walter detected the lovely fragrance, and he later discovered that his grand-daughter was pregnant. A week later he smelt the very same scent, and won £4,000 on the bingo. The sweet phantom smell always seem to be the precursor of good news in Walter's case.

SKIRMISHES WITH
SUPERNATURAL ABDUCTIONS

I have written about the so-called 'Thing on Higher Lane' in previous *Haunted Liverpool* books. The 'Thing' in question has been described as having various forms, ranging from an amorphous, shapeless black pool which crawls along Fazakerley's Higher Lane, to a black humanoid figure which melts away into a dark tar-like mass. In 2005, a seventy-year-old man named Robert Smith contacted me via his nephew Darren, to tell me of a terrifying encounter with an entity he believes to have been the 'Thing' in 1946, when Robert was eleven years of age. Robert lived on Walton Hall Avenue East at the time of this strange incident with his mother, father, three brothers and his grandfather. He was just a rather mundane schoolboy who was more concerned with sweets and football than the supernatural, and on the evening the incident took place, he was returning home from the house of his best mate, another 11-year-old lad named Billy Morris. Robert left Billy's house near the junction of Aintree Lane and Longmoor Lane at 10pm, and instead of going the shortest way home down Lower Lane, Robert went down Higher Lane because he had heard that a certain hard knock of a kid nicknamed "Bully" was hanging round with his gang on Lower Lane. It was a moonlit night, and as Robert walked along he was more scared of encountering Bully and his gang than a ghost, but then suddenly, as he was passing Sparrow Hall Playing fields, the boy thought he saw something dark move up the road towards him and stop dead. He assumed it was the shadow of one of the clouds scudding against the face of the full moon, and nothing more. At this point, Robert suddenly remembered that he had left his older brother Terry's brand new leather football at Billy's house. Now he had two things to worry about. Robert's parents, and his mother in particular, would tell him off because he wasn't supposed to stay out later than 9pm on these wintry nights, and now Terry would throttle him when he learned that Robert had not only 'borrowed' his new football, but had also left in Billy Morris's house. The boy wondered if he should run back to Billy's house, just over half a mile away, but then something took place which made Robert's earthly worries pale into insignificance.

The ground gave away under Robert's feet, and he found himself sinking into what felt like a deep lukewarm pool of quicksand. The boy looked about as he sank into the black viscous goo and let out a cry. At this time of night in 1946, this stretch of Higher Lane was deserted. Robert instinctively tried to lay on his back, as he had seen the people do in films when they fell into quicksand. As he tried to lift his arm, he heard a squelching noise from the suction, perhaps caused by the vacuum he was creating by the very act of lifting a limb. Within seconds he was in the strange out-of-place swamp up to his shoulders, and now he could definitely feel something under the black sludge pulling at his feet. Robert let out a terrible scream, and believed he was about to die. He was naturally confused; how on earth could there be quicksand on Higher Lane? It didn't make any sense, and yet here he was, about to meet a terrible fate.

'Rob!' shouted a voice in the darkness somewhere nearby. It was the voice of his best friend Billy, who had been on his way to Robert's house with the new football he had left in Billy's garden.

Robert turned his head slightly, and spat out the black sticky sludge which was now up to his lips. Billy Morris was running towards him, about seven feet away. 'Billy! Help me! Help me!' screamed Robert, and he tried to lift his arm, but the suction was too great to allow even that.

Billy bravely took off his jacket and lay it across the black slithery pool, and he lay on it and thrust out the football towards Robert, but the lad couldn't even lift his hands out of the swampy mass to grab the ball. Robert was now in tears, and Billy suddenly got Robert in a headlock, and began to pull him with such force, he must have cut off the blood coursing through his doomed friend's carotid artery, because Robert fainted. At this point, a car came down the road, and caught the whole surreal scene in its headlamps. The car came to an abrupt halt, and a man in a trilby and a belted long coat got out the vehicle and rushed to the aid of the children. As this man came upon the scene, the mysterious black quicksand literally faded away, and all that was left were the two schoolboys lying on the pavement. But Robert Smith had no shoes on and was also missing a sock. The motorist lifted unconscious Robert to his feet and took him to the car with Billy, intending to take the lad to hospital, but Robert came around and began to cry his eyes out. Billy Morris had seen the 'phantom quicksand' and so had the motorist, and he drove Robert to his home and told the boy's parents what had happened, but they found the bizarre story hard to accept, even though Billy and the motorist backed up the story. After that night, Robert Smith refused to go anywhere near Higher Lane, and of course many years later, when he was in his sixties, he heard me on a local radio station talking about the many reports I had collected about the weird amorphous black entity that had been seen on Higher Lane over the decades, and he realised that he had almost been swallowed up by this thing back in 1946. Robert was also shocked when he read about the reports of the Thing in my books, because a number of the sightings of the black fluidic creature occurred close to Sparrow Hall Playing Fields. The reports of the Thing have thinned out in recent years, but, whatever it is; it may make a comeback yet.

Another supernatural abduction almost took place in Daulby Street, off Pembroke Place, near the Royal Liverpool Teaching Hospital. This incident took place in 1981, and like the Thing on Higher Lane, cannot be rationally explained. A 13-year-old boy we shall call Phillip, who lived on Marmaduke Street, near Wavertree Road, was gallivanting around the city centre with his friend Ben (also aged 13) one autumn evening. Phillip and Ben were walking up London Road after their aimless walkabout when Ben saw his older sister, Patty and her new boyfriend, Keith, in the latter's new car, which was waiting at the traffic lights near the junction of Daulby Street, Moss Street and Prescot Street. Ben knocked on the window of the car, startling his sister and her boyfriend, and asked if they would give him a lift home. The couple were headed for Patty's home in Kensington, so Keith wound down the window and said, 'Hurry up then before the lights change!'

Ben got into the car, and the lights changed, and Phillip sulkily walked away up Daulby Street because he had not been invited into the car. He marched along, feeling rather hurt by Ben's selfish action, when suddenly, a tall, rather skinny but smart-looking man in a pin-striped suit came up behind Phillip and grabbed the collar of his coat. He dragged the startled boy to a white transit van, and as Phillip tried to free himself from the stranger's clutches, one of the doors in the back of the van flew open, and Phillip was thrown inside. In the back of the van was a terrifying scene which was bathed in the faint glow from a solitary small lightbulb in the roof of the interior. A woman with the strangest-looking face was sitting on a crate, and against the walls of the van sat four or five little children, all crying their eyes out with looks of pure terror on their faces. The woman sitting on the crate had a massive head of purplish-red curly hair, and her face was abnormally long. Her eyes were black with golden pupils, and this creepy-looking woman began to scream at Phillip. He saw the woman's mouth open vertically and stretch. It opened much wider than a normal human mouth could possibly do. The screams from the unearthly woman deafened Phillip, and he turned and somehow managed to open the doors and run off towards Pembroke Place. As he ran up Pembroke Place, the white transit van sped past him, and as it curved into Crown Street, Phillip saw the vehicle fade away into nothing. The sound of the vehicle's engine faded away at the same moment.

Phillip ran all the way home to Marmaduke Street in

a terrible state, and when his mother came to the door, she saw her son in a terrible state, bent over clutching the side of his abdomen because he had developed an agonising stitch with all of the non-stop running. That night, the boy's auntie May paid a visit to the house on Marmaduke Street. May was a rather stone-faced woman who said little and was not very animated in conversation. When Phillip's mother told May about her son's 'far-fetched story' May said: 'A few people have seen that van and the children in it over the years. John saw them in 1977, just before he died.'

The dry and monotonous way May imparted this piece of information chilled Phillip's parents to the bone; they realised that their son was telling the truth after all, but they and others who have seen that phantom transit van over the years remain baffled as to the motive and identity of the weird-looking woman with the huge mouth, the man in the pinstriped suit (who was presumably the driver of the ghostly van) and the poor little terrified children in the back of the white transit. I had déjà vu when I heard Phillip's recollections of this chilling encounter; the scenario seems very familiar as if I have heard of something similar a long time back, but I cannot find any such references to the incident in my case notes.

EVE & LIV

Everton and Liverpool at Wembley is, without a doubt, a landmark fixture and a sporting event (dare I say it?) to even eclipse that other local but global event of the sporting calendar– the Grand National. As fiercely rival clubs that live within a mile of each other in this football-crazed city, the polarising pull of Everton and Liverpool can divide families and even the closest, most intimate couples in a way that defies any anthropological analysis. I have even seen priests in heated arguments after a Derby game. Most people in Liverpool are born Red or Blue, and should a geneticist scrutinise the Human Genomes of the people of this city closely enough he will see 'Nil Satis Nisi Optimum' or 'YNWA' encoded in their DNA. To say football is a passion in Liverpool is a clichéd understatement – it's a religion – possibly a throwback to the ancient Celtic Druids. Long before St Augustine brought Christianity to these shores, the Roman vanguard saw mad-looking ancient tattooed Britons, one group with their skins dyed blue with Woad and the other tribe stained red with an iron-based pigment called vitrum, and they were kicking animal-hide prototype footballs about under the supervision of a druidic overseer (a referee). Football then, is part of the shared race memory, embedded in the collective unconscious, a metaphysical ritual, a devotion, and that often misquoted line about Shankly saying football is much more important than a simple matter of life and death is truer than we think: he was citing a scripture.

The love of the game even transcends death itself.

Many years ago in 1984, the year the Reds and The Toffees met twice at that cathedral of sport, Wembley, there lived two friends, Matty and Stan, red and blue respectively, both aged 22, who were the closest of friends, but their families, took their love of their team to extremes. Their houses faced one another, and a fortnight before the FA Charity Shield game at Wembley, things escalated. Matty was forbidden to associate with Stan, and vice versa. However, the lads bumped into one another in town one Saturday night in the Philharmonic pub, where they met the most beautiful girls they had ever seen. Eve was a supermodel in the eyes of Matty, and Liv was like some sultry Hollywood starlet to Stan, and the foursome went to all the clubs, and love really was in the air. 'We'll take them to Wembley,' Stan told Matty, after escorting the girls home, and Matty said: 'Played! Good idea Stan, lad.'

The families of Stan and Matty yawned when the lads told them they had each found 'the one'. There was talk of marriages at Anfield and Goodison, and then one day, in Hardman Street's Kirklands wine bar over lager and 'expensive scran' as Matty called it. Eve revealed her name was short for Everton, and Liv then laughed with a startled expression at this disclosure, because her name was short for Liverpool, not Olivia as Stan and most people had assumed. The girls' fathers had been fundamentalist football fanatics. Stan and Matty were struck dumb by the revelations and almost cried. They went the toilet together and were both sick in the cubicles. They had to go home and 'come out' about the situation, but in the end their families supported them. On the morning the couples were ready to go down to Wembley, Stan found his front door had been painted royal blue, and Matty's door had been painted LFC red. This spooked both families because their long deceased warring grandfathers used to paint their teams' colours on the front doors when a Derby was due. The milk man deepened the mystery because he had passed both doors at 7.30 am, and when he passed those same doors ten minutes later, they had been painted, yet he had seen and heard no one on the doorsteps. Despite the spooky goings-on the lads and lasses married anyway – and are still together, and their children are a mixture of reds and blues!

EAVESDROPPING ON HELL

The following story, which took place in 1985, was reported to me a few years ago, and like a lot of tales in this book, it's hard to explain in rational terms, although I will present a few possible explanations at the end of the story.

Chris dearly loved his grandmother Elsie, and now she seemed to be having difficulty hearing things, but was too proud to go for a hearing test. Elsie's daughter Joan had told her she would probably qualify for a free hearing aid, but Elsie would shake her head and say, 'My hearing's okay, don't you worry; I can hear the grass grow; it's just a bit of wax.'

So one day, 30-year-old Chris, who was something of an electronics hobbyist, decided he'd build an hearing aid for his beloved Gran. It wouldn't be one of those sleek state-of-the-art models; it would have to be about the size of a pack of cigarettes with a PP3 battery and a simple earphone Elsie could stick in her ear, but it would have the best amplification Chris could achieve with his electronic components. At the time, Chris lived in Tuebrook near Lisburn Lane, and his Gran lived by Mab Lane in the West Derby district of the city. Chris had been going to her house ever since he was six, and loved nothing better than sitting with her watching the match or a good film on the telly with her. Now she was turning the volume up on the TV and asking Chris what someone in *Coronation Street* or *Columbo* had said, and her nephew found it quite saddening to see her struggling to hear things.

Chris sat in the little hut in his garden where he had cabinets of electronic components, soldering irons, oscilloscopes, voltmeters and all of the paraphernalia which goes with electronics. He decided he would build a sensitive 'electronic ear' circuit based around an integrated circuit called an LM380 and a few transistors. In less than 90 minutes the circuit and the PP3 Ever Ready battery was built and housed in a small plastic box. The microphone in the box was a miniature loudspeaker, and two twisted wires led from the box to a simple crystal earphone which would hopefully convey the amplified sounds of the world to Elsie's good ear (which was her right one). On the box was the knob of a little potentiometer so Elsie could turn the sensitivity up to the desired level. Just turning the knob a quarter of the way was sufficient, Elsie discovered.

Chris's home-made hearing aid worked quite well, and Elsie was really chuffed with it. She watched a wildlife programme called *The World About Us*, and could hear every word the narrator spoke. Then Elsie enjoyed an episode of the anarchic military hospital comedy *M*A*S*H*, before turning over to BBC 1 to watch the detective agency drama *Remington Steele*. Christmas wasn't that far off and all the good films would be coming on the telly soon, and this time, Elsie would be able to hear them instead of lip-reading the actors and actresses and turning the volume up to provoke thumps on the walls from the irritated neighbours. Around 11pm, Elsie decided to call it a day, and looked forward to using her thoughtful nephew's hearing aid device in the morning when she was due to go shopping. She had missed out on so much gossip from her friends who were not willing to speak up as they jangled about various people in the neighbourhood. Elsie switched off the telly, and was just about to switch off the hearing aid when she heard whispers. She stopped and looked towards the bay window, then reached under the big amber shade of the floor lamp and switched off the bulb. She went to the net curtains and peeped through them. There was no one there. Not a soul. The street was empty and the pavement and roads were glossy with a coating of rain. And yet she could still hear the voices. What were they saying? Elsie listened intently then recalled the volume control on the hearing aid, and she turned it past the quarter mark to about twenty-five per cent. Now she could really hear the voices. It was two men, and they were crying as they tried to speak. They both sounded as if they were in great distress.

'I'm burning, please stop! Please stop! I can't breathe!' said a deep male voice. Elsie thought the voice belonged to a man in his forties, perhaps a bit older – but then she knew how deceptive voices were. DJ's on the radio she listened to sounded as suave as Roger Moore but when she saw what they really looked like, most of them looked more like Patrick Moore on a bad day. Elsie herself had been told she had a young-sounding voice on the telephone. But where were these tortured voices coming from?

A younger, much higher-pitched voice screamed, startling Elsie, and then this voice moaned: 'Oh Joe, Hell is a horrible place! Joe! Where are you? Are you still there?'

Elsie was a little scared and yet she couldn't switch off the hearing device because her curiosity always got the better of her. She turned the volume up by a few more degrees, and now she could hear a woman, perhaps of about thirty-something, who sounded hysterical. She yelled: 'Why is there no light? I can't see! Where am I? I want to go home! Where am I?'

And another male voice, much lower and sounding a lot older than the other voices, answered: 'You're in Hell, that's where you are my dear!'

'Who's that? Who are you?' the female voice asked, sounding as if she had been startled by the reply she had heard.

'Hell!' said a group of voices in unison.

'I can't be,' the unseen lady answered, 'I've done nothing wrong! I want to go home! Why can't I see? Help me someone!'

There was an outbreak of jeers and vile swear-words levied at the woman, and then a mocking voice said: 'You will never see your home again, love! You are stuck here for ever, and that is a very very very very long time!'

'Shut up! Shut up! Please stop it, please!' an agonised male voice pleaded. 'I've been here for years! Years! You just got here! Wait till you've been here as long as I have you moaning bastard!'

There was another barrage of laughs and hurtful jibes, this time directed at the last speaker.

Another voice, this time an elderly female one, announced: 'We're forgotten here, and no amount of shouting and screaming will save you. You're better just trying to think of nothing!'

'I shouldn't even be here!' said a voice with an Irish lilt to it. It continued: 'My family will be saying prayers for me now; I'll soon be delivered!'

A raspy ancient-sounding voice swore in response to the Irishman and told him, 'You killed someone, and

283

now you're going to pay in this blackness for ever and ever. No prayers by your family can save you now! I've been here for fifty years! Fifty years of this!'

An unnerving cacophony of wailing and screaming and laughter erupted. Elsie had heard enough, and she felt physically sick. She switched off the hearing aid, and listened. Now all Elsie could hear was the old German clock on the mantelpiece, which had always ticked rather loudly. Nothing more was heard. Those horrible quarrelling voices had gone. On the following day at noon, Elsie returned from the shops with a satisfied smirk on her face, because the hearing aid had allowed her to participate in all of the jangling at the supermarket and also at the post office, where she had gone to buy some postage stamps for the Christmas cards she'd be sending off soon. Chris called round with his best friend Tony, and Elsie told her nephew about the odd argumentative people she had heard the night before. At first Chris assumed the hearing aid's amplifier had perhaps picked up stray radio signals or even VHF broadcasts of a television programme's audio channel, but Elsie was adamant that the voices had used swear words, and she had felt as if there was something – well – supernatural about them.

'Nah, it won't be anything like that Gran,' Chris reassured Elsie, 'let me have a listen,' he said, and Elsie handed him the hearing aid. Chris switched it on and put the earphone to his right ear. Everything sounded too amplified, even his own breathing, so he turned down the volume and listened. 'Testing, testing, one two three!' he intoned, and heard nothing strange.

'Is there anybody there?' Tony joked, and Chris glared at him and gave a slight shake of the head, meaning 'Shut up!'

A male voice replied: 'Yes, who is that?'

Tony and Elsie didn't hear it, just Chris, and that voice was coming through on the hearing aid.

Chris was stuck for words for a few moments, and then he said, 'Hello, who's that?'

'Oh God you can hear me, I don't believe it! Oh –' the overemotional voice replied. It begged Chris to go to a certain priest and request a Mass to be held. 'Tell him to say a Mass for me, and tell him that my wife [and a name was given here] will pay him whatever he wants. Please tell him to pray for me!'

'Who are you talking to Chris?' Tony asked, and he and Elsie looked at Chris with intrigued expressions.

'Where are you and what's your name?' Chris asked the man, ignoring Tony's question.

The man gave a name, and the surname was quite unusual - and then he said: 'I think I'm in Hell, in fact I'm sure of it, and its horrible here. Please tell the priest, and then will you keep talking to me? Please don't go!'

Chris was not only creeped out by the conversation from a man he could not see; he was also worried that this affair about the eerie voices could frighten his grandmother. He turned off the hearing aid, and made up a cock and bull story about the hearing aid acting as a type of walkie-talkie, but Elsie could tell Chris was fibbing; he always had been a bad liar. Chris took the hearing aid home under the impression that he would fix it and return it. When he got home, he and Tony took turns listening out for the voice via the device's earphone, but heard nothing but the normal hissing sound one normally hears when the volume of an amplifier is turned up. It was soon ascertained that the voices were only heard when the hearing aid was used in Elsie's house, and especially near the bay window for some reason. Elsie became afraid to use her nephew's home-built hearing aid and decided to go to the doctor's to have her ears checked. The result of the visit was the GP sending her to a hearing specialist, and he supplied Elsie with a proper hearing aid, and this one did not pick up any uncanny voices.

Chris could not explain what the voices where, and Elsie would not allow him to bring a tape-recorder to her house to capture the voices for future analysis. Just what the voices were is still unknown. I wonder if they were perhaps a form of what is now known as EVP – Electronic Voice Phenomena, which was probably discovered by Friedrich Jurgenson, a Swedish opera singer, musician, painter, and film producer. In 1959, Jurgenson recorded birdsong in the country near his villa in Sweden one day, but when he played back the tape-recording he was intrigued to hear voices talking about birdsong in Swedish and Norwegian. Jurgenson's first natural assumption was that he had somehow picked up a stray transmission from a radio station, but if that was so, it seemed somewhat coincidental how the speakers were talking about birdsong – the very thing Jurgenson was recording. Jurgenson made further recordings, and always, when the recordings were being made, he and others who were present heard nothing except mundane noises such as birds tweeting or various natural background noises, but when the tapes were played back, voices were heard, and it soon became clear that these invisible speakers were not transmissions from a radio station being picked up by the recording equipment, because the voices responded to questioning from Jurgenson. Jurgenson could hear his dead father's voice during one session, and he also heard his late wife calling his name and allegedly received a message from his dead mother. In 1965, Jurgenson worked with Dr Konstantin Raudive, a Latvian psychologist (who had studied under Jung) who had escaped from his native country because of the 1945 Soviet invasion. Raudive made thousands of recording in very tightly-controlled conditions in an effort to eliminate hoaxing and the accidental recording of radio transmissions. Even under these controlled conditions where factory-clean tapes were used in soundproof chambers, whispering voices were still captured. The origins of these so-called 'Raudive voices' have never been traced or explained. Some believe they are the voices of the dead. One of the earliest attempts at contacting the dead through electronic means supposedly took place in 1920 when the extraordinary inventor Thomas Edison (the man who came up with the light bulb and the forerunner of the record player amongst many other things) embarked on an invention of his to bridge the apparent gulf which seems to exist between those who have passed on and those who are still living in a flesh and blood body. Edison, the self-taught genius and most eminent practical scientist of his day, made several statements which generated headlines around the world. Edison said of a life after death: 'If our personality survives, then it is strictly logical and scientific to assume that it retains memory, intellect and other faculties and knowledge that we acquire on this earth. Therefore if personality exists after what we call death, it is reasonable to conclude that those who leave this earth would like to communicate with those they have left here. I am prompted to believe that our personality hereafter will be able to affect matter. If this reasoning be correct, then, if we can evolve an instrument so delicate as to be affected, or moved, or manipulated, as it exists in the next life, such an instrument, when available, should be able to record something.'

Edison rarely talked of his beliefs about the possibility of a life after death, but it is known he was a type of agnostic – which means he sat on the fence, neither believing or disbelieving, but waiting for the evidence to convince him either way. However, in 1916, it is known that Edison told a friend named Allan L Benson (a presidential candidate and author) that he believed a Creator was behind everything in the universe. Edison believed that a form of intelligence, present in everything from an amoeba to a neuron in the brain, possessed intelligence, and could not die. Where did this intelligence come from? According to Edison: 'It is drawn from some common source; a reservoir to which it returns after each individual life ends, to be used again and again forever. Intelligence, like energy is indestructible and immortal. Each cell is intelligent, but some are more intelligent than others and develop the ability to do some things that others cannot do. Some of the cells of a tree, for instance, know how to pump water from the earth into the branches, while others conduct the intricate chemical processes involved in the metabolism of the leaf. My stomach knows how to make hydrochloric acid; I don't.'

So, in Edison's view, when a person dies and decays or is cremated, all of the cells die or are burned, and all of the intelligence of that person remains in some limbo-like dimension, ready to be recycled. Edison's machine for contacting the dead, if it ever got off the drawing board at all, has never been found, but the voices later discovered by Jurgenson and Raudive, are still being picked up by sensitive recorders. It's relatively easy to record EVP yourself, using either the classic audio cassette recorder (fairly hard to come by in this digital day and age), or a digital recorder of the type found in pocket digital dictaphones. You can even use the recorder built into your mobile phone, and I imagine there are probably EVP apps which should be treated with caution. The best times to attempt an EVP recording are between sunset and sunrise, preferably in the wee small hours of the morning when there is less noise about. Raudive said a person trying to record EVP should recite the date and time into the recorder, followed by a solemn invitation for the 'spirits' to speak. Keep each recording session under two minutes if possible, as intense concentration is required during the playback of the recording as you scan for voices.

What of the voices heard by Elsie and her nephew Chris? Are they really the sounds of people in Hell? Every culture, across the world, claims there is a place where sinners are punished after death for sins committed during their lifetimes. Even the Buddhists state that there are a number of hells where sinners are subjected to freezing cold and searing temperatures. The Ancient Egyptians and the Greeks believed in various hells, and even the great philosopher Plato wrote about souls being punished after death in a grim hell called Tartarus. Perhaps there is a punishment system which we enter after death if we have committed sins, and perhaps Elsie and Chris picked up the voices of the damned through some anomaly, some weak part of our dimension which occasionally touches upon some infernal region we would term as Hell. That's a lot of suppositions. The philosopher C. D. Broad (1887-1971) once postulated that when a person dies, he or she leaves a shell of psychic energy behind containing all of our expectations, fears and beliefs, but the real soul goes on to wherever its supposed to go, leaving this shell of energy which Broad termed the "Mindkin". The Mindkin would exist for quite some time after the person's real soul and personality had passed on, so it would seem alive to mediums and would even enter into a two-way conversation – a bit like an artificial intelligence computer program – giving the medium the impression he was talking to a real deceased person. Broad believed that such Mindkins would fabricate Heaven and Hell depending on the religious persuasion of the mind they had come from. This theory could explain the voices as nothing but an energy shell left behind by someone who has shuffled off their mortal coil and progressed to a higher level. Or, perhaps Hell is a reality and some reading these words may one day find themselves in the place of eternal damnation and endless torment in the not-too-distant future…best be good eh?

SOME CARNATE AND
DISCARNATE GHOSTS

Without a doubt, some of the worst hauntings in Liverpool – and anywhere for that matter – are the ones in which nothing is seen, but sensed instead. I remember as a child, playing in a 'toyroom' in a certain old house in Garston which belonged to a relative, and I had no idea the house was haunted at the age of six. My cousin went out the room for a while, and I sat there, playing with various toys and modelling clay, when all of a sudden, I just knew something else was in that room with me. I felt something touch my shoulder and heard the floorboard creak, and then I saw a little red Dinky car move along on its own. I heard a faint chuckle, and I ran straight out the room.

Many years later, after the house had changed hands, I happened to be called upon to investigate an alleged ghost that had been resorting to some terrifying antics at the place. I realised this was the very house I had sensed the presence in when I was a child. The present owner, a Mrs Richardson, told me how, one evening, she was about to go up the staircase to her 16-year-old daughter's room when powerful invisible arms embraced her and prevented her from ascending the stairs. Mrs Richardson began to scream – and the invisible assailant clamped a cold moist hand over her mouth. She heard it chuckle: a deep male snigger, and the entity gave off a ghastly musky aroma. Somehow

Mrs Richardson managed to break free and ran screaming up to the room of her daughter Penny – with the sounds of heavy footsteps following her on the stairs. Mother and daughter hugged one another as they stood there, shaking, watching the handle of the bedroom door turning slowly, accompanied by that sinister chortling sound of the thing on the other side of the door.

There was a heavy knocking at the front door, and immediately the ghostly attacker let go of the bedroom handle and it was heard to run away along the landing. The caller was Mrs Richardson's friend, Mrs Abbot, who came round each week for a natter and a cup of tea. Mrs Richardson and her daughter hurried out of the bedroom and went down to answer the door, and were so afraid, they went to Mrs Abbot's house and stayed there for hours until they returned with several relatives for 'back up'. I mentioned the house in question on my website and received many emails and letters from previous occupants who had lived there before and after my relatives had owned the place. In the 1950s, a woman named Hilda had awakened in her bed one morning at around four o'clock to feel her hand, which was sticking out from under the blankets, being held by an invisible cold hand. She tried to withdraw her hand from the eerie grip, but found it very difficult, and the discarnate presence actually pulled her clean out of the bed. Once again, subdued laughter was heard. When Hilda went downstairs, she found a bunch of plucked daffodils in the middle of her table – even though it was early December.

In the end, I consulted a Catholic priest, who came to the house and blessed it. He said prayers in each room, and this priest had a cast-iron faith, and the thing eventually departed from the house. As far as I know, it has not returned, but ghosts can often leave a dwelling for years, even decades, only to return with a vengeance.

So much for the discarnate ghost which has no solid-looking physical body, but what of the carnates? These are a type of ghost that look as real and solid as you and I, and when they are encountered, people often assume the spook is a real, living person. Here are a few local cases of carnate hauntings.

In 2009 at a certain well-known supermarket in Liverpool, a 41-year-old woman named Pauline was consulting her shopping list as her 17-year-old daughter Alexis listened to various songs on her iPhone via her earphones. Pauline noticed she was by the clothing section of the supermarket, and so she went in search of a top. An old smartly-dressed woman approached, looking very concerned. She was aged about seventy-something and wore a beige coat, a 'pill-box' hat, and her lipstick was a vivid scarlet colour. She had a small envelope style handbag in her left arm. The woman halted by Alexis and parked her trolley by the girl; a trolley which contained eggs, a newspaper, a packet of fish fingers and several other items which Pauline can't recall now. The woman said something to Alexis, but the teen didn't hear what it was because she was listening to her iPhone songs, so she took the earphones out and said, 'What, sorry?'

At this point, Pauline, who had been leafing through a rack of clothes-hangers for a size 14 top, also noticed the elderly lady, and turned fully to see what she wanted.

'I'm really worried about something,' the refined old lady said in a well-spoken voice, and she turned to look towards the toilets near the entrance to the supermarket. 'May I just leave this trolley with you for a moment?'

'Yeah,' said Alexis, baffled.

'Yes,' Pauline also said in reply, 'is everything okay love?'

'Don't let them take the trolley away,' the woman said, 'tell them the lady will be back for it in a moment.'

Pauline and Alexis then watched the old woman head towards the toilets. Minutes crawled past, and Pauline and Alexis kept waiting for the woman to come out of the toilets, but she never came out again. Pauline went to the customer services desk in the supermarket and told the woman there she was concerned about the elderly lady who had left her trolley to go to the toilets. Pauline and the Customer Services woman went into the ladies toilets – and the old lady was not there. A security guard went into the male toilets just in case the old woman had gone in there by mistake. She wasn't there either. Some time later a senior member of the supermarket staff came on the scene, and in a matter-of-fact way he told Pauline and the lady from the Customer Services counter that the old woman they were looking for was a ghost.

'What?' Pauline said, with a shocked look. The Customer Services lady and Alexis threw nervous glances at one another. The senior staff member nodded with a smile, then said. 'Yeah, she's done this before. Always the same items as well; eggs, fish fingers, newspaper. I don't know why she does it.' The ghost of the old lady with the trolley apparently dates back to around the mid 1990s, and she has even been seen on the supermarket's security cameras, but on some occasions, an empty trolley has been seen wheeling itself down an aisle near to the pharmacy section around 11pm. What frightened Pauline and her daughter in particular was the way they took the ghost to be a living person. 'She looked so real and solid, and me and Alex never dreamt we were talking to something supernatural,' Pauline told me.

In 2002, a 65-year-old woman named Helen was walking her dog in Wavertree Playground one sunny afternoon when she was approached by a young man of about twenty to twenty-five years of age. He had short black hair that looked as if it was slicked back with oil, and he wore a dark blue suit and black brogue shoes. 'Excuse me,' he said to Helen, 'but could you direct me to Abbeyholme School?'

Helen was not a Wavertree woman; she had moved to the area from Old Swan, and so she wasn't aware of any school named Abbeyholme. Before she could tell the young man she hadn't a clue where the school was, he said: 'I have an appointment with a Mister Veltcamp at half-past four you see and he's a stickler for punctuality.'

Helen smiled faintly and shook her head, and as she said, 'I'm sorry, I've never heard of Abbeyholme School,' her dog – a little Yorkshire Terrier named Bob, began to snap at the young man. 'Bob! Stop that!' Helen scolded her pet and dragged him away from the young man who was now heading towards the gates on Prince Alfred Road. Helen turned to see where the young man was going – and saw no one. He had been there literally a second or so ago, and now he was nowhere to be seen. Helen wondered if he had walked behind the huge pillars of the gates, and she went to look, but he was not there, and Bob began to act very out of character; he was normally a very sociable well-behaved dog, but Helen had to drag him to the gates, and the collar almost slipped off at one point.

Helen returned to her home on nearby Newcastle Road, and that evening she was visited by Valerie, a former neighbour who was now living on Menlove Gardens North. Valerie had lived in Wavertree all of her life, and so Helen mentioned the young man who had been looking for Abbeyholme School. Valerie said such a school had existed on Church Road, not far from the Wavertree Playground park, and Valerie recalled that a gentleman named Veltcamp (possible spelt Veltkamp) had been a headmaster at the school, and possibly owned the property as well. Valerie knew this because her cousin had attended the school in the late 1950s and early 1960s. 'Perhaps Mr Veltcamp is at another school in the area now, if he's still alive,' Valerie mused.

Three days later, Helen was once again in Wavertree Playground walking Bob, when who should she see walking towards her but the very same young man in the dark-blue suit who had asked her for directions to the school, only this time he walked past Helen (who said hello to the man but received no acknowledgement) and on this occasion he went to an elderly bald-headed man who was smoking his pipe has he sat on a park bench . Helen could faintly hear the young man asking the same question – word for word – that he had asked three days before. The man sitting on the bench nodded in response to the question and began to make gestures with his hands and point towards the Wavertree Blind School as he gave directions. The young man then turned and walked past Helen again – and a growling Bob – and slipped out of the gates of the park. This time, Helen could see the stranger walking up Fir Lane outside the park. Out of curiosity, she went to the old man who was seated on the bench, and he smiled when he saw Bob and asked how old he was. Helen told him, and then she said: 'I couldn't help overhearing the young man asking you for directions to Abbeyholme School before – '

'Ah, yes, said the man with a half smile.

'He asked me the same question three days back, and I had no idea where it was – ' Helen was explaining, when the man cut through her words with a shocking statement.

'He's a ghostie,' the man said, and he nodded, his vague smile had gone now.

Helen was speechless. She thought she had misheard the man. 'He's a what, sorry?'

'A ghost. He's asked me that same question now, let's see – for about ten years.'

'A ghost?' Helen tried to force a smile.

'Yes, I'm serious. A a lot of people have been approached by him. He always asks the same question about a meeting with a Mr Veltcamp. That school he's looking for was demolished years ago. I don't know who that lad is, or who he was.'

'But,' Helen struggled to find the words, 'he – he seemed so real. He can't be a –'

The old man puffed on his pipe and nodded with a serene but sure look on his face. And of course, he was right. That young man in the dark blue suit and black brogues has indeed been encountered by many people, always in the vicinity of Wavertree Playground, except for one encounter on nearby Hunter's Lane, where a postman was approached early one morning by the ghost, who asked the same old hackneyed question. I have researched the case and have no idea who the man was, and even several psychics I have employed in an effort to home in on the ghost have failed to come up with anything in the way of a name or surname. We started this section of the book looking into discarnate ghosts – ghost that have no physical body and no visual image that accompanies their manifestation, which can be an electrifying presence or a slight breeze on the face, or a gentle stirring of the curtains. One night at a house on Dodd's Lane, Maghull, in 2009, a discarnate ghost allegedly entertained two boys (both aged 9) named Eddy and Milesh in a very unusual way. Milesh was allowed to stay over at his schoolfriend Eddy's home once a week, usually on a Friday night, and on this evening, both boys played FIFA and several other games on Eddy's Playstation until midnight, when Eddy's mother said it was time they got some sleep. The boys slept top-tail in Eddy's bed, and they both chatted away and told jokes until they began to doze off. Then, around 2.30 am, Milesh woke up with an urge to go the toilet, and he crept out of the bedroom, went to the loo, and returned to Eddy's bedroom about three minutes later, but when he entered the room he saw something on the wall which made him think he was dreaming. On a blank part of the bedroom wall that was not adorned with posters and pinned-up drawings, there was a disc of yellowish light with a face on it – a smiling face – and one of the eyes winked at Milesh, who was naturally a bit scared of the luminous apparition. He poked Eddy in the shoulder with his finger repeatedly until his friend woke in a rather grumpy mood. 'What? What do you want?' Eddy moaned.

'Eddy, look!' Milesh pointed to the 'moon face' smiling on the wall, and he rubbed the sleep from his eyes and then he sat up as Milesh crouched at the side of the bed, spellbound by the weird 'projection'.

'What is it?' Eddy asked, and suddenly the disc with the smiling face moved up and down with a bouncing movement. And then it faded, and in its place a square of multicoloured shapes appeared on the wall – just as if some cartoon was being projected from somewhere. Faint flute music could be heard, and then all sorts of cartoon animals appeared on the wall. Milesh turned on the bedroom light because he found the cartoon show quite eerie, and as soon as the light was switched on, the music and the cartoon stopped being projected on the wall.

'Turn it off!' Eddy urged Milesh, and looked back to the space on the wall where the moon face and cartoon film had been. There was nothing there now.

'I'm scared,' Milesh admitted, and stood there with his hand still on the light switch. He looked at the spot on the wall with a worried expression.

'Don't be scared,' Eddy tried to reassure his best friend. 'Turn the light off and see if it comes back.'

Milesh just stood there, then reluctantly switched the

bedroom light off.

A square of light slowly reappeared on the wall in the same place as before, and this time a piano was playing somewhere in the distance. Both boys could plainly hear it jangling away. A black and white scene of a typical wild west town appeared this time, and the swinging doors of a saloon burst open and out came a clown dressed as a cowboy, firing a gun which emitted clouds of smoke with each shot. The clown did cartwheels across the street, and narrowly missed a stagecoach, and then the scene changed to show an evil looking cowboy in a black hat with a black curled up moustache and chalk white face. His eyes darted sideways to look at Milesh and Eddy, and they could see from the silver star he wore on his chest that he was some sheriff. He began to fire his gun at the camera, and the scene changed back to the clown cowboy, who now had five black circular holes in his chest where the bullets had hit him. Dark grey blood spurted out of these holes in this bizarre flickering monochrome film. The clown staggered about, and his cowboy hat fell off, revealing a white bald head. He aimed his gun at the camera and fired, and then the scene changed to show the sheriff – with a bullet hole – depicted as a circular black disc over his left eye, which began to spurt out inky black blood. There was then a close-up of the clown's face as blood trickled out of his mouth. Milesh let out a scream and turned the light on, then ran out the bedroom and went straight to the bedroom of Eddy's parents to tell them about the strange upsetting film being show in their son's bedroom. Eddy's father went to see what all the fuss was about, and found Eddy crying in his bed. The boy had seen a horse being shot full of arrows by stereotypical 'red Indians' and then the sheriff had been hanged by a posse and his head had come off.

Eddy's father turned the light off and sat and looked at the wall where this distressing show was supposed to be projected by someone, but nothing appeared. As soon as the boys had settled down and Eddy's father had gone back to bed, there came a faint echoing sound of a badly-tuned honky-tonk piano being played by some manic pianist. The boys froze for a moment, and then Eddy peeped over the edge of his duvet at the wall, and there was the moon face character, bouncing up and down on the wall. Eddy shouted for his father once again, and on this occasion, Eddy's father, and his mother - who had left her bed to see what all the screaming was about – both heard the ghostly ethereal pianist for about a minute. When Milesh's parents heard about the strange goings on, they didn't let their boy stay over any more, and Eddy's father put a bookcase against the wall where the weird show had been projected, and to date, the moon face character and the bizarre 'films' have not been shown.

I looked into this case and discovered that a cinema projectionist lived close to the house where Eddy lives, and he died in the 1970s. I wondered if the projectionist had perhaps returned from beyond the grave as a discarnate form to 'entertain' the boys with his surreal and macabre 'shows' which might have been a creation of his own mind, but of course, any evidence to back up this theory is sadly lacking.

Printed in Great Britain
by Amazon